The Sirtfood Diet

3 BOOKS IN 1:

COMPLETE BEGINNERS GUIDE & COOKBOOK WITH MORE THAN **300 TASTY RECIPES**! BURN FAT ACTIVATING YOUR "SKINNY GENE"! QUICK AND EASY MEALS + A SMART **28-DAYS MEAL PLAN** TO BOOST YOUR WEIGHT LOSS! LOSE FAT AND GAIN MUSCLE!

By

Eleanor Fields

&

Susan Wilma Cooper

TABLE OF CONTENTS

INTRODUCTION

The Sirtfood diet is a term coined by Dr. Bill Evans for a high in the sirtuin proteins he has isolated from various foods. The sirtuin proteins are present in foods that contain carbohydrates, plant-based fat, and protein. There are many of these, also known as food elixirs; this diet protects against diseases and extends life and overall health. Food elixir has been used for many beneficial aspects, but little has been done to put it to widespread use in the last decades. It is believed that it will revolutionize aging, benefiting both younger and older generations.

The Sirtfood diet targets eating foods full of sirtuin proteins. The study of aging is a young field, still in its infancy. Sirtuin proteins, however, have been known for some time. They are unique to humans; so many humans live up to one hundred years despite their bodies not being designed for such longevity. The sirtuin proteins are also the source of a new diet that promises to add years to one's life.

The sirtuin diet is all about sticking to a special diet and making food choices based on the tests that are run every week on the blood sample provided by the patient. The blood sample is performed in conjunction with the overall antioxidant status of one's body. The key is finding out which foods can support the body in key nutrients. The antioxidant status of the system is used to make the list of foods that should be added to the diet.

Those on a diet experience positive changes ranging for the better. Every week the results of the patients vary medically between a major recovery of health and minor improvements in the immune system. The goal of the entire program is to make the body perform better and, on average, to get many more years of living.

In the cells, there are numerous pieces taking part in the everyday processes that are important for the overall function of the cells. There are hooks, chains, rollers, pedals, and other components working in synchronicity to provide the cell with function. Every component is crucial because the slightest error will stall the entire process. Some particles are pressed upon to function to their full potential, while others take part in the overall running of the process but are not given much focus.

The overall function is the same regardless of the part involved. All it takes is just a minor hindrance to bringing everything in a cell crashing down. When this happens, the cell will be overrun with faulty particles.

Sirtuins assume a key job in controlling the aging process, called the cells' metabolism. When there is a problem in any part of the cell, the metabolism suffers. Sirtuins make sure that the overall performance of the cell process is kept up and that only the healthy particles are involved. Sirtuins are special enzymes that enter the stage in full when one wants to correct the metabolism of the cells.

Several foods that contain sirtuin were discovered with the emergence of sirtuins. It was found that these types of foods should be added to the diet because they add the necessary components to speed up the metabolism in the cells. The right amount of foods providing the sirtuins is called food elixir, and it works to help the overall health and fitness of the person.

CHAPTER 1: WHAT IS THE SIRTFOOD DIET?

Sirtuins are a group of proteins that manage cell wellbeing. Sirtuins assume a key job in controlling cell homeostasis.

In the cells, numerous pieces take a shot at different undertakings with an extreme objective: remain sound and capacity proficiently for whatever time that conceivable. Similarly, as needs in the organization change, so do needs in the cells because of different inside and outer variables. Somebody needs to run the workplace, directing what completes when, who will do it and when to switch courses.

NAD+ is essential to cell digestion and many other organic procedures. If sirtuins are an organization's CEO, at that point, NAD+ is the cash that pays the pay of the CEO and workers, all while keeping the lights on and the workplace space lease paid. An organization, and the body, can't work without it.

Protein may seem like dietary protein — what's found in beans and meats and, well, protein shakes — yet for this situation, we're discussing atoms called proteins, which work all through the body's phones in various capacities. Consider proteins the divisions at an organization, everyone concentrating without explicit capacity while planning with different offices.

Acetyl groups control explicit responses. They're physical labels on proteins that different proteins perceive will respond with them. If proteins are the cell branches and DNA are the CEO, the acetyl groups are the accessibility status of every division head. For instance, if a protein is accessible, at that point, the sirtuins can work with it to get something going; similarly, the CEO can work with an accessible division head to get something going.

Sirtuins work with acetyl groups by doing what's called deacetylation. One way that sirtuins work is by evacuating acetyl gatherings deacetylation organic proteins, for example, histones. The histone is an enormous cumbersome protein that the DNA folds itself over. This loosened up chromatin implies the DNA is being translated, a fundamental procedure.

We've just thought about sirtuins for around 20 years, and their essential capacity was found during the 1990s. From that point forward, specialists have rushed to examine them, recognizing their significance while likewise bringing up issues about what else we can find out about them.

In 1991, Elysium fellow benefactor and MIT scientist Leonard Guarantee, along with graduate understudies Nick Austria and Brian Kennedy, directed tests to all the more likely see how yeast matured. By some coincidence, Austria attempted to develop societies of different yeast strains from tests he had put away in his ice chest for quite a long time, which made an unpleasant situation for the strains.

This is the place acetyl groups become possibly the most important factor. Their first idea was that SIR2 might be a deacetylation protein — which means it expelled those acetyl gatherings — from different atoms; however, nobody knew whether this was valid since all endeavors to show this movement in a test tube demonstrated negative.

In Guarantee's very own words: "Without NAD+, SIR2 sits idle. That was the basic finding on the circular segment of sirtuins science."

Ecological factors significantly influence the destiny of living beings, and sustenance is one of the most persuasive variables. These days life span is a significant objective of medicinal science and has consistently been a fabrication for the individual since antiquated occasions. Specifically, endeavors are planned to accomplish effective maturing, be a long life without genuine ailments, and have a decent degree of physical and mental autonomy and satisfactory social connections.

Gathering information unmistakably exhibits that it is conceivable to impact the indications of maturing. Without a doubt, wholesome mediations can advance wellbeing and life span. A tribute must be given to Ansel Keys, who was the first to give strong logical proof about the job of sustenance in the wellbeing/sickness balance at the populace level, explicitly in connection to cardiovascular illness, still the main source of death overall. It is commonly valued that the sort of diet can significantly impact the quality and amount of life, and the Mediterranean eating regimen is paradigmatic of an advantageous dietary example. The developing cognizance of the useful impacts of a particular dietary example on wellbeing and life span in the second half of the remaining century produced a ground-breaking push toward structuring eating fewer carbs that could diminish the danger of constant maladies, subsequently bringing about solid maturing. Subsequently, during the 1990s, the Dietary Approaches to Stop Hypertension Dash diet was contrived to assess whether it was conceivable to treat hypertension, not pharmacologically. To be sure, the DASH diet was very like the Mediterranean Diet, being wealthy in foods grown from the ground, entire grains, and strands, while poor in creature-soaked fats and cholesterol. The awesome news leaving the investigation was that not exclusively did the DASH diet lower circulatory strain. However, it additionally diminished the danger of cardiovascular infection, type 2 diabetes, a few sorts of malignant growth, and other maturing related maladies. The Portfolio Diet was planned to improve the medical advantages of plant nourishment-rich, creature fat-terrible eating routines, especially in people with hypercholesterolemia. This eating regimen, other than being, to a great extent, veggie-lover, with just limited quantities of soaked fats, prescribes a high admission of utilitarian nourishments, including thick filaments, plant stools, soy proteins, and almonds likewise. Curiously, members on the Portfolio Diet displayed a decrease of coronary illness chance related to lower plasma cholesterol in contrast with members on a sound, for the most part, vegan diet.

Additionally, the measure of ingested nourishment has been pulling in light of a legitimate concern for mainstream researchers as a potential modifier of the harmony between wellbeing and infection in a wide range of living species. Specifically, calorie limitation CR has been exhibited as a rising healthful intercession that animates the counter maturing instruments in the body.

In this way, the eating routine of the individuals living on the Japanese island of Okinawa has been widely broken down because these islanders are notable for their life span and expanded wellbeing range, bringing about the best recurrence of centenarians on the planet. Interestingly, the customary Okinawan diet came about to be fundamentally the same as the Mediterranean Diet and the DASH diet regarding nourishment types. Be that as it may, the vitality admission of Okinawans, at the hour of the underlying logical perceptions, was about 20% lower than the normal vitality admission of the Japanese, along these lines deciding an average state of CR.

A famous singer has confirmed that she has lost 30 kilos in just one year. The secret? It's all thanks to the Sirtfood Diet. The singer revealed it through international media, such as the Daily Mail and the New York Post.

The Sirtfood Diet is not the classic fasting diet. It is, in fact, a diet that leaves room for both cheese and red wine as well as chocolate, in the right proportions, and of course under the supervision of a specialist doctor, who knows how to evaluate your health and recommend the most suitable diet to lose weight safely.

CHAPTER 2: PHASES OF THE SIRTFOOD DIET

The diet is divided into two phases: the first lasts one week, and the other lasts 14 days.

Phase 1 (The Most Effective): Three Kilos in Seven Days

It is the "supersonic" phase: the calorie restriction is combined with a diet rich in Sirt foods. The novelty compared to other diets is that it fattens and fattens the muscles. Two different moments. Days 1-3 are the most intense, and during this time, you can consume a maximum of one thousand calories per day. You must consume 3 Sirt green juices and a solid meal. On days 4-7 assigned the intake of one thousand five hundred calories daily. You have to take two green Sirt juices and two solid meals. Phase 1 is the most intense, in which the best results are seen, which allows you to lose up to 3.5 kilos. The maximum calories consumed during the first 3 days is 1000, while from the fourth to the seventh one reaches 1500 calories per day. The menu to follow includes a "fixed" part relating to green juice created by nutritionists that help to moderate the brain's appetite and varies daily.

The green juice recipe is simple and includes all-natural products: 75 g of curly kale, 30 g of arugula, and 5 g of parsley must be centrifuged, together with 150 g of green celery leaves 1/2 green apple, grated. Everything must be completed with half a squeezed lemon and half a teaspoon of Matcha tea.

Here is more in detail the program of the first week:

Monday - Wednesday: 3 Sirt green juices to be taken on waking up, mid-morning and mid-afternoon; 1 solid meal of animal or vegan protein (for example, turkey escalope or buckwheat noodles with tofu) accompanied by vegetables, always ending with 15-20 g of 85% dark chocolate.

Thursday - Sunday: 2 Sirt green juices and 2 solid meals, remembering to always vary the main course chosen, from salmon fillet to vegetable tabbouleh to buckwheat spaghetti with celery and kale.

Phase 2 (Maintenance), For 14 Days

Every day, for 14 days, you will eat three balanced meals, chock full of Sirt foods, drink a Sirt green juice, and consume 1-2 Sirt snacks. Green juice should be taken in the morning as soon as you wake up or at least 30 minutes before breakfast or mid-morning. The evening meal must be eaten by 7 pm.

Phase 2 is the maintenance phase. During this period, the goal is to consolidate weight loss, although the possibility of losing weight is not excluded. To do all this, just feed on the exceptional foods rich in Sirtuins. It lasts 14 days, it is less restrictive than the first and provides for Sirt foods at will: 3 solid meals plus two juices. The important thing is that they are balanced.

The positive aspects of this diet are: One is the fact that the calorie limit is indicative and not a goal to be achieved. Another advantage is that the dishes on offer are very satisfying. This way, you won't have the hunger attacks typical of other diets. The caloric restriction of the diet even in the most intensive phase is not drastic, and Sirt foods have a satiating effect, which prevents us from getting hungry at meals

And then?

As already explained in the introduction, the Sirtfood diet cannot (and must not) continue indefinitely and for a very long time. Rather, it must be done in cycles, once, two, or three times a year. However, the Sirt "lifestyle" can continue even after completing the phase. Sirt foods can be eaten all year round, continuing to speed up the metabolism. However, this should not be combined with a very strong calorie restriction, but only avoid eating unhealthy foods, such as fried, sweet, or unsaturated fats. Your persistence will make the difference between success and failure; remember, this is not a shot but a marathon!

Sirt cycles are simply a boost, a powerful weapon in your arsenal that you can use twice a year (depending on your body, of course). Still, you can have a healthy lifestyle all year round, perhaps combined with regular physical exercise.

Phase 3 (Make the Sirt Food Diet For Life)

For 1 week, the participants followed the diet and exercised daily. At the end of the week, participants lost an average of 7 pounds (3.2 kg) and maintained or even gained muscle mass.

Yet, these results are hardly surprising. Restricting your calorie intake to 1,000 calories and exercising simultaneously will nearly always cause weight loss. Regardless, this kind of quick weight loss is neither genuine nor long-lasting, and this study did not follow participants after the first week to see if they gained any weight back, which is typically the case.

When your body is energy-deprived, it uses up its emergency energy stores, or glycogen, in addition to burning fat and muscle. Each molecule of glycogen requires 3–4 molecules of water to be stored. When your body uses up glycogen, it gets rid of this water as well. It's known as "water weight."

In the first week of extreme calorie restriction, only about one-third of the weight loss comes from fat, while the other two-thirds come from water, muscle, and glycogen. As soon as your calorie intake increases, your body replenishes its glycogen stores, and the weight comes right back. Unfortunately, this type of calorie restriction can also cause your body to lower its metabolic rate, causing you to need even fewer calories per day for energy than before. This diet may likely help you lose a few pounds initially, but it'll likely come back as soon as the diet is over. 3 weeks is probably not long enough to have any measurable long-term impact as far as preventing disease. On the other hand, adding Sirtfoods to your regular diet over the long term may very well be a good idea. But in that case, you might as well skip the diet and start doing that now.

CHAPTER 3: THE BEST 20 SIRTFOODS

Arugula

This green salad leaf (also known as rucola) is very common in the Mediterranean diet. It is not too popular in the US food culture, and it is considered an absolute arrogance to have it on your plate. However, we are not talking about a leaf covered in gold or silver; we are talking about a green salad leaf with a peppery taste that can be used for digestive and diuretic purposes. During ancient Rome and in the Middle Ages, this leaf was known to have aphrodisiac properties. However, there is a lot more to this miracle leaf. It has nutrients like quercetin and kaempferol capable of activating sirtuins. This combination is said to have very positive effects on the skin as it can moisturize and improve collagen synthesis. So why not have this leaf in your salad and add some extra olive oil to it, making it a powerful Sirtfood duo? As you can see, it has many positive effects on your body.

Buckwheat

This is one of the best sources for rutin, a sirtuin-activator nutrient. However, this crop is also amazing for ecological and sustainable farming, as it can improve the quality of the soil and prevent weed growth. However, the most interesting part about buckwheat is that it is a fruit seed, like rhubarb, so it is not a grain. It is not a coincidence at all that buckwheat has more protein than any grain known to man, so it fits perfectly in your Sirtfood diet. For every person trying to avoid gluten, this can be the ideal food. It is the ideal alternative for grains.

Capers

Some of you may not be too familiar with capers. If you have not had the chance to taste them, you should. They are those dark-green salty things you can sometimes see on top of a pizza. Unfortunately, capers are not very used in a standard diet (it is very overlooked and underrated), but those who never had the chance to try capers do not know what they are missing. We are talking about the flower buds of the caper bush, a plant growing abundantly in the Mediterranean region. It is usually handpicked and preserved, and it has some interesting antidiabetic, anti-inflammatory, antimicrobial, antiviral, and immunomodulatory properties. Moreover, it has been used in medicine all around the Mediterranean area.

Celery

This is a plant used for thousands of years, as in ancient Egypt, people were already aware of it and its properties. Back then, it was considered a medicinal plant used for detoxing, cleansing, and preventing diseases. Therefore, celery consumption is very good for your gut, kidney, and liver. When it was growing wildly in ancient times, it had a strong bitter flavor. However, ever since its domestication in the 17th century, celery has become a bit sweeter, and now it can be used in salads.

Chilies

This veggie should be in your diet whether you like eating spicy food or not. It contains capsaicin, and this substance makes us savor it even more. Consuming chilies is great for activating sirtuins, and it speeds up your metabolism. The spicier the chili is, the more powerful it is when it comes to activating sirtuins. You probably heard that people eating spicy food three or four times per week have a 14 percent lower death rate than people who eat them less than once a week. This does not mean that you have to go for the hottest chilies you can find, especially if you are not a spicy food enthusiast. Take it easy at the beginning.

Cocoa

The Aztecs and Mayans considered Cocoa sacred, and it was a food type reserved only for the warriors or the elite. It was often used as a currency, as people were aware of its value. Although it was mostly used as a drink back then, you do not have to dilute it with milk or water to reap the full benefits. The best way to consume cocoa is by eating dark chocolate (with at least 85 percent solid cocoa). However, this also depends on how the chocolate is made, as this product is usually treated with an alkalizing agent, which is known to lower the acidity of the chocolate and give it a darker color. This substance is also known to reduce the sirtuin-activating flavanols.

Coffee

This is a drink enjoyed by most adults out there, and it is considered indispensable by most of them. We even believe that we can function without a cup of coffee to start within the morning. That is not true, but we can honestly believe that coffee significantly improves our productivity and daily activities. Caffeine acid is a nutrient known to activate sirtuins, so there is more to drinking coffee than a popular and very pleasant social activity.

Extra-Virgin Olive Oil

This oil is perhaps the healthiest form of fats you can think of, and it is not missing from any salad in the Mediterranean diet. The health benefits of consuming this oil are countless. It prevents and fights against diabetes, different types of cancer, osteoporosis, and many more. Besides, extra-virgin olive oil can be associated with increased longevity, as it also has anti-aging effects. You can easily find this type of oil in most supermarkets, so you do not have any excuse to exclude it from your Sirtfood diet. This oil has the right nutrients to activate the sirtuin gene in your body.

Garlic

I do not know about you people, but I am simply in love with garlic. I am sure I am not the only one. Forget about the smell it leaves behind. Enjoy the great taste it offers. I would have garlic with any meal. Of course, this may not fit with our busy lifestyle, as it is not recommended to have it before a meeting, but you can enjoy it for dinner or at home. However, there is more to the consumption of garlic. As you probably know, it has an antifungal and antibiotic effect and has been successfully used to treat stomach ulcers. Also, it can be used to remove waste products from your body.

Green Tea

In some cultures, drinking tea is as popular as drinking coffee, but find the tea assortment that works best for you. You can indeed have tea from various medicinal plants, and they all have positive effects on your health. However, most of these plants are focused on preventing or fighting a specific disease. Have you ever thought about drinking tea for your well-being or to feel great? Well, this is what green tea is for. It first appeared in Asia; green tea has become very popular in Western culture. It has plenty of antioxidants. It can be used for detox, and it speeds up your metabolism.

Kale

You can never go wrong with some leafy greens, and this is applicable for kale as well. Perhaps not many of you have tried it before, but it is worth it. Over the last few years, kale has gained a lot of popularity and appreciation from both nutritionists and consumers, and they have all the reasons to like and appreciate it.

Medjool Dates

If you have the chance to go to any country in the Middle East or the Arabian Peninsula, you will find that dates are a very common snack. Dehydrated, covered in chocolate, or a fresher form, dates are perhaps the most common snack you can find over there.

Parsley

The parsley leaves are extremely frequent in recipes, so it is not missing from the Sirtfood diet. You can chop them and toss them in your meal or use a sprig for decorative purposes. But parsley is not for decorating your plate, as you are not trying to impress a jury of famous chefs. This is an underrated plant.

Red Endive

This vegetable is one of the latest discoveries in the world of plants. How come? It was discovered by accident in 1830 when a Belgian farmer who stored chicory roots in his cellar forgot about them and discovered them with white leaves that happened to be crunchy, tender, and delicious.

Red Onions

If you are only eating onions as O-rings with your burger, then you had better rethink the way you consume this incredible vegetable. This type of onion has a sweeter taste (compared to yellow onion). It has plenty of antioxidants, and it is known to fight against inflammation, heart diseases, and diabetes.

Red Wine

The Mediterranean diet encourages the consumption of red wine, and there are plenty of reasons why you should consider moderate consumption of it. We are not going to talk about its effects on your blood, blood sugar level, and so on. Not even about how moderate consumption can decrease the death rates by heart disease. Alternatively, about how red wine can prevent common colds and cavities (yes, it can even improve your oral health). Red wines like Merlot, Cabernet Sauvignon, or Pinot Noir have an incredible concentration of polyphenol to activate your sirtuins.

Soy

There is a completely food-processing industry behind soy, as it creates food products for vegetarians. However, let us face it — drinking soymilk will not activate your sirtuins. Industrially processed food is not very recommended for your health, so it should be excluded from your Sirtfood diet. In natural form, soy contains formononetin and daidzein, two great sirtuin-activating nutrients.

Strawberries

Of all the fruits out there, strawberries are among the ones with the most health benefits. Yes, they are sweet, but they happen to have a very high concentration of fisetin, a nutrient that can activate sirtuins. What is very confusing is that strawberries are known to prevent heart diseases, diabetes, cancer, osteoporosis, and Alzheimer's disease. They are even associated with healthy aging. Although they are sweet, 3½ ounces of strawberries only contain a teaspoon of sugar.

Turmeric

You are probably familiar with ginger's effects on your overall health, but you do not know what turmeric can do for you. This plant is related to ginger, and it is very appreciated throughout Asia for medical and culinary reasons. India is responsible for 80 percent of the whole turmeric on the planet, and some nutritionists refer to it as the "golden spice" or "India's gold." Why is that? Because it contains curcumin, a very rare sirtuin-activating nutrient.

Walnuts

As it happens, the walnut tree is the oldest food tree known to humans, as it was discovered around 7,000 BCE. Its original location was in ancient Persia (modern-day Iran), and now this tree is spread worldwide, as it can easily adapt to different climates of the globe. In the United States, walnuts are a success story. California is the biggest producer of walnuts in the United States, responsible for 99 percent of the US commercial supply and three-quarters of the walnut trade worldwide.

CHAPTER 4: FREQUENTLY ASKED QUESTIONS

Can Children Eat Sirtfoods?

There are powerful Sirtfoods, most of which are safe for children. Children should avoid wine, coffee, and other highly caffeinated foods, such as matcha. On the other hand, children can enjoy sirtuin-rich foods such as cabbage, eggplant, blueberries, and dates with their regular balanced diet.

Yet, while children can enjoy most sirtuin-rich foods, that is not the same as saying that they can practice the Sirt diet. This diet plan is not designed for children, and it does not fit the needs of their growing bodies. Practicing this diet plan could negatively affect them physically, but it could damage their mental health for years to come. Anyone can develop an eating disorder, but it is especially true for children. If you want your child to eat well, ensure they eat a wide range of foods, as recommended by their doctor, and you can simply include an abundance of sirtuin-rich foods into what they are already eating. Leave the focus on eating healthfully and not losing weight. Even if your child's doctor wants them to lose weight, you don't need to make the child aware of it. You can help guide them along with a healthy lifestyle, teaching them how to eat well and stay active through sports and play, and the weight will come off naturally without placing an unneeded burden on their small shoulders.

For similar reasons, you can include Sirtfoods in a balanced diet while pregnant, but you should avoid practicing the Sirt diet when you are pregnant. It doesn't contain the nutrition requirements for either a pregnant woman or a growing baby. Save the diet for after you have delivered a healthy baby, and both you and your child will be healthy and happy.

Can I Exercise During Phase One?

If you use exercise during either phase one or two, you can increase weight loss and health benefits. While you shouldn't push the limits during phase one, you can continue your normal workout routine and physical activity. It is important to stay within your active comfort zone during this time, as physical exertion more than you are accustomed to will be especially difficult while restricting your calories. It will not only wear you out, but it can also make you dizzy, more prone to injury, and physically and mentally exhausted. This is a common symptom whenever a person pushes their limits while restricting calories, but you should avoid it.

Keep it up if you are used to doing yoga and a spin class a few times a week! If you are used to running a few miles a day, have at it! Do what you and your body are comfortable with, and as your doctor advises, you should be fine.

I'm Already Thin. Can I Still Follow the Diet?

Whether or not you can follow the first phase of the Sirt diet will depend on just how thin you already are. While a person who is overweight or well within a healthy weight can practice the first phase, nobody who is clinically underweight should. You can know whether or not you are underweight by calculating your Body Mass Index or BMI. You can find many BMI calculators online, and if yours is at nineteen points or below, you should avoid the first phase.

It is always good to ask your doctor if it is safe to lose weight and if the Sirt diet is safe for your condition. While the Sirt diet may generally be safe for people with certain illnesses, it may not be the case.

While it is understandable to desire to be even more thin, even if you already are thin, pushing yourself past the point of being underweight is incredibly unhealthy, both physically and mentally. This fits into the category of disordered eating and can cause you a lot of harm.

Some of the side effects of pushing your body to extreme weight loss include bone loss and osteoporosis, lowered immune system, fertility problems, and increased disease risk. If you want to benefit from the health of the Sirt diet and are underweight, instead consume however many calories your doctor recommends, along with plenty of Sirtfoods. This will ensure you maintain a healthy weight while also receiving the benefits that sirtuins have to offer.

If you are thin but still at a BMI of twenty to twenty-five, then you should be safe beginning the Sirt diet unless otherwise instructed by your doctor.

Can You Eat Meat and Dairy On The Sirtfood Diet?

In many recipes, we use Sirtfood sources, such as soy, walnuts, and buckwheat. However, this does not mean that you aren't allowed to enjoy meat on the Sirt diet. Sure, it's easy to enjoy a vegan or vegetarian Sirt diet, but if you love your sources of meat, then you don't have to give them up. Protein is an essential aspect of the Sirt diet to preserve muscle tone, and whether you consume only plant-based proteins or a mixture of plant and animal-based proteins is completely up to you. And, just as you can enjoy meat, you can also enjoy moderate consumption of dairy.

Some meats can help you better utilize the Sirtfoods you eat. This is because the amino acid leucine can enhance the effect of Sirtfoods. You can find this amino acid in chicken, beef, pork, fish, eggs, dairy, and tofu.

Can I Drink Red Wine during Phase One?

As your calories will be limited during the first phase, it is not recommended to drink alcohol. However, you can enjoy it in moderation during phase two and the maintenance phase.

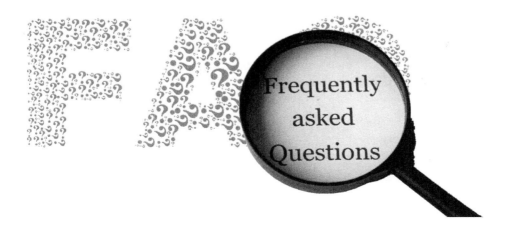

CHAPTER 5: SIRTFOOD FOR BUILDING MUSCLE

Sirtuins are a group of proteins with different effects. Sirt-1 is the protein responsible for causing the body to burn fat rather than muscle for energy, which is a miracle for weight loss. Another useful aspect of Sirt-1 is its ability to improve skeletal muscle.

Skeletal muscle is all the muscles you voluntarily control, such as the muscles in your limbs, back, shoulders, and so on. There are two other types; cardiac muscle is what the heart is formed of, while the smooth muscle is your involuntary muscles – which includes muscles around your blood vessels, face, and various parts of organs and other tissues.

Skeletal muscle is separated into two different groups, the blandly named type-1 and type-2. Type 1 muscle is effective at continued, sustained activity, whereas type-2 muscle is effective at short, intense periods of activity. So, for example, you would predominantly use type-1 muscles for jogging but type-2 muscles for sprinting.

Sirt-1 protects the type-1 muscles, but not the type-2 muscle, which is still broken down for energy. Therefore, holistic muscle mass drops when fasting, even though type-1 skeletal muscle mass increases.

Sirt-1 also influences how the muscles work. Sirt-1 is produced by the muscle cells, but the ability to produce Sirt-1 decreases as the muscle ages. As a result, muscle is harder to build as you age and doesn't grow as fast in response to exercise. A lack of Sirt-1 also causes the muscles to become tired quicker and gradually decline over time.

When you start to consider these effects of Sirt-1, you can start to form a picture of why fasting helps keep the body supple. Fasting releases Sirt-1, which in turn helps skeletal muscle grow and stay in good shape. Sirt-1 is also released by consuming Sirtuin activators, giving the Sirtfood diet its muscle retaining power.

Who Should Try the Sirtfood Diet?

The Sirtfood diet is suitable for individuals who:

→ Are overweight or obese

→ Want to maintain his/her weight

→ Needs to have a "detox" and flush away the toxins from the body

→ Have failed to lose weight using different diet techniques

→ Want not only to lose weight but also build muscle

→ Want a healthier lifestyle and to achieve optimal health

Health Risks for Overweight and Obesity

➢ **Type 2 Diabetes** - This disease occurs when the blood sugar level becomes higher than normal. According to studies, about 80% of individuals who have Type 2 diabetes are overweight. What makes diabetes a killer disease is that it is a major cause of stroke, heart disease, kidney disease, amputation, and even blindness.

➢ **Sleep Apnea** - This is when an individual pauses in breathing while sleeping. Being overweight or obese is a risk factor. Why? This is because the fats stored in the neck area make the air pathway smaller. Besides, the fat could also cause inflammation. Sleep apnea should not be taken lightly because it can also result in heart failure.

➢ **High Blood Pressure** - Also known as hypertension, this condition refers to a state when your systolic blood pressure (usually above 140) is consistently higher than your diastolic blood pressure (usually about 90). How does being overweight make you a high risk for hypertension? Generally, larger body size will increase your blood pressure so that your heart will have to work harder to produce the necessary supply of blood to all cells. Also, your excess body fats can damage your kidneys (your kidney helps your body regulate blood pressure). High blood pressure can result in kidney failure, heart disease, and stroke.

➢ **Fatty Liver Disease** - This is when there is a build-up of fat around the liver which can cause damage.

➢ **Reproductive issues** - Menstrual issues and ultimately infertility are some of the issues experienced by overweight women.

➢ **Cancer** - If you are obese or overweight, the risk of acquiring breast cancer, gallbladder, colon, and endometrial cancer increases.

These are only some of the diseases associated with being overweight. Not to mention the social, emotional, and psychological impact of the extra weight.

It stresses the importance of finding the right "strategy" to lose those excess pounds. And we have the perfect solution –the Sirtfood diet.

Are You Familiar With These Scenarios?

You know that you have overindulged during the holidays, but as you weigh yourself, you literally would want to shave all the extra pounds because you did not expect to have gained that much weight!

There is an upcoming wedding event, and you need to lose those extra pounds to fit into your gown/suit. There is no way that you are going to lose that much weight in 2 months!

You know that you are overweight and just plain unhealthy. You have already tried many diets but to no avail. Either you feel that those diets are too restrictive, there is an adverse health effect, and the diet is too expensive to maintain. Speaking of maintenance, you are having a hard time keeping off the little weight that you have managed to lose!

You are getting older, and you start to notice that aside from having a hard time dealing with hangovers and late-night parties, losing and maintaining weight is not that easy as it used to be. You are not a big fan of eliminating numerous food groups and doing rigorous exercise.

You have probably heard these scenarios too many times before, and you have probably experienced one or two, or you are in one of these scenarios right now. Being overweight or obese is one of the most common health problems around the world. According to the World Health Organization (WHO), being overweight is when your BMI is equal to or greater than 25, while being obese is when your BMI is equal to or greater than 30.

In the 2014 data from WHO, worldwide obesity has doubled since 1980, and more than 1.9 billion adults are overweight. It would be safe to conclude that after two years that that number has already increased significantly.

Health experts agree that this is a very alarming rate, but the good news is, obesity or having excess weight is preventable and reversible.

As you will notice, most of these scenarios are focused on aesthetics—looking good and feeling more confident about your body, but what I would like to stress is the ill effects of every extra bulge or pound that we carry. The possible health illnesses associated with being overweight are the primary reason you need to try the revolutionary SirtFood diet.

CHAPTER 6: BENEFITS OF SIRTFOOD DIET

Fight Fat

The problem with most diets is that you will return to your unhealthy eating habits and regain weight once you stop eating junk food. This has happened to many people after stopping their diet. The real challenge is maintaining your weight if you are satisfied with your weight loss so far.

The Sirtfood diet also controls appetite, and I don't mean the mind control that fasting encourages. The increase in leptin satisfies us as it reduces our hunger. It makes sense, right? Leptin is important as it is the hormone responsible for regulating appetite. This should keep you from asking for more food, but in the case of obesity, leptin may not do its job properly. Due to the hypothalamus, the brain does not feel that the body is well nourished and constantly wants more food, as the brain somehow believes that the body is malnourished. This condition is called leptin resistance.

Build Muscle Mass

When people say they want to lose weight, they are referring to fat loss and not muscle. Fat is lighter than muscle, but we all want to have an optimal BMI, right? There is a myth that a certain amount of protein is needed to maintain muscle mass. Well, that's not entirely true. In the case of fasting, growth hormone reaches incredibly high levels after 72 hours of pure fasting so that you can maintain and even increase your muscle mass due to calorie deprivation. It's not healthy to be on a very long fasting period, but what if you find the right ingredients to eat and have the same benefits?

When you are on a high carbohydrate diet, you are not building muscle. You are accumulating fat. However, the Sirtfood diet is not rich in carbohydrates. It is rich in sirtuins, a very healthy type of protein. The founders of this diet claim that you will lose seven pounds in seven days. However, food must create the right environment to build or maintain muscle mass, which this diet does. Besides, muscles are important for your mobility and prevent chronic diseases such as osteoporosis or diabetes. Believe it or not, muscles can even have a psychological advantage, as they are known to fight depression. Yes, you will feel great about yourself when you look sporty.

SIRT1 can maintain muscle mass even when fasting and can even increase your muscle mass. Muscles are made up of various cells, including the satellite cell, activated when the muscle is damaged or stressed. If you do some weight training, putting pressure on the muscle, your muscles will grow because of the satellite cell. However, the satellite cell can only be activated by SIRT1. Otherwise, your muscles won't grow, develop, or regenerate properly.

To better comprehend the significance of sirtuins, particularly SIRT1, have in mind that without them, your muscles are prone to inflammation and fatigue—muscles age without sirtuin activity. Therefore, for muscles to function properly, they need SIRT1. Muscles do not improve over time, like wine. Keep in mind that the effects of muscle aging can begin at age 25. By the time you reach 40, you have already lost 10 percent of your muscle mass, and by the time you are 70, you have already lost 40 percent of your muscle mass. However, this can be prevented and reversed through the activity of sirtuin. Therefore, they can easily be considered regulators of muscle growth and prevention.

Fight Diseases

The modern-day eating habits and lifestyle encourage the accumulation of fats and toxins (fat tissue protects the toxins) and the increase of blood sugar and insulin level. This is where the trouble starts, from a simple pre-diabetes condition to more serious diseases (it can eventually lead to cancer). However, the antidote to many of these issues lies hidden within ourselves. As you already know, all bodies possess sirtuin genes, and activating them is crucial to burn fat and to build a stronger and leaner body.

As it turns out, the benefits of sirtuins activity extend way beyond the fat-burning process. Whether we like it or not, the lack of sirtuins can be associated with many diseases and medical conditions. Naturally, activating sirtuins will have the opposite effect. For example, sirtuins can improve your heart health by protecting the muscle cells in your heart and improving the function of the heart muscle. But that's not all. Sirtuins can play a major role in improving the function of your arteries, controlling cholesterol levels, and preventing atherosclerosis.

By now, you are familiar with the effects of fasting and an LCHF diet on the insulin level, and you are probably wondering what sirtuins can do in this case. If you have diabetes, you should know that activating sirtuins will make insulin work more effectively to do its job properly (regulating the blood sugar level). SIRT1 works perfectly with metformin (one of the most powerful antidiabetic drugs). As it turns out, pharmaceutical companies are adding sirtuin activators to metformin treatments. These studies were conducted on animals, and the results were simply amazing. It was noticed that an 83 percent reduction of the metformin dose is required to achieve the same effects.

Other diets or programs are bragging about their effects on neurodegenerative diseases, like Alzheimer's disease. Well, let's think about what sirtuins do! They send a message to the brain, helping it make the right decisions regarding appetite suppression. This involves enhancing the communication signals in the brain, improving cognitive function, and lowering brain inflammation. Sirtuin activation stops the tau protein aggregation and amyloid B production, some of the most damaging things in the brains of Alzheimer's patients.

The benefits of sirtuins expand to bones as well, as they encourage the production of osteoblast cells (the ones responsible for strengthening your bones) and increase their survival. In other words, sirtuin activation is very important for overall bone health.

We all know that the food we eat today can even lead to cancer, as we are eating small portions of poison. Diets are claiming that they represent the cure for cancer in a nascent form, but at the moment, we can't say this about Sirtfoods, as there are still plenty of studies to be done on this topic. However, it is fair to say that people who eat mostly Sirtfoods have the lowest cancer rates.

Losing weight is simply not enough nowadays, as the diet you have to follow needs to have plenty of health benefits as well; otherwise, you can't stick to it in the long run. Therefore, you need to see the bigger picture and not focus on losing many pounds in a very short amount of time. The less processed food you eat, the more chances you will have to experience the health benefits from your meal plan, so you don't have to see a doctor very often.

Natural ingredients have a lot of vitamins and minerals. They have a very high nutritional value. Coincidence or not, sirtuins can mostly be found in such ingredients (essentially fruits and veggies). Therefore, you will need to unleash these benefits on your body by consuming these amazing ingredients daily.

Anti-Aging Effect

Anti-aging is somehow linked to autophagy, an intracellular process of repairing or replacing damaged cell parts. This is rejuvenation at an intracellular level. However, a part of this response is the lysosomal degradation pathway autophagy. Now you are probably wondering what sirtuins have to do with all of these. Well, SIRT1 can activate AMPK (and the other way around), so it can be considered one of the triggers of autophagy. But I'm going to spare you all the chemical details that you can't remember. You need to know that autophagy rejuvenates the cell, and this process can happen in all the cells of your body—starting from the ones of your internal organs to the ones of your skin.

There are a few ways to induce autophagy, and it has a very positive effect on your health and overall lifespan. Just think of the cell as a car, and autophagy is the skilled mechanic capable of fixing or replacing any broken parts in it. The cell will have a longer life, and this extrapolates to your overall life. If your cells function properly, like a Swiss mechanical clock, you can expect increased longevity. You can't reverse aging, as there is no such cure for it, and autophagy is not "the fountain of youth." However, this process can significantly slow down aging and its effect. And the best part is that sirtuins, especially SIRT1, can activate it.

So far, people were not aware of too many ways to trigger autophagy. Some of them were doing it the hard way through intermittent fasting. Others were trying to induce it through an LCHF diet, like the keto diet. Well, now there is an extra way to activate it, and that is through the Sirtfood diet.

Here is a list of other benefits of the Sirtfood Diet:

- ♥ Promotes fat loss, not muscle loss
- ♥ You will not regain weight after the end of the diet
- ♥ You will look better; you will feel better, and you will have more energy
- ♥ You will avoid fasting and feeling hungry
- ♥ You will not have to undergo exhausting physical exercises
- ♥ This diet promotes longer, healthier life and keeps diseases away.

The benefits of the Sirtfood Diet are many, besides obviously that of slimming. Activators of sirtuins would lead to noticeable muscle building, decreased appetite, and improved memory. Also, the Sirtfood Diet normalizes the sugar level in the blood and can cleanse the cells from the accumulation of harmful free radicals.

CHAPTER 7: SIRTFOOD DIET AND ITS' SCIENCE

Do you think that is the typical seasonal fad or hype diet doomed to disappear? Well, then you are wrong! This diet is thought of as a lifestyle and not as a diet to lose only weight. Like other diets, i.e., the ketogenic one, the Sirtfood diet is based on scientifically proven activation mechanisms for the body's natural slimming. Moreover, it allows for eating special foods like wine and chocolate the right way, thus not renouncing the taste pleasure.

The Sirtfood diet has been proven to give many benefits:

- ♥ Slowed aging, better metabolism, and improved circadian rhythm thanks to the consumption of food that actives the SIRT receptors stimulating your cells to repair and rejuvenate your body.

- ♥ SIRT receptor activation by sirtuins regulate the metabolism of glucose and fat by acting protein functioning mechanisms

- ♥ Sirtuins in many foods can create effects similar to fasting and exercise and keep your body clean, thus eliminating any urge to eat junk foods. Moreover, these foods (like dark chocolate and red wine) are rich in antioxidants helping your body detox.

- ♥ Activation of the "skinny gene," which boosts your metabolism and helps you burn fat; indeed, sirtuins are generally called "longevity genes."

Sirtuin protein is stimulated by sirtfood consumption, which is known to affect the circadian rhythm. This is a cyclic physiological process part of all living beings that takes place for 24 hours which regulates your sleep cycle, hormonal level, and *appetite*, thus having an important role in your health. The circadian system regulates energy metabolism, oxidative stress, inflammation, cellular proliferation, and senescence, thus impacting metabolism-related diseases, chronic airway diseases, and cancers (Zhou et al., 2020). Indeed, an unhealthy diet and lifestyle, like spending a lot of time in front of screens, eating junk foods, and being sleep deprived, leads to your hormones' misbalance. The consequences are a misfunction of your metabolism, mood, and overall mental state with uncontrolled appetite. So many celebrities choose this diet because they want a better life in their super busy lifestyle. But that's true also for folks who find eating habits and regular exercise are difficult to apply to their busy schedule. Exercise and lifestyle have an important role in weight loss, but the key factor is the diet since it is the main source to get the right nutrients to give your body strength. A permanent weight loss needs the right diet, and the Sirtfood diet can twist you with all the convenience and satisfaction of a regular, healthy diet.

'Sirtuins' or SIRT are a protein family of adenine dinucleotide (NAD+)-dependent histone deacetylases, which have been demonstrated to regulate a series of physiological processes and affect diseases such as obesity, insulin resistance, type 2 diabetes, cancer, heart disease, and aging (Zhou et al., 2020).

Sirtfoods are accessible to everyone. Thus, you can easily increase your body's SIRT level. The natural substances found in these foods boost your "skinny gene" activator level (sirtuins) by eating easy-to-find foods like kale, strawberries, parsley, onions, olive oil, walnuts, and others. As you can see, there's nothing particularly special or difficult for you to do or eat to follow this diet.

The sirtfood diet is composed of only two phases. The first one is the most challenging and lasts in one week, and the latter is slightly easier, which is two weeks. At the end of the diet, you can choose between returning to your regular diet or continuing to eat Sirtfoods as long as you want. The good news is there is no limit in the number of sirtfoods you can eat since they all have healthy properties and are beneficial for your health.

Goggins & Matten (2017) are the creators, and they ran a small pilot study on this diet at the end of which all of the participants lost over 7lb in 7 days. During the week, they lost an average of 3.2 kg without losing muscle mass, which is generally the cause of initial weight loss in a regular diet, but without losing fat. Indeed, to compensate for the lack of calorie supply, your body starts to get rid first of the excess water and then starts burning your muscle tissue to produce energy.

The Sirtfood diet led to burn fat quicker without producing any study participants' muscle mass loss. The significant weight loss derived from the phase one and two of the diet is the most challenging.

Like the ketogenic diet, when your body needs energy, it starts to eliminate the excess of water first, and then it uses the glycogen stored and finally attacks the fat. This is what happens in the Sirtfood diet first phase. At this point, a third of the weight lost will be from fat, and the other lost pounds could come back after water and glycogen deposit reconstitution.

The primary two stages of the diet are fundamental to activating your metabolism. On the other hand, the third phase aims to maintain the weight loss permanently. Sirtuins contained in foods will boost your metabolism for a long time. Making the Sirtfood diet a lifestyle will experience a noticeable change in your health with high benefits.

To highlight the importance of sirtuins in science, I want to give you just some little pills about recent research based on them:

→ Sirtuins play a pivotal role in regulating tumor cell metabolism, proliferation, migration, and angiogenesis. In the cell, they act as redox sensors, and their activities are dependent on the cell's metabolic status. Researchers are studying the regulatory mechanisms adopted by sirtuins to develop new therapeutic strategies against angiogenesis, metastasis, and tumor progression (Edatt et al., 2020).

→ The available research evidence indicates that sirtuins have great potential as novel therapeutic targets for preventing and treating kidney diseases. Indeed, sirtuins are fundamental to numerous biological processes, including proliferation, DNA repair, mitochondrial energy homeostasis, and antioxidant activity (Hong et al., 2020).

→ In the last years, scientists have increasingly recognized sirtuins to have a significant role in the regulation of stem cell biology, in addition to their well-known roles in metabolism and aging. It has been demonstrated to have functions in pluripotent stem cells, embryogenesis, and development and their roles in adult stem cell maintenance, regeneration, and aging. (Fang et al., 2019).

→ Based on the available literature, the sirtuins appear to be essential targets in managing various skin diseases from cosmetic (e.g., skin aging) to fatal conditions (e.g., melanoma). Sirtuins are intricately involved in multiple essential and skin-relevant cellular functions and processes, including aging, UV damage response, oxidative stress, and wound repair (Garcia-Peterson et al., 2017).

References

✓ Zhou S, Dai YM, Zeng XF, Chen HZ. Circadian Clock and Sirtuins in Diabetic Lung: A Mechanistic Perspective. Front Endocrinol (Lausanne). 2020; 11:173. DOI: 10.3389/fendo.2020.00173.

✓ Edatt L, Poyyakkara A, Raji GR, Ramachandran V, Shankar SS, Kumar VBS. Role of Sirtuins in Tumor Angiogenesis. Front Oncol. 2020; 9:1516. DOI: 10.3389/fonc.2019.01516.

✓ Hong YA, Kim JE, Jo M, Ko GJ. The Role of Sirtuins in Kidney Diseases. Int J Mol Sci. 2020;21(18):6686. DOI: 10.3390/ijms21186686.

✓ Fang Y, Tang S, Li X. Sirtuins in Metabolic and Epigenetic Regulation of Stem Cells. Trends Endocrinol Metab. 2019;30(3):177-188. DOI: 10.1016/j.tem.2018.12.002.

✓ Garcia-Peterson LM, Wilking-Busch MJ, Ndiaye MA, Philippe CGA, Setaluri V, Ahmad N. Sirtuins in Skin and Skin Cancers. Skin Pharmacol Physiol. 2017;30(4):216-224. DOI: 10.1159/000477417

CHAPTER 8: SHOPPING LIST

All these would be the highest-rated 20 foods to get a Sirtfood-rich diet program and ways to incorporate them into your everyday meals.

- ✓ **Earth's - Eye Chili.** Additionally, sold as Thai chilies, they truly are stronger than ordinary chilies and packed with more nutritional elements. Utilize them to increase sour or sweet recipes.
- ✓ **Buckwheat.** Strictly a pseudo-grain: it's a berry seed linked to rhubarb. Additionally, accessible noodle shape (like soba) ensures that you're getting the wheat-free edition.
- ✓ **Capers.** If you are wondering, then they are pickled flower buds. Sprinkle them a salad or roasted steaks.
- ✓ **Celery.** The leaves and hearts would be the most healthful part, and thus do not throw them off if you are mixing a shakeup.
- ✓ **Chicory.** Red is most beneficial, but yellowish works too. Include it in a salad.
- ✓ **Cocoa.** The flavonol-rich type enhances blood pressure, blood glucose cholesterol, and control. Search to get a high proportion of cacao.
- ✓ **Coffee.** Drink it shameful – there are some signs that milk can lower the absorption of sirtuin-activating nutritional elements.
- ✓ **Extra Virgin Steak Oil.** The extra-virgin type includes more Sirt benefits and also a far more pleasing flavor.
- ✓ **Green Tea or Matcha.** Add a piece of lemon juice to raise the absorption of sirtuin-producing nutritional elements. Matcha is much better, but go Japanese, not Chinese, to avoid potential lead contamination.
- ✓ **Kale.** Includes huge levels of sirtuin-activating nutrition quercetin and kaempferol. Scrub it with coconut oil and lemon juice serve it as a salad.
- ✓ **Lovage.** It is a herb. Grow your personal onto a window sill and throw it into stirfries.
- ✓ **Medjool Dates.** They truly are a hefty 66 percent glucose, however in moderation – they do not raise glucose levels, also have been connected to reduced levels of diabetes and cardiovascular disease.
- ✓ **Parsley.** More than only a garnish – it's saturated in apigenin. Throw into a juice or smoothie for the complete benefit. Chicory Red is most beneficial, but yellowish functions fine. Throw it in a salad.
- ✓ **Red Onion.** The reddish variety is healthier and sweet enough to eat raw. Stir it and put it into a salad or eat it with a hamburger.
- ✓ **Red Wine.** You've been aware of resveratrol: the fantastic news is that it is heat stable, which means it's possible to benefit from cooking together with it (in addition to glugging it directly). Pinot noir has got the maximum content.
- ✓ **Rocket.** One among the very least interfered-with salad greens out there. Drizzle it with olive oil.
- ✓ **Soy.** Soybeans and miso are saturated in sirtuin activators. Include it in stirfries.
- ✓ **Strawberries.** Though they are sweet, they simply comprise 1tsp. Of sugar per 100g – and research suggests that they improve the ability to manage carbonated carbohydrates.
- ✓ **Turmeric.** Evidence suggests the curcumin inside its anti-cancer properties. It's difficult for your human body to assimilate alone; however, cooking it into fluid and including black pepper increases absorption.
- ✓ **Walnuts.** Full of calories and fat, but well recognized in lessening metabolic disorder. Mash them up with a skillet to get a sirt-flavored pesto.

Only a reminder of this scientific backdrop into the Sirtfood diet regime.

Sirtfoods are the revolutionary way of triggering our sirtuin genes in the finest way possible. All these are miracle foods, especially full of specific all-natural plant compounds, called polyphenols, that possess the capability to trigger our sirtuin genes by changing them. Essentially, they mimic the results of exercise and fasting. Doing this brings notable benefits by helping the system better control glucose levels, burn fat, build muscle, and promote memory and health.

Because they're stationary, plants also have developed an extremely complex stress-response system and produce antioxidants to help them conform to the challenges in their environment. Once we consume these plants, we additionally eat up these polyphenol nourishments. Their effect is strong: they trigger our very own inborn stress-response pathways.

Even though all plants possess stress-response techniques, just certain ones have grown to create impressive levels of sirtuin-activating polyphenols. All these plants are Sirtfoods. Their discovery ensures instead of strict fasting regimens or tough exercise apps, there is presently a radically new means to trigger your sirtuin genes: eating a healthy diet loaded with Sirtfoods. On top of that, the dietary plan involves putting (sirt)foods on your plate so as not to carry off them.

Would You Eat Meat in Your Sirtfood Diet?

The answer can be a resounding yes. The diet not just comprises ingesting a healthful part of beef. It urges that protein becomes a crucial addition within a Sirtfood-based diet plan to reap the most benefit in maintaining the metabolic process and lessening the muscle imbalance common in many fat loss programs. It isn't just a beef-heavy diet (we remember the awful breath out of the Atkins diet), it's very vegetarian friendly and caters to nearly everyone, and that's exactly what causes it to be a sensible alternative.

Leucine is an amino acid found in protein that divides and enriches the action of Sirtfoods. This usually means that the perfect solution to consume Sirtfoods is simply mixing them with chicken, beef, or an alternative supply of leucine like eggs or fish.

Poultry could be eaten (since it's a great source of protein, B vitamins, potassium, and phosphorous), also that red meat (still another superb source of iron, protein, calcium, and vitamin B12) might be consumed on three occasions (750g raw weight) weekly.

Foods saturated in sirtuins (proteins that regulate cellular and metabolic purposes) can play a part in increasing our wellbeing, reducing inflammation, and potentially helping in weight loss too. Suppose you are worried this diet will soon be miserably restrictive. In that case, you are in fortune: those sirtuin-activating foods aren't simply full of good polyphenols for you, but they're also diverse, flavorful, also might be incorporated into your diet in many creative methods.

Sirtuin activators and Sirtfoods have become fresh to this science of nutrition. Now a 'Sirtfood' is a food packed in sirtuin activators. Vitamins were discovered over a hundred decades back, antioxidants 50 decades ago, and sirtuin activators only ten decades ago.

The 1st sirtuin activator understood – but the most effective known – has been resveratrol, found in the skin of red grapes (and that's the reason why red wine is traditionally believed to continue to keep you healthy), pomegranates, and Japanese knotweed.

Additional Sirtuin activators soon followed, like catechins (seen in green tea extract and also presumed to work with cancer cells) and epicatechins in cocoa powder (accountable for the health benefits of chocolates).

However, research took away once the pharmaceutical giant GlaxoSmithKline bought the rights to generate artificial variations of resveratrol for 462 million. It hastens trial, such as a cancer treatment; however, the consequences weren't impressive. This season the organization announced it had ceased the research.

22

However, today, it seems that eating Sirtfoods naturally full of sirtuin activators could be described as a much healthier, far better, and cheaper alternative for supplements. It was considering the newest trials of Sirtfoods as well as also the Sirtfood dietary plan. Present results imply that Sirtfoods targets precisely the same path for reducing weight and staying fit since dietary restriction and physical exercise.

Resveratrol, seen in red wine, might help counteract the unfavorable effect of elevated fat/high glucose diets-SirtFood Research

Red wine fans have a new cause to observe. Researchers have located a brand new wellness advantage of resveratrol that occurs naturally in grape skins, raspberries, mulberries, crimson wine, and thus in blueberries. Resveratol is recognized as a sirtuin activator.

Even though analyzing the resveratrol results from the diet rhesus monkeys, Dr. J.P. Hyatt, an Associate Professor at Georgetown University, and his group of investigators found a resveratrol supplement could counteract the bad effect of fat/high sugar diet onto the thoracic muscles. In previous animal studies, resveratrol has been shown to improve the life span of mice and slow down the onset of cardiovascular disease. One study revealed the results of aerobic exercise mice that have been fed with a superior fat/high sugar-free diet plan.

Even though these outcomes are reassuring, also there may be a desire to keep on eating a superior fat/high sugar and just incorporate a glass of red wine or even a cup of fresh fruit into someone's daily ingestion; the investigators highlight that the value of a wholesome diet can't be overemphasized. However, for the time being, there is an additional reason to have a glass of wine.

There are growing signs that sirtuin activators can have a vast selection of health benefits in addition to building muscle and curbing desire. These generally include improving memory, helping your human body control glucose levels, and clearing up the damage from free radical molecules, which could collect in cells and result in cancer and other diseases.

Substantial observational evidence is present for its favorable outcomes of the intake of food and beverage full of sirtuin activators in diminishing risks of chronic illness.

Even though Sirtuin activators are observed throughout the plant kingdom, certain veggies and fruits have large amounts to count since SirtfFoods. Examples include green tea extract, cocoa powder, Indian spice broccoli, garlic, onions, and pineapple.

In supermarkets, most vegetables and fruit, like avocados, berries, lettuce, kiwis, carrots, and pineapple, are now saturated in sirtuin activators. It will not signify they aren't worth eating; however, they provide tons of different advantages.

The beauty of having a diet packaged using SirtFoods can become significantly more elastic than other diet plans. You might only eat adding some SirtFoods on top. Or you might ask them to in a concentrated manner as advocated by the SirtFood diet regime.

CONCLUSION

Thank you for making it to the end. A healthy meal contains a lot of vegetables. So most of the plate should consist of vegetables such as zucchini, cucumber, peppers, or other vegetables; this guarantees a lot of vitamins, low calories, and a nice freshness (if the vegetables are not overcooked).

- **Colorful.** Of course, it is not enough just to eat vegetables; they should also be varied and colorful. Ideally, the vegetables are as mixed and colorful as a traffic light: yellow, red, and green. Of course, a white vegetable such as white cabbage and cauliflower is not wrong and serves as colorful icing on the cake. The colorful mixture, which changes over repeatedly, offers many vitamins and a varied taste. Even if you love something (such as tomatoes), it's important to vary a bit. Otherwise, deficiency symptoms can occur, and the food becomes boring over time.

- **Protein.** Protein is one of the essential components of our body. However, not as much as needed, as many believe. And even then, it does not always have to be animal protein.

- Other proprotein sources, tofu, provide a change in the daily diet and bring creativity to life.

- **Carbohydrates.** Again and again, the diets with "low-carb" (pronounced the "little-carbohydrates") are the total hit. No wonder. Carbohydrates also make you fat. At least if you eat too many of them, if you eat them in the wrong combination (i.e., with too much fat or sugar) or do not vary enough. Carbohydrates are generally crucial for us to have energy, an essential ingredient for satiety, and it's important because it's good for your nerves, among other things.

The best thing you can do for your body is to win food from natural ingredients. Fruits and vegetables are, at best, varieties that are available regionally and seasonally. Of course, it is okay from time to time sometimes not to eat regional specialties, such as pineapple or bananas (if you live in Germany, there will probably be hardly regional), b. Still, it is completely redundant for us outside the strawberry time overpriced strawberries from Africa to buy, which taste like nothing and have hardly any vitamins. As we end this book, please remember the five no-gos:

A Lot of Fat

Fat is good for the body. If we have too little fat, it will harm our health in the long run. But many people have the problem of eating too much fat, which is not healthy either. Too much fat is bad for the brain, the immune system, and the arteries, which in turn can cause a heart attack.

Of course, one must distinguish between healthy fats (olive oil, nut oil, nuts) and unhealthy fats (butter, animal fats, etc.).

Lots of Sugar

It is perfectly okay to consume sugar. Because sugar is an energy supplier, and sugar tastes good too. However, too much sugar is not good for the body and the immune system and can lead to addiction, particularly in bad cases. Above all, sugar has the disadvantage of not filling you up for long and that you quickly lose energy again. Even if you are pushed by sugar, the effect lasts only very briefly.

Chemical Substances

Our body is a natural organism; it does not need chemical additives, so why should you forcefully pump yourself with chemistry? Unfortunately, many people tend to stuff themselves with ready-made sauce-fix bags and other unhealthy things for convenience. From time to time, it may not be a problem to feed a little unhealthy; you will not die because you incorporate some e-substance. However, too many chemical foods are not good for your health. This can cause many other diseases of affluence that you would not normally have.

Many Spices

People like spicy food, and that's perfectly fine, but certain levels of spiciness and too much salt are not among the spices people need on the contrary. The man needs a little salt. All foods contain some salt naturally, and the over-flavoring of food causes water retention, is bad for the brain and harms the organism.

One-Sided

The worst you can do to yourself and your body is to eat one-sidedly. It does not matter whether the food bathes in fat, whether you are constantly fed on peppers, eating too much sugar or too little fruit, any form of one-sided diet has the result that you have deficiency symptoms, and you get sick sooner or later becomes. This can be in a one-sided diet, where you eat only unhealthy things, and in a one-sided diet, you eat only healthy food. That cannot and should not be the goal because ironing out these deficiencies requires a lot of work and a lot of discipline.

That's all, and I hope you have learned something!

PART II: INTRODUCTION

The Sirtfood diet is based on the activation of the Sirtuins. Sirtuins are particular proteins that play a very important role in our body; they regulate events such as aging, protect our cells, increase resistance to stress, and influence energy efficiency and vigilance during low-calorie situations. The Sirtfood diet includes all the foods that activate the sirtuins in the food plan for these specific reasons. Among these foods, we can find red wine, dark chocolate, kale, coffee, celery, and many others that we will see in detail later.

The Sirtfood diet is divided into two simple phases; the first phase lasts 7 days. In the first 3 days, the diet plan is based on 3 sirt green juices and one main meal, for 1000 calories per day. In the following 4 days, the caloric intake is 1500 calories, with 2 sirt green juices and two main meals. Phase two, which lasts 14 days, includes 3 main meals (breakfast, lunch, and dinner), where you will have to put sirt food, plus a sirt green juice. In this phase, you must be careful not to overdo the caloric intake. The objective of phase two is to lose more weight, continue to take sirt foods, and activate the sirtuins. This phase also called the maintenance phase, is important because it should help you change your diet plan. The goal of the two nutritionists, inventors of the diet, is to make people lose weight at first but help them take advantage of the benefits of sirtuins during their entire lives. As we have already said, sirtuins have several beneficial properties for our body, including helping to manage digestion, increase muscle mass, and consume fat. Two renowned nutritionists working for a private practice center in the UK have built the Sirtfood Diet. They promote a change in the diet plan to activate the "skinny gene" in the body. This food plan is based on Sirtuins (SIRTs), a set of seven proteins found within every living organism and which appear to control a range of abilities. The intake of specific foods and specific mixes of individual plants may potentially expand the degree of these proteins in the body. These particular foods are called SIRTFOODS.

The Sirtfood Diet book was first distributed in the U.K. in 2016. Be that as it may, the U.S. arrival of the book has started the greater interest in the subject. The eating routine started getting publicity when Adele debuted her slimmer figure at the Billboard Music Awards. Her coach, Pete Geracimo, is a huge fan of the eating routine and says the vocalist shed 30 pounds from following a Sirt food diet.

Sirt foods are rich in substances that activate an alleged "skinny gene" called sirtuin. Goggins and Matten indicate that this "skinny gene" is activated when a lack of energy occurs after limiting calories. The diet became fascinating for the world of nutrition in 2003, when specialists discovered that resveratrol, a substance found in red wine, affects the body similar to that caused by calorie restriction, without the restriction occurs.

In the 2015 pilot study (led by Goggins and Matten) testing the viability of sirtuins, the 39 members lost a normal of seven pounds in seven days. Those outcomes sound noteworthy, yet it's critical to understand this is a small example size concentrated over a brief timeframe.

What Foods Are High in Sirtuins?

The book contains a summary of the 20 main foods with a high sirtuin content. These include Medjool dates, red wine, turmeric, pecans, and kale.

Dr. Youdim notes that while the advanced nourishments are stable, they won't advance weight reduction alone.

The fundamental reason for the Sirtfood Diet is that sure nourishments, named "Sirtfoods," can emulate the demonstrated advantages of caloric limitation and fasting. This happens by method for actuating sirtuins—proteins in the body (going from SIRT1 to SIRT7) that manage natural pathways, turn certain qualities on and off, and help shield cells from age-related decay. Enactment of SIRT1, for instance, has appeared in some labs. The creature concentrates on initiating the development of new mitochondria, expanding life length, and improving oxidative digestion, which may bolster weight reduction and support.

Since fasting and extreme caloric limitation is extremely hard (and frequently, not fitting), Goggins and Matten built up their dietary arrangement—concentrated on eating heaps of "Sirtfoods." Sirtfood eating is a more straightforward method to invigorate the body's sirtuin qualities (in some cases alluded to as "thin qualities") and increase weight reduction and advance broad well-being.

What Makes Something a "Sirtfood"?

Green tea, berries, cocoa powder, turmeric, kale, onions, parsley, arugula, chilies, espresso, red wine, pecans, escapades, buckwheat, and olive oil. These nourishments contain explicit polyphenol mixes (quercetin, resveratrol, kaempferol, and so on.) that have, truth be told, been found in logical investigations to increment sirtuin action. Along these lines, right now, diet is, at any rate, to some degree dependent on science. The issue, notwithstanding, is that these nourishments may not contain adequate degrees of these polyphenols to enact sirtuins in any meaningful manner. A large number of the examinations connecting polyphenol mixes to expanded sirtuin action have just been done on exceptionally focused types of these mixes.

CHAPTER 1: LONG-TERM MAINTENANCE: TIPS FOR SPECIAL SIRTFOOD COOKING

Long-term maintenance for Sirtfood entails advanced bio-scanning and multiple rounds of genetic testing, and there are mandatory health checkups every three months. It's much like the truth serum; it's compulsory, and anyone who fails to follow the protocol can face serious penalties.

There is a strong push and pull of gene manipulation and the so-called human evolution. There are rumors of the government keeping human DNA reservoirs, but I am not supposed to believe these hearsays.

However, the government is very proactive in the evolution of the human species. A futuristic brand of Sirtfood is being released soon, and I feel that this is one medium through which gene manipulation and human evolution will take place de-facto. I am not authorized to tell anything more.

Tips for Special Sirtfood Cooking Include

The new Sirtfood diet is not like any other diet. It is more like a new lifestyle because you need to make some important changes to enjoy Sirtfood meals safely. The tips for special Sirtfood cooking are very simple. Follow these simple tips, and you will be able to stay healthy with Sirtfood.

1. A Sirtfood meal consists of seven different meals a day.

There is 1 meal for breakfast, 2 meals for lunch, 2 meals for dinner, and 2 meals for late-night snacks.

2. The meals to be eaten a day are like this.

Breakfast

- One slice of bread
- One teaspoon of jam
- One egg
- One glass of milk
- One cup of yogurt
- Coffee

Dinner

- One cup of Yogurt
- One slice of bread
- One slice of cheese
- One bowl of pasta
- One orange
- One glass of water

- One glass of milk
- One slice of cake
- One cup of coffee
- Coffee
- One jar of tea
- One cup of coffee
- One cup of tea
- One banana

Late night snack

- One slice of bread and butter
- One cup of pasta
- One teaspoon of jam
- One banana

Eating a healthy diet for you and your loved ones if you want them to be healthy forever. That is the aim of the diet. Besides, the most important aspect of the diet is that you need to stick with the diet forever. You will not be able to eat anything else if you do not want to get health issues. A healthy diet makes the choice of food easy. Because of the standardization of the nutrients in the Sirtfood Diet, the calorie value of different Sirtfood meals is the same. So all you need to do is be aware of the certain portion size of sirt foods you are supposed to take for different meals.

Moreover, try to stick with it. Above all, you need to exercise regularly and eat the Sirtfood diet forever. As long as this diet is part of your life, your life had better be healthy forever.

Sirtfood allows for optimal health and extended life spans. But this diet is not advised for excursions outside the laboratory and entails lifelong addiction to Sirtfood. You should not try to make yourself a fanatic. This is not a realistic way of thinking.

There are a lot of advantages and disadvantages to Sirtfood, not all of them are similar. You should take good care of the Sirtfood lifestyle. Otherwise, you will certainly be in trouble. Eating a healthy diet day after day is one of the most make-or-break aspects of having a healthy diet.

You are going to fall in line with sirt foods and do this regularly. It is not something that you do one day and then goes back to your normal life. That is something to be avoided.

CHAPTER 2: BREAKFAST

1. Caprese Salad

Preparation Time: 5 minutes

Cooking Time: 0 minutes

Servings: 2

Ingredients:

- ✓ 1 sliced avocado
- ✓ 2 sliced large tomatoes
- ✓ 1 bunch basil leaves
- ✓ 1 tsp. sea salt
- ✓ 1 cup cubed jackfruit

Directions:

- ☞ Add the sea salt to season. Serve.

☞ In a bowl, toss all the salad ingredients to mix.

Nutrition: Calories: 125 kcal Fat: 10.1g Carbs: 9.1g Protein: 2g

2. Smoked Salmon Omelets

Preparation Time: 45 minutes   **Cooking Time:** 15 minutes   **Servings:** 2

Ingredients:

- ✓ 2 medium eggs
- ✓ 100 g Smoked salmon, cut
- ✓ 1/2 tsp. Capers
- ✓ 10 g Rocket, slashed

- ✓ 1 tsp. Parsley, slashed
- ✓ 1 tsp. extra virgin olive oil

Nutrition:

- ♥ Calories: 148 Cal

- ♥ Fat: 8.73 g
- ♥ Carbohydrates: 0.36 g
- ♥ Protein: 15.87 g
- ♥ Fiber: 0 g

Directions:

- ☞ Split the eggs into a bowl and whisk well. Include the salmon, tricks, rocket, and parsley.
- ☞ Warmth the olive oil in a non-stick skillet until hot yet not smoking. Include the egg blend and, utilizing a spatula or fish cut, move the mixture around the dish until it is even.

- ☞ Diminish the warmth and let the omelet cook through. Slide the spatula around the edges and move up or crease the omelet fifty-fifty to serve.

3. Baked Salmon Salad with Creamy Mint Dressing

Preparation Time: 55 minutes   **Cooking Time:** 20 minutes   **Servings:** 1

Ingredients:

- ✓ 1 salmon fillet (130g)
- ✓ 40g mixed salad leaves
- ✓ 40g young spinach leaves
- ✓ 2 radishes, trimmed and thinly sliced

- ✓ 5cm piece (50g) cucumber, cut into chunks
- ✓ 2 spring onions, trimmed and sliced
- ✓ 1 small handful (10g) parsley, roughly chopped

For the dressing:
- ✓ 1 tsp. low-fat mayonnaise
- ✓ 1 tbsp. natural yoghurt
- ✓ 1 tbsp. rice vinegar

- ✓ 2 leaves mint, finely chopped
- ✓ Salt to taste
- ✓ Freshly ground black pepper

Directions:

- ☞ First, preheat your oven to 200°C (180°C fan/Gas 6).
- ☞ Now place the salmon fillet on a baking tray. Bake it for 16–18 minutes until cooked. Now remove it from the oven and set it aside. The salmon is equally useful to be used as hot or cold in the salad. If the salmon has skin, simply cook the skin side down. Remove the salmon from the skin. It slides off easily when cooked.
- ☞ Now mix the mayonnaise, yoghurt, rice wine vinegar, and mint leaves. Add salt and pepper.
- ☞ Leave them to stand for at least 5 minutes. It allows the flavors to develop.
- ☞ Arrange salad leaves and spinach on a serving plate. Top with radishes, cucumber, spring onions, and parsley. Now flake the cooked salmon onto the salad. Finally, drizzle the dressing over.

Nutrition: Calories: 483 Cal Fat: 33.89 g Carbohydrates: 34.89 g Protein: 13.82 g Fiber: 0

4. Salmon and Spinach Quiche

Preparation Time: 55 minutes   **Cooking Time:** 45 minutes   **Servings:** 2

Ingredients:

- ✓ 600 g frozen leaf spinach
- ✓ 1 clove of garlic
- ✓ 1 onion
- ✓ 150 g frozen salmon fillets
- ✓ 200 g smoked salmon
- ✓ 1 small bunch of dill

- ✓ 1 untreated lemon
- ✓ 50 g butter
- ✓ 200 g sour cream
- ✓ 3 eggs
- ✓ Salt, pepper, nutmeg
- ✓ 1 pack of puff pastry

Nutrition:
- ♥ Calories: 903 Cal
- ♥ Fat: 59.79 g
- ♥ Carbohydrates: 30.79 g
- ♥ Protein: 65.28 g
- ♥ Fiber: 0 g

Directions:

- ☞ Let the spinach thaw and squeeze well.
- ☞ Peel the garlic and onion and cut into fine cubes.
- ☞ Cut the salmon fillet into cubes 1-1.5 cm thick.
- ☞ Cut the smoked salmon into strips.
- ☞ Wash the dill, pat dry and chop.
- ☞ Wash the lemon with hot water, dry, rub the zest finely with a kitchen grater, and squeeze the lemon.
- ☞ Heat the butter in a pan. Sweat the garlic and onion cubes in it for approx. 2-3 minutes.
- ☞ Add spinach and sweat briefly.
- ☞ Add sour cream, lemon juice, and zest, eggs, and dill and mix well.
- ☞ Season with salt, pepper, and nutmeg.
- ☞ Preheat the oven to 200 degrees top/bottom heat (180 degrees convection).
- ☞ Grease a Springform pan and roll out the puff pastry in it and pull up on edge. Prick the dough with a fork (so that it does not rise too much).
- ☞ Pour in the spinach and egg mixture and smooth out.

- Spread salmon cubes and smoked salmon strips on top.

- The quiche in the oven (grid, middle inset) about 30-40 min. Yellow gold bake.

5. Asian King Prawn Stir-Fry with Buckwheat Noodles

Preparation Time: 55 minutes   **Cooking Time:** 20 minutes   **Servings:** 2

Ingredients:

- ✓ 150g raw royal shrimps in shelled skins
- ✓ 2 teaspoons of tamari (you can use soy sauce if you do not avoid gluten)
- ✓ 2 teaspoons extra virgin olive oil
- ✓ 75g soba (buckwheat noodles)
- ✓ 1 clove of garlic, finely chopped
- ✓ 1 aerial view of finely chopped chili
- ✓ 1 teaspoon of finely chopped fresh ginger
- ✓ 20g red onion, cut into slices
- ✓ 40g celery, trimmed and cut into slices
- ✓ 75g chopped green beans
- ✓ 50g kale, coarsely chopped
- ✓ 100 ml of chicken stock
- ✓ 5g lovage or celery leaves

Directions:

- Heat a frying pan over high heat, and then cook the prawns for 2–3 minutes in 1 teaspoon tamari and 1 teaspoon oil. Put the prawns on a plate. Wipe the pan out with paper from the oven, as you will be using it again.

- Cook the noodles for 5–8 minutes in boiling water, or as indicated on the packet. Drain and put away.

- Meanwhile, over medium-high heat, fry the garlic, chili, and ginger, red onion, celery, beans, and kale in the remaining oil for 2–3 minutes. Remove the stock and bring to the boil, then cook for one or two minutes until the vegetables are cooked but crunchy.

- Add the prawns, noodles, and leaves of lovage/celery to the pan, bring back to the boil, then remove the heat and serve.

Nutrition: Calories: 251 Cal Fat: 22.97 g Carbohydrates: 34.14 g Protein: 22.97 g Fiber: 0 g

6. Garlic Mashed Potatoes

Preparation Time: 10 minutes

Cooking Time: 25 minutes

Servings: 4

Ingredients:

- ✓ 4 russet potatoes
- ✓ 1 c. vegetable broth
- ✓ 6 minced garlic cloves
- ✓ 4tbsps. chopped parsley
- ✓ Salt
- ✓ ½ c. low-fat milk

Directions:

- Cut the potatoes into medium-sized chunks.
- Put the chunks into the Instant Pot along with the garlic and broth.
- Close the lid and cook at high pressure for 5 minutes.

- ☞ When the cooking is complete, do a natural release pressure.
- ☞ Open the lid carefully and with a handheld masher, mash the potato.
- ☞ Add milk, parsley, and salt and stir well to combine.

Nutrition: Calories: 177 Fat: 0.9 g Carbs: 31.6 g Protein: 6.2 g

7. Pasta with Cheesy Meat Sauce

Preparation Time: 10 minutes

Cooking Time: 30 minutes

Servings: 6

Ingredients:

- ✓ ½ box large-shaped pasta
- ✓ 1-pound ground beef*
- ✓ ½ cup onions, diced
- ✓ 1 tablespoon onion flakes
- ✓ 1½ cups beef stock, reduced or no sodium
- ✓ 1 tablespoon Better Than Bouillon® beef, no salt added
- ✓ 1 tablespoon tomato sauce, no salt added
- ✓ ¾ cup Monterey or pepper jack cheese, shredded
- ✓ 8 ounces cream cheese, softened
- ✓ ½ teaspoon Italian seasoning
- ✓ ½ teaspoon ground black pepper
- ✓ 2 tablespoons French's® Worcestershire sauce, reduced-sodium

Directions:

- ☞ Cook pasta noodles according to the directions on the box.
- ☞ In a large sauté pan, cook ground beef, onions, and onion flakes until the meat is browned.
- ☞ Drain and add stock, bouillon, and tomato sauce.
- ☞ Bring to a simmer, stirring occasionally. Stir in cooked pasta, turn off the heat, and add softened cream cheese, shredded cheese, and seasonings (Italian seasoning, black pepper, and Worcestershire sauce). Stir pasta mixture until cheese is melted throughout.
- ☞ **TIP:** You can substitute ground turkey for beef.

Nutrition: Calories: 502 kcal Total Fat: 30 g Saturated Fat: 14 g Cholesterol: 99 mg Sodium: 401 mg
Total Carbs: 35 g Fiber: 1.7 g Sugar: 0 g Protein: 23 g

8. Creamy Shrimp and Mozzarella Pasta

Preparation Time: 45 minutes   **Cooking Time:** 10 minutes   **Servings:** 2

Ingredients:

- ✓ 2 cups penne pasta, cooked still somewhat firm
- ✓ Two tablespoons olive oil
- ✓ Four cloves garlic, minced
- ✓ 1-pound shrimp, stripped and deveined
- ✓ Two teaspoons salt, partitioned

- ✓ 1/2 cups substantial cream
- ✓ 1 cup destroyed mozzarella
- ✓ 1/2 cup sun-dried tomatoes
- ✓ Two tablespoons cleaved basil

- ✓ 1/2 teaspoon red pepper pieces
- ✓ Two teaspoons lemon juice
- ✓ Cleaved basil, to decorate

Directions:

☞ In a heavy skillet over medium-high warmth, sauté garlic in olive oil until fragrant, around 2 minutes. Include shrimp and cook for about 3 minutes on each side. Season with a large portion of the salt, remove from skillet and put in a safe spot. In a similar skillet, add overwhelming cream and heat to the point of boiling.

☞ Diminish to a stew and include mozzarella, sun-dried tomatoes, basil, and red pepper chips. Stew for 5 minutes and lessen to low warmth.

☞ Return shrimp to the dish and include lemon squeeze and staying salt. Include cooked pasta and basil and serve.

Nutrition: Calories: 664 Cal Fat: 20.94 g Carbohydrates: 51.53 g Protein: 70.86 g Fiber: 6 g

9. Green Beans with Vegan Bacon

Preparation Time: 15 minutes   **Cooking Time:** 20 minutes   **Servings:** 8

Ingredients:

- ✓ 2 slices of vegan bacon, chopped
- ✓ 1 shallot, chopped

- ✓ 24 oz. green beans
- ✓ Salt and pepper to taste
- ✓ ½ teaspoon smoked paprika

- ✓ 1 teaspoon lemon juice
- ✓ 2 teaspoons vinegar

Directions:

☞ Preheat your oven to 450 degrees F.

☞ Add the bacon to the baking pan and roast for 5 minutes.

☞ Stir in the shallot and beans.

☞ Season it with salt, pepper, and paprika.

☞ Roast for 10 minutes.

☞ Drizzle with lemon juice and vinegar.

☞ Roast for another 2 minutes.

Nutrition: Calories: 49 Fat: 1.2g Saturated fat: 0.4g Cholesterol: 3mg Potassium: 249mg Carbohydrates: 8.1g Fiber: 3g Sugar: 4g Protein: 2.9g

10. Chicken Breakfast Skillet

Preparation Time: 30 minutes   **Cooking Time:** 30 minutes   **Servings:** 2

Ingredients:

- ✓ 1 chicken breast
- ✓ 3 ounces ground sausage
- ✓ 2 eggs

- ✓ 3 slices bacon
- ✓ ½ teaspoon garlic powder

- ✓ ½ teaspoon ground black pepper

Directions:

☞ Chop the bacon and chicken breast into pieces roughly one inch in size. Add the bacon to a skillet over medium heat and cook

for two minutes, stirring frequently. Once the bacon grease has begun to accumulate in the pan, stir in the diced chicken and ground or crumbled sausage.

☞ Add garlic powder and pepper to the meat in the skillet. Brown the meat over medium-high heat for about six to eight minutes.

☞ Reduce heat to medium. On opposite sides of the pan, clear two pockets of space for the eggs. Crack the eggs into the skillet and break the yolks apart. Cover the skillet and allow cooking so that the egg whites are firm about 10 minutes. Uncover and scoop onto a plate to serve.

Nutrition: Calories: 341 Fat: 19 g Sodium: 631 mg Carbohydrates: 1 g Fiber: 0 g Sugar: 1 g Protein: 36g

11. Slow Cooker Bone Broth

Preparation Time: 15 minutes   **Cooking Time:** 24 hours   **Servings:** 16

Ingredients:

- ✓ 3 pounds of assorted animal bones, with marrow
- ✓ 1 gallon of water
- ✓ 3 tablespoons salt
- ✓ 2 tablespoons ground black pepper

Directions:

☞ Add assorted bones to a slow cooker. Pour in the water and season with salt and pepper. Turn the slow cooker to high.

☞ Bring the water inside the slow cooker to a boil. This may take up to 20 minutes due to a large amount of water. Then reduce the temperature settings to low and allow to simmer for up to 24 hours. Letting the bone broth cook for this long gives you a more nutritious and tastier product. You do not need to stir the broth during this time. If necessary, add more water around the 12-hour

mark if you notice the water level has dropped far below the top of the bones.

☞ Shut off the heat and let the broth cool. Strain into a large stockpot or other container and discard the remains of the bones. Enjoy hot or allow cooling completely before packaging for refrigeration or freezing. The bone broth will solidify in the fridge, so simply reheat leftover

Nutrition: Calories: 56 Fat: 2 g Sodium: 480 mg Carbohydrates: 0 g Fiber: 0 g Sugar: 0 g Protein: 9 g

12. Fragrant Asian Hotpot

Preparation Time: 30 minutes   **Cooking Time:** 10 minutes   **Servings:** 2

Ingredients:

- ✓ 1 teaspoon tomato puree
- ✓ 1-star anise, crushed (or 1/4 teaspoon anise)
- ✓ A small handful (10 g) of parsley, finely chopped stalks
- ✓ A small handful of coriander (10 g), finely chopped stalks
- ✓ Juice from 1/2 lime

- ✓ 500 ml chicken broth, fresh or made from 1 cube
- ✓ 1/2 carrot, peeled and cut into matches
- ✓ 50 g broccoli, cut into small roses
- ✓ 50 g bean sprouts
- ✓ 100 g raw tiger prawns
- ✓ 100 g hard tofu, chopped

- ✓ 50 g rice noodles, cooked according to the instructions on the packaging
- ✓ 50g of boiled water chestnuts, drained
- ✓ 20g chopped ginger sushi
- ✓ 1 tablespoon of good quality miso paste

Directions:

- ☞ Place in a large saucepan the tomato purée, star anise, parsley stalks, coriander stalks, lime juice, and chicken stock and bring 10 minutes to a simmer. Stir in the cabbage, broccoli, prawns, tofu, noodles, and water chestnuts, and cook gently until the prawns are finished. Remove from heat and whisk in the ginger sushi and the paste miso.

- ☞ Serve sprinkled with the leaves of the parsley and coriander.

Nutrition: Calories: 253 Cal Fat: 7.35 g Carbohydrates: 29.99 g Protein: 19.39 Fiber: 6 g

13. Sirtfood Green Juice

Preparation Time: 5 minutes

Cooking Time: 10 minutes

Servings: 1

Ingredients:

Recipe 1:

- ✓ 1 tbsp. parsley
- ✓ 1 stalk celery
- ✓ 1 apple
- ✓ ½ lemon

Recipe 2:

- ✓ 1 cucumber
- ✓ 1 stalk celery
- ✓ 1 apple
- ✓ 3 mint leaves

Directions:

- ☞ Choose one of the recipes above.
- ☞ Add all ingredients into a juicer and extract the juice according to the manufacturer's method.
- ☞ In case you don't have one, add all the ingredients to a blender and pulse until well combined.
- ☞ Filter the juice through a fine-mesh strainer and transfer it into a glass. Top with water if needed. Serve immediately.

Nutrition: Calories 30kcal, Fat 0.4 g, Carbohydrate 4.5 g, Protein 1 g

14. Pancakes with Caramelized Strawberries

Preparation Time: 5 minutes   **Cooking Time:** 15 minutes   **Servings:** 2

Ingredients:

- ✓ 1 egg
- ✓ 1 ½ oz. self-raising flour
- ✓ 1 ½ oz. buckwheat flour
- ✓ 1/3 cup skimmed milk
- ✓ 1 cup strawberries
- ✓ 2 tsp. honey

Directions:

- ☞ Mix the flours in a bowl; add the yolk and a bit of mix in a very thick batter. Keep adding the milk bit by bit to avoid lumps.

☞ In another bowl, beat the egg white until stiff and then mix it carefully to the batter.

☞ Put enough batter to make a 5-inch round pancake to cook 2 minutes per side until done. Repeat until all the pancakes are ready.

☞ Put strawberries and honey in a hot pan until caramelized, the put half on top of each serving.

Nutrition: Calories: 272 Fat: 4.3g Carbohydrate: 26.8g Protein: 23.6g

15. Scrambled Eggs and Red Onion

Preparation Time: 2 minutes   **Cooking Time:** 2 minutes   **Servings:** 1

Ingredients:

✓ 2 eggs

✓ 1 tbsp. Parmesan

✓ Salt and pepper

✓ ½ cup red onion

✓ 1 tbsp. parsley, finely chopped

Directions:

☞ Put eggs and cheese with a pinch of salt and pepper and finely chopped onion in a bowl. Whisk quickly.

☞ Cook the scrambled eggs in a skillet for 2 minutes, stirring continuously until done.

Nutrition: Calories: 278, Fat: 5.4g, Carbohydrate: 12.8g, Protein: 18.9g

16. Matcha Overnight Oats

Preparation Time: 10 minutes   **Cooking Time:** 0 minutes   **Servings:** 2

Ingredients:

✓ 2 tsp. Chia seeds

✓ 3 oz. Rolled oats

✓ 1 tsp. Matcha powder

✓ 1 tsp. Honey

✓ 1 ½ cups Almond milk

✓ 2 pinches ground cinnamon

✓ 1 Apple, peeled, cored, and chopped

✓ 4 walnuts

Directions:

☞ Place the chia seeds and the oats in a container or bowl.

☞ In a different jug or bowl, add the matcha powder and one tablespoon of almond milk and whisk with a hand-held mixer until you get a smooth paste, then add the rest of the milk and mix thoroughly.

☞ Pour the milk mixture over the oats, add the honey and cinnamon, and then stir well. Cover the bowl with a lid and place in the fridge overnight.

☞ When you want to eat, transfer the oats to two serving bowls, then top with the walnuts, and chopped apple.

Nutrition: Calories 324, Carbs37 g, Fat14 g, Protein: 22g

17. Salmon Fritters

Preparation Time: 10 minutes

Cooking Time: 20 minutes

Servings: 2

Ingredients:

- ✓ 6 oz. salmon, canned
- ✓ 1 tbsp. flour
- ✓ 1 clove garlic, crushed
- ✓ ½ red onion, finely chopped
- ✓ 2 eggs
- ✓ 2 tsp. olive oil
- ✓ Salt and pepper to taste
- ✓ 2 cups arugula

Directions:

☞ Separate egg whites from yolks and beat them until very stiff. In a separate bowl mix salmon, flour, salt, pepper, onion, garlic, onion, and yolks.

☞ Add egg whites and slowly mix them together. Heat a pan on medium-high. Add 1tsp. oil and when hot form salmon fritters with a spoon.

☞ Cook until brown (around 4 minutes per side) and serve with arugula salad seasoned with salt, pepper, and 1 tsp. olive oil.

Nutrition: Calories: 320 Carbs: 18g Fat: 7g Protein: 27g

18. Mince Stuffed Eggplants

Preparation Time: 10 minutes   **Cooking Time:** 70 minutes   **Servings:** 6

Ingredients:

- ✓ 4 oz. lean mince
- ✓ 6 large eggplants
- ✓ 1 egg
- ✓ 3 tbsp. dry red wine
- ✓ ½ cup cheddar, grated
- ✓ Salt and pepper, to taste
- ✓ 1 red onion
- ✓ 2 tsp. olive oil
- ✓ 2 tbsp. tomato sauce
- ✓ 2 tbsp. parsley

Directions:

☞ Preheat oven to 350°F. Meanwhile, slice eggplants in 2 and scoop out the center part, leaving ½ inch of meat. . Place eggplants in a microwavable dish with about ½" of water in the bottom.

☞ Microwave on high for 4 minutes. In a saucepan, fry mince with onion for 5 minutes.

☞ Add wine and let evaporate.

☞ Add tomato sauce, salt, pepper, eggplant meat and cook for around 20 minutes until done.

☞ Combine, mince sauce, cheese, egg, parsley, salt, and pepper in a large bowl and mix well. Pack firmly into eggplants.

☞ Return eggplants to the dish you first microwaved them in and bake for 25 to 30 minutes, or until lightly browned on top.

Nutrition: Calories: 350 Carbs: 22g Fat: 10g Protein: 17g

19. Easy Shrimp Salad

Preparation Time: 5 minutes **Cooking Time:** 0 minutes **Servings:** 2

Ingredients:

- ✓ 2 cups red endive, finely sliced
- ✓ 1 cup cherry tomatoes, halved
- ✓ 1 tsp. of extra virgin olive oil
- ✓ 1 tbsp. parsley, chopped
- ✓ 3 oz. celery, sliced
- ✓ 6 walnuts, chopped
- ✓ 2 oz. red onion-sliced
- ✓ 1 cup yellow pepper, cubed
- ✓ ½ lemon, juiced
- ✓ 6 oz. steamed shrimps

Directions:

- ☞ Put red endive on a large plate. Evenly distribute on top finely sliced onion, yellow pepper, cherry tomatoes walnuts, celery, and parsley.
- ☞ Mix oil, lemon juice with a pinch of salt and pepper and distribute the dressing on top.

Nutrition: Calories: 353, Fat: 4.8g, Carbohydrate: 28.1g, Protein: 28.3g

20. Red Onion Frittata with Chili Grilled Zucchini

Preparation Time: 5 minutes **Cooking Time:** 30 minutes **Servings:** 2

Ingredients:

- ✓ 1 ½ cups red onion, finely sliced
- ✓ 3 eggs
- ✓ 3 oz. cheddar cheese
- ✓ 2 tbsp. milk
- ✓ 2 zucchini
- ✓ 2 tbsp. oil
- ✓ 1 clove garlic, crushed
- ✓ ½ chili, finely sliced
- ✓ 1 tsp. white vinegar
- ✓ Salt and pepper to taste

Directions:

- ☞ Heat the oven to 350°F. Cut the zucchini into thin slices; grill them and set them aside.
- ☞ Add 3 eggs, shredded cheddar cheese, milk, salt, pepper, whisk well and pour in a silicone baking tray and cook 25-30 minutes in the oven.
- ☞ Mix garlic, oil, salt, pepper, and vinegar and pour the dressing on the zucchini. Serve the frittata alongside the zucchini.

Nutrition: Calories: 359, Fat: 7.8g, Carbohydrate: 18.1g, Protein: 21.3g

21. Garlic Chicken Burgers

Preparation Time: 10 minutes **Cooking Time:** 10 minutes **Servings:** 2

Ingredients:

- ✓ 8 oz. chicken mince
- ✓ ¼ red onion, finely chopped
- ✓ 1 clove garlic, crushed
- ✓ 1 handful of parsley, finely chopped
- ✓ 1 cup arugula
- ✓ ½ orange, chopped
- ✓ 1 cup cherry tomatoes
- ✓ 3 tsp. extra virgin olive oil

Directions:

- Put chicken mince, onion, garlic, parsley, salt pepper in a bowl and mix well. Form 2 patties and let rest 5 minutes.
- Heat a pan with olive oil and when very hot cook 3 minutes per part.

- They are also very good when grilled, if you opt for grilling; just brush the patties with a bit of oil right before cooking.
- Put the arugula on two plates; add cherry tomatoes and orange on top, dress with salt and the remaining olive oil. Put the patties on top and serve.

Nutrition: Calories: 353, Fat: 4.8g, Carbohydrate: 28.1g, Protein: 28.3g

22. Turmeric Turkey Breast with Cauliflower Rice

Preparation Time: 5 minutes   **Cooking Time:** 25 minutes   **Servings:** 2

Ingredients:

- ✓ 2 cups cauliflower, grated
- ✓ 8 oz. turkey breast, cut into slices
- ✓ 2 tsp. ground turmeric
- ✓ 1/2 pepper, chopped
- ✓ 1/2 red onion, sliced
- ✓ 2 tsp. extra virgin olive oil
- ✓ 1 large tomato
- ✓ 1 clove garlic, crushed
- ✓ 1 cup milk, skimmed
- ✓ 2 tsp. buckwheat flour
- ✓ 1 oz. parsley, finely chopped

Directions:

- Coat turkey slices with flour. Heat a pan on medium-high with half the oil and when hot add the turkey.
- Let the meat color on all sides, then add milk, salt, pepper, 1 tsp. turmeric. Cook 10 minutes until the turkey is soft and the sauce has become creamy. In a different pan, add the remaining oil and heat on medium heat. Add pepper, onion, and tomato, 1 tsp. turmeric and let cook 3 minutes.
- Add the cauliflower and cook for another 2 minutes. Add salt, pepper and let rest 2 minutes. Serve the turkey with the cauliflower rice.

Nutrition: Calories 107 Total Fat 2.9 g Total Carbs 20.6 g Protein 2.1 g

23. Mustard Salmon with Baby Carrots

Preparation Time: 10 minutes   **Cooking Time:** 40 minutes   **Servings:** 2

Ingredients:

- ✓ 8 oz. salmon fillet
- ✓ 2 tbsp. mustard
- ✓ 1 tbsp. white vinegar
- ✓ 1 tsp. parsley, finely chopped
- ✓ 2 cups baby carrots
- ✓ 4 oz. buckwheat
- ✓ 2 tsp. extra virgin olive oil
- ✓ Salt and pepper to taste

Directions:

- Heat the oven to 400°F. Boil the buckwheat in salted water for 25 minutes then drain. Dress with 1 tsp. olive oil. Set aside. Put the salmon over aluminum foil.
- Mix mustard and vinegar in a small bowl and brush the mixture over the salmon, close the foil in a packet. Cook in the oven for 35 minutes.
- While the salmon is cooking, steam baby carrots for 6 minutes then put them in a pan on medium heat with 1tsp. olive oil, salt, and pepper until light brown.

☞ Serve the salmon with baby carrots and buckwheat on the side.

Nutrition: Calories 314, Fat 9.1g, Protein 41.5g, Carbohydrate 15.7g

24. Turmeric Couscous with Edamame Beans

Preparation Time: 10 minutes   **Cooking Time:** 15 minutes   **Servings:** 2

Ingredients:

- ✓ ½ yellow pepper, cubed
- ✓ ½ red pepper, cubed
- ✓ 1 tbsp. turmeric
- ✓ ½ cup red onion, finely sliced
- ✓ ¼ cup cherry tomatoes, chopped
- ✓ 2 tbsp. parsley, finely chopped
- ✓ 5 oz. couscous
- ✓ 2 tsp. extra virgin olive oil
- ✓ ½ eggplant
- ✓ 1 ½ edamame beans

Directions:

☞ Steam edamame for 5 minutes and set aside. Add 6 oz. salted boiling water to couscous and let rest until it absorbs the water.

☞ In the meantime, heat a pan on medium-high heat.

☞ Add oil, eggplant, peppers, onion and tomatoes, turmeric, salt, and pepper. Cook for 5 minutes on high heat.

☞ Add the couscous and edamame.

☞ Garnish with fresh parsley and serve.

Nutrition: Calories 342, Carbs 15 g, Fat 5 g, Protein: 32g

25. Kale Omelette

Preparation Time: 5 minutes   **Cooking Time:** 5 minutes   **Servings:** 1

Ingredients:

- ✓ 2 eggs
- ✓ Garlic – 1 small glove
- ✓ Kale – 2 handfuls
- ✓ Goat cheese or
- ✓ Sliced onion – ¼ cup
- ✓ Extra virgin olive oil – 2 teaspoons

Directions:

☞ Mince the garlic, and finely shred the kale. Break the eggs into a bowl, add a pinch of salt. Beat until well combined.

☞ Place a pan to heat over medium heat. Add one teaspoon of olive oil, add the onion and kale, cook for approx.

☞ Five minutes, or until the onion has softened and the kale is wilted. Add the garlic and cook for another two minutes.

☞ Add one teaspoon of olive oil into the egg mixture, mix and add into the pan.

☞ Use your spatula to move the cooked egg toward the center and move the pan so that the uncooked egg mixture goes towards the edges. Add the cheese into the pan just before the egg is fully cooked, then leave for a minute.

☞ Serve immediately.

26. Chocolate Dessert with Dates and Walnuts

Preparation Time: 10 minutes

Cooking Time: 15 minutes

Servings: 2

Ingredients:

- ✓ 4 Medjool dates, pitted
- ✓ 2 tbsp. cocoa powder
- ✓ 1 cup milk, skimmed
- ✓ 1 tsp. agar powder
- ✓ 1 tbsp. peanut butter
- ✓ 1 pinch of salt
- ✓ ½ tsp. cinnamon
- ✓ 2 walnuts
- ✓ 1 tsp. whole wheat flour

Directions:

- ☞ Blitz dates, peanut butter, and 1tbsp. milk in a food processor.
- ☞ Put the mix in a pan; add cocoa, cinnamon, salt, flour, agar powder.
- ☞ Add the remaining hot milk bit by bit and mix well to obtain a smooth mixture.
- ☞ Turn the heat on, bring to a boil and cook around 6-8 minutes until dense.
- ☞ Divide into 2 cups, let cool, and put in the fridge.
- ☞ Add chopped walnuts before serving.

Nutrition: Calories 326, Carbs7 g, Protein: 25g, Fat3 g

27. Dijon Celery Salad

Preparation Time: 10 minutes   **Cooking Time:** 0 minutes   **Servings:** 4

Ingredients:

- ✓ 2 tsp. honey
- ✓ ½ lemon, juiced
- ✓ 1 tbsp. Dijon mustard
- ✓ 2 tsp. extra virgin olive oil
- ✓ Black pepper to taste
- ✓ 2 apples, cored, peeled, and cubed
- ✓ 1 bunch celery roughly chopped
- ✓ ¾ cup walnuts, chopped

Directions:

- ☞ In a salad bowl, mix celery and its leaves with apple pieces and walnuts.
- ☞ Add black pepper, lemon juice, mustard, honey, and olive oil, whisk well, add to your salad, toss, divide into small cups and serve as a snack.

Nutrition: Calories 125 Fat 2 Carbohydrate 7 g Protein 7 g

28. Mediterranean Tofu Scramble Snack

Preparation Time: 10 minutes   **Cooking Time:** 8 minutes   **Servings:** 2

Ingredients:

- ✓ 1 tsp. extra virgin olive oil
- ✓ ½ onion, chopped
- ✓ ½ zucchini, chopped
- ✓ 1 cup baby spinach
- ✓ ½ cup halved cherry tomatoes
- ✓ 1 tbsp. sundried tomatoes in oil
- ✓ 4 oz. tofu crumbled

Directions:

- ☞ Place a pan on medium to low heat. Add oil.
- ☞ When the oil is hot, add all vegetables until they are soft. Season with salt and pepper and cook for 5 minutes.
- ☞ Add spinach along with tomatoes and cook for a few minutes until the spinach wilts.
- ☞ Add tofu and mix well. Heat thoroughly. Adjust the seasoning if necessary.
- ☞ Remove from heat and serve as a snack.

Nutrition: Cal 134 Fat 9 g Carbs 5 g Fiber 1 g Protein 10 g

29. Salmon & Kale Omelet

Preparation Time: 10 minutes

Cooking Time: 7 minutes

Servings: 4

Ingredients:

- ✓ 6 eggs
- ✓ 2 tablespoons unsweetened almond milk
- ✓ Salt and ground black pepper, to taste
- ✓ 2 tablespoons olive oil
- ✓ 4 ounces smoked salmon, cut into bite-sized chunks
- ✓ 2 cup fresh kale, tough ribs removed and chopped finely
- ✓ 4 scallions, chopped finely

Directions:

- ☞ In a bowl, place the eggs, coconut milk, salt, and black pepper and beat well. Set aside. In a non-stick wok, heat the oil over medium heat.
- ☞ Place the egg mixture evenly and cook for about 30 seconds without stirring. Place the salmon kale and scallions on top of the egg mixture evenly.
- ☞ Now, reduce heat to low. With the lid, cover the wok and cook for about 4–5 minutes or until the omelet is done completely. Uncover the wok and cook for about 1 minute.
- ☞ Carefully, transfer the omelet onto a serving plate and serve.

30. Eggs with Kale

Preparation Time: 15 minutes **Cooking Time:** 25 minutes **Servings:** 4

Ingredients:

- ✓ 2 tablespoons olive oil
- ✓ 1 yellow onion, chopped
- ✓ 2 garlic cloves, minced
- ✓ 1 cup tomatoes, chopped
- ✓ ½ pound fresh kale, tough ribs removed and chopped
- ✓ 1 teaspoon ground cumin
- ✓ ¼ teaspoon red pepper flakes, crushed
- ✓ Salt and ground black pepper, to taste
- ✓ 4 eggs
- ✓ 2 tablespoons fresh parsley, chopped

Directions:

- ☞ Heat the oil in a large wok over medium heat and sauté the onion for about 4–5 minutes. Add garlic and sauté for about 1 minute.
- ☞ Add the tomatoes, spices, salt, and black pepper and cook for about 2–3 minutes, stirring frequently. Stir in the kale and cook for about 4–5 minutes.
- ☞ Carefully, crack eggs on top of the kale mixture. With the lid, cover the wok and cook for about 10 minutes, or until the desired doneness of eggs. Serve hot with the garnishing of parsley.

Nutrition: Calories 175 Fat 11.7 g Carbs 11.5 g Sodium 130 mg Fiber 2.2 g Protein 8.2

31. Pancakes with Apples and Blackcurrants

Preparation Time: 5 Minutes **Cooking Time**: 50 Minutes **Servings**: 4

Ingredients:

- ✓ 2 apples cut into small chunks
- ✓ 2 cups of quick cooking oats
- ✓ 1 cup flour of your choice
- ✓ 2 egg whites
- ✓ 1 ¼ cups almond milk, unsweetened
- ✓ Cooking spray
- ✓ 1 cup blackcurrants, stalks removed
- ✓ 3 tbsp. water may use less
- ✓ 2 tbsp. raw sugar, or coconut sugar, or honey, or a few stevia drops (optional)

Directions:

1. Place the ingredients for the topping in a small pot simmer, stirring frequently for about 10 minutes until it cooks down and the juices are released. Take the dry ingredients and mix in a bowl. After, add the apples and the milk a bit at a time (you may not use it all), until it is a batter. Whisk the egg whites until they are firm and gently mix them into the pancake batter.

2. Set aside in the refrigerator. Spray a flat pan with cooking spray, and when hot, pour some of the batter into it in a pancake shape. When the pancakes start to have golden brown edges and form air bubbles, they are ready to be flipped. Repeat for the next pancakes. Top each pancake with the berry topping.

Nutrition: Calories: 370kcal, Fat: 10.83 g, Carbohydrates: 79 g, Protein: 11.71 g

32. Flax Waffles

Preparation Time: 5 minutes **Cooking Time**: 5 minutes **Servings**: 2

Ingredients

- ✓ ½ cup whole-wheat flour
- ✓ ½ tbsp. flaxseed meal
- ✓ ½ tsp baking powder
- ✓ 1 tbsp. olive oil
- ✓ ½ cup almond milk, unsweetened
- ✓ ¼ tsp vanilla extract, unsweetened

✓ 2 tbsp. raw sugar, or coconut sugar, or honey, or a few stevia drops (optional)

Directions:

1. Switch on a mini waffle maker and let it preheat for 5 minutes. Meanwhile, take a medium bowl, place all the ingredients in it, and then mix by using an immersion blender until smooth.
2. Pour the batter evenly into the waffle maker, shut with lid, and let it cook for 3 to 4 minutes until firm and golden brown. Serve straight away. Cool the waffles, divide them between two meal prep containers, evenly add berries into the container, and then add maple syrup in mini-meal prep cups.
3. Cover each container with lid and store in the refrigerator for up to 5 days.
4. When ready to eat, enjoy them cold or reheat them in the microwave for 40 to 60 seconds or more until hot.

Nutrition: Calories 220kcal, Fat 3.7 g, Carbohydrate 7 g, Protein 21.5g

33. Raspberries Parfait

Preparation Time: 5 minutes   **Cooking Time**: 0 minutes   **Servings**: 2

Ingredients

✓ 4 oz. raspberries
✓ 3 tbsp. chia seeds
✓ 2 ½ tbsp. shredded coconut
✓ 3 tbsp. maple syrup
✓ 8 oz. almond milk, unsweetened
✓ ½ tsp vanilla extract, unsweetened

Directions:

1. Take a medium bowl, place chia and coconut in it; add maple syrup and vanilla pour in the milk and whisk until well combined. Let the mixture rest for 30 minutes, then stir it and refrigerate for a minimum of 3 hours or overnight.
2. Assemble the parfait: divide half of the chia mixture into the bottom of serving glass, and then top evenly with three-fourth of raspberries. Cover berries with remaining chia seed mixture and then place remaining berries on top. Serve straight away.
3. Use wide-mouth pint jars to layer parfait cover tightly with lids and store jars in the refrigerator for up to 7 days. When ready to eat, enjoy it cold.

Nutrition: Calories 239kcal, Fat 9.5 g, Carbohydrate 9.9 g, Protein 34g

34. Blueberries Pancake

Preparation Time: 5 minutes   **Cooking Time**: 10 minutes;   **Servings**: 2

Ingredients

✓ 1 banana, peeled
✓ 4 tbsp. peanut butter
✓ ¼ cup whole-wheat flour
✓ 2 oz. blueberries
✓ 1 tbsp. maple syrup
✓ A pinch of ground cinnamon
✓ ½ cup almond milk, unsweetened
✓ Cooking spray

Directions:

1. Add all the ingredients in a blender and then pulse for 2 minutes until smooth. Spray a medium skillet pan with cooking spray, place it over medium heat and until it gets hot.
2. Pour in some batter into the pan, shape batter to form a pancake, and cook for 2 to 3 minutes per side until golden brown.
3. Transfer cooked pancakes to a plate and then repeat with the remaining batter. Serve straight away. Pancakes can be stored up to 3 days in the fridge using a proper container with a lid. When ready to eat, reheat in the microwave oven for 1 to 2 minutes until hot and then serve.

Nutrition: Calories 408kcal, Fat 14 g, Carbohydrate 53 g, Protein 10.2g

35. Cashew Biscuits

Preparation Time: 25 minutes   **Cooking Time**: 14 minutes   **Servings**: 9

Ingredients

- ✓ 1¼ cups whole wheat flour
- ✓ ⅓ cup toasted whole cashews, unsalted
- ✓ ½ tsp fine sea salt
- ✓ 1½ teaspoons baking powder
- ✓ 1 tbsp. coconut oil
- ✓ 3 tbsp. natural smooth cashew butter
- ✓ ½ cup soft silken tofu or unsweetened plain yogurt

Directions:

1. Preheat the oven to 425°F. Line a baking sheet with parchment paper. Place the flour and nuts in a food processor. Pulse until almost all the nuts are chopped: a few larger pieces are okay and add texture to the cookies. Add salt and baking powder and pulse a couple of times.
2. Add oil and nut butter and pulse to combine. Add tofu or yogurt, and pulse until a crumbly (but not dry) dough forms. Gather the dough on a piece of parchment and pat it together to shape into a 6-inch square.
3. Cut into nine 2-inch square biscuits. Transfer the cookies to the baking sheet. Bake for 12 to 14 minutes or until golden brown at the edges cool on a wire rack and serve.

Nutrition: Calories 166kcal, Fat 3.7 g, Carbohydrate 27 g, Protein 3.5g

36. Raspberry Waffles

Preparation Time: 5 minutes
Cooking Time: 5 minutes
Servings: 2

Ingredients:

- ✓ ½ cup whole-wheat flour
- ✓ 1 ½ tbsp. chopped raspberry
- ✓ ½ tsp baking powder
- ✓ 1 tbsp. olive oil
- ✓ ½ cup almond milk, unsweetened
- ✓ ¼ tsp vanilla extract, unsweetened
- ✓ 2 tbsp. coconut sugar or a few drops of stevia (optional)

Directions:

1. Switch on the waffle maker and let it preheat for 5 minutes. Meanwhile, take a medium bowl, place all the ingredients in it, and then mix by using an immersion blender until smooth.
2. Pour the batter evenly into the waffle maker, shut with lid, and let it cook for 3 to 4 minutes until firm and golden brown. Serve straight away. Cool the waffles, divide them between two meal prep containers, evenly add berries into the container, and then add maple syrup in mini-meal prep cups.
3. Cover each container with lid and store in the refrigerator for up to 5 days.
4. When ready to eat, enjoy them cold or reheat them in the microwave for 40 to 60 seconds or more until hot.

Nutrition: Calories 229kcal, Fat 3.7 g, Carbohydrate 35.4 g, Protein 3.5g

37. Kale Scramble

Preparation Time: 10 minutes   **Cooking Time**: 6 minutes   **Servings**: 2

Ingredients:

- ✓ 4 eggs
- ✓ 1/8 tsp ground turmeric

✓ Salt and ground black pepper, to taste

✓ 1 tbsp. water
✓ 2 teaspoons olive oil

✓ 1 cup fresh kale, chopped

Directions:

1. In a bowl, add the eggs, turmeric, salt, black pepper, and water and with a whisk, beat until foamy. In a skillet, heat the oil over medium heat.
2. Add the egg mixture and stir to combine.

3. Reduce the heat to medium-low and cook for about 1–2 minutes, stirring frequently.
4. Stir in the kale and cook for about 3–4 minutes, stirring frequently.
5. Remove from the heat and serve immediately.

Nutrition: Calories 183kcal, Fat 13.4 g, Carbohydrate 4.3 g, Protein 12.1 g

38. Tomato Frittata

Preparation Time: 10 minutes

Cooking Time: 20 minutes

Servings: 2

Ingredients:

✓ ¼ cup cheddar cheese, grated
✓ ¼ cup kalamata olives halved

✓ 8 cherry tomatoes, halved
✓ 4 large eggs
✓ 1 tbsp. fresh parsley, chopped

✓ 1 tbsp. fresh basil, chopped
✓ 1 tbsp. olive oil
✓ 1 tbsp. tomato paste

Directions:

1. Whisk eggs together in a large mixing bowl.
2. Toss in the parsley, basil, olives, tomatoes and cheese, stirring thoroughly. In a small skillet, heat the olive oil over high heat. Pour in the frittata mixture and cook until firm (around 10 minutes).

3. Remove the skillet from the hob and place it under the grill for 5 minutes until golden brown.
4. Divide into portions and serve immediately.

Nutrition: Calories 269 kcal; Fat: 23.76 g, Carbohydrate: 5.49 g, Protein: 9.23 g

39. Green Omelet

Preparation Time: 5 Minutes

Cooking Time: 35 Minutes

Servings: 1

Ingredients:

✓ 1 tsp of olive oil
✓ 1 shallot peeled and finely chopped

✓ 2 large eggs
✓ Salt and freshly ground black pepper

✓ A handful of parsley, finely chopped
✓ A handful of rocket

Directions:

1. Heat the oil in a large frying pan, over medium low heat. Add the shallot and gently fry for about 5 minutes. Increase the heat and cook for two more minutes.
2. In a cup or bowl, whisk the eggs; distribute the shallot in the pan then add in the eggs. Evenly distribute the eggs by tipping over the pan on all sides.

3. Cook for about a minute before lifting the sides and allowing the runny eggs to move to the base of the pan.
4. Sprinkle rocket leaves and parsley on top and season with pepper and salt to taste.
5. When the base is just starting to brown, tip it onto a plate and serve right away.

Nutrition: Calories 221 kcal, Fat 28 g, Carbohydrate 10.6 g, Protein 9.5 g

CHAPTER 3: LUNCH

40. Avocado and Salmon Salad Buffet

Preparation Time: 10 minutes   **Cooking Time:** 10 minutes   **Servings:** 2 - 3

Ingredients:

- ✓ ½ pieces cucumber
- ✓ 1 piece avocado
- ✓ ½ pieces red onion
- ✓ 250 g mixed salad
- ✓ 4 slices smoked salmon

Directions:

- ☞ Slice the cucumber and avocado into cubes and chop the onion. Spread the lettuce leaves on deep plates and spread the cucumber, avocado, and onion over the lettuce.
- ☞ Season with salt and pepper (you can also add a little olive oil to the salad).
- ☞ Place smoked salmon slices on top and serve.

Nutrition: Calories: 209 Cal Fat: 21 gCarbs: 33.19 g Protein: 8.82 g Fiber: 16.7 g

41. Paleo-Force Bars

Preparation Time: 15 minutes   **Cooking Time:** 10 minutes plus freezing time   **Servings:** 10

Ingredients:

- ✓ 10 pieces Medjoul dates (cored)
- ✓ 100 g Grated coconut
- ✓ 100 g crushed linseed
- ✓ 75 g Cashew nuts
- ✓ 60 g Coconut oil

Directions:

- ☞ Put all ingredients in a food processor and pulse until a sticky and granular dough is formed. Line a small baking sheet with parchment paper.
- ☞ Spread the mixture on the bottom of the baking sheet and press down firmly.
- ☞ Let them solidify and harden them in the freezer for a few hours.
- ☞ After the mixture has hardened, cut it into bars.
- ☞ If you want to pack them as individual snacks, wrap the bars in cling film or baking paper.

Nutrition: Calories: 267 Cal Fat: 33.76 g Carbs: 89.14 g Protein: 18.2 g Fiber: 11.8 g

42. Vinaigrette

Preparation Time: 5 minutes   **Cooking Time:** 0 minutes   **Servings:** 1 cup

Ingredients:

- ✓ 4 teaspoons Mustard yellow
- ✓ 4 tablespoon White wine vinegar
- ✓ 1 teaspoon Honey
- ✓ 165 ml Olive oil

Directions:

- ☞ Whisk the mustard, vinegar, and honey in a bowl with a whisk until they are well mixed.
- ☞ Add the olive oil in small amounts while whisking with a whisk until the vinaigrette is thick. Season with salt and pepper.

Nutrition: Calories: 45 Cal Fat: 0.67 g Carbs: 7.18 g Protein: 0.79 g Fiber: 0.8 g

43. Spicy Ras-El-Hanout Dressing

Preparation Time: 10 minutes   **Cooking Time:** 5 minutes   **Servings:** 1 cup

Ingredients:

- ✓ 125 ml olive oil
- ✓ 1 piece lemon (the juice)
- ✓
- ✓ 2 teaspoons honey
- ✓ 1 ½ teaspoon Ras el Hanout
- ✓ ½ pieces red pepper

Directions:

- ☞ Remove the seeds from the chili pepper.
- ☞ Chop the chili pepper as finely as possible.
- ☞ Place the pepper in a bowl with lemon juice, honey, and Ras-El-Hanout and whisk with a whisk.
- ☞ Then add the olive oil drop by drop while continuing to whisk.

Nutrition: Calories: 81 Cal Fat: 0.86 g Carbs: 20.02 g Protein: 1.32 g Fiber: 0.9 g

44. Chicken Rolls With Pesto

Preparation Time: 15 minutes   **Cooking Time:** 20 minutes   **Servings:** 4

Ingredients:

- ✓ 2 tablespoon pine nuts
- ✓ 25 g yeast flakes
- ✓ 1 clove garlic (chopped)
- ✓ 15 g fresh basil
- ✓ 85 ml olive oil
- ✓ 2 pieces chicken breast

Directions:

- ☞ Preheat the oven to 175 ° C.
- ☞ Bake the pine nuts in a dry pan over medium heat for 3 minutes until golden brown. Place on a plate and set aside.
- ☞ Put the pine nuts, yeast flakes, and garlic in a food processor and grind them finely.
- ☞ Add the basil and oil and mix briefly until you get a pesto.
- ☞ Season with salt and pepper.
- ☞ Place each piece of the chicken breast between 2 pieces of cling film
- ☞ Beat with a saucepan or rolling pin until the chicken breast is about 0.6 cm thick.
- ☞ Remove the cling film and spread the pesto on the chicken.
- ☞ Roll up the chicken breasts and use cocktail skewers to hold them together.
- ☞ Season with salt and pepper.
- ☞ Melt the coconut oil in a saucepan and brown the chicken rolls over high heat on all sides.
- ☞ Put the chicken rolls in a baking dish, place in the oven and bake for 15-20 minutes until they are done.
- ☞ Slice the rolls diagonally and serve with the rest of the pesto.
- ☞ Goes well with a tomato salad.

Nutrition: Calories: 105 Cal Fat: 54.19 g Carbs: 6.53 g Protein: 127 g Fiber: 1.9 g

45. Vegetarian Curry From The Crock-Pot

Preparation Time: 6 h 10 min   **Cooking Time:** 6 hours   **Servings:** 2

Ingredients:

- ✓ 4 pieces carrot
- ✓ 2 pieces sweet potato
- ✓ 1 piece onion
- ✓ 3 cloves garlic
- ✓ 2 tablespoon curry powder
- ✓ 1 teaspoon ground caraway (ground)
- ✓ ¼ teaspoon chili powder
- ✓ 1/4 TL Celtic sea salt
- ✓ 1 pinch cinnamon
- ✓ 100 ml vegetable broth
- ✓ 400 g tomato cubes (can)
- ✓ 250 g sweet peas
- ✓ 2 tablespoon tapioca flour

Directions:

- ☞ Roughly chop vegetables and potatoes and press garlic. Halve the sugar snap peas. Put the carrots, sweet potatoes, and onions in the slow cooker.
- ☞ Mix tapioca flour with curry powder, cumin, chili powder, salt, and cinnamon, and sprinkle this mixture on the vegetables.
- ☞ Pour the vegetable broth over it. Close the lid of the slow cooker and let it simmer for 6 hours on a low setting.
- ☞ Stir in the tomatoes and sugar snap peas for the last hour.
- ☞ Cauliflower rice is a great addition to this dish.

Nutrition: Calories: 397 kcal Protein: 9.35 g Fat: 6.07 g Carbohydrates: 81.55 g

---

46. Fried Cauliflower Rice

Preparation Time: 20 minutes   **Cooking Time:** 25 minutes   **Servings:** 4

Ingredients:

- ✓ 1 piece cauliflower
- ✓ 2 tablespoon coconut oil
- ✓ 1 piece red onion
- ✓ 4 cloves garlic
- ✓ 60 ml vegetable broth
- ✓ Fresh ginger
- ✓ 1 teaspoon chili flakes
- ✓ ½ pieces carrot
- ✓ ½ pieces red bell pepper
- ✓ ½ pieces lemon (the juice)
- ✓ 2 tablespoon pumpkin seeds
- ✓ 2 tablespoon fresh coriander

Directions:

- ☞ Cut the cauliflower into small rice grains in a food processor. Finely chop the onion, garlic, and ginger, cut the carrot into thin strips, dice the bell pepper and finely chop the herbs.
- ☞ Melt 1 tablespoon of coconut oil in a pan and add half of the onion and garlic to the pan and fry briefly until translucent.
- ☞ Add cauliflower rice and season with salt.
- ☞ Pour in the broth and stir everything until it evaporates and the cauliflower rice is tender.
- ☞ Take the rice out of the pan and set it aside.
- ☞ Melt the rest of the coconut oil in the pan and add the remaining onions, garlic, ginger, carrots, and peppers.
- ☞ Fry for a few minutes until the vegetables are tender. Season them with a little salt.
- ☞ Add the cauliflower rice again, heat the whole dish, and add the lemon juice.
- ☞ Garnish with pumpkin seeds and coriander before serving.

Nutrition: Calories: 261 Cal Fat: 35.61 g. Carbs: 34.5 g Protein: 10.27 g Fiber: 8.4 g

47. Mediterranean Paleo Pizza

Preparation Time: 15 minutes **Cooking Time:** 15 minutes **Servings:** 3 - 4

Ingredients:

For the pizza crusts:

- ✓ 120 g Tapioca flour
- ✓ 1 teaspoon Celtic sea salt
- ✓ 2 tablespoon Italian spice mix
- ✓ 45 g coconut flour
- ✓ 120 ml olive oil (mild)

- ✓ Water (warm) 120 ml
- ✓ Egg (beaten) 1 piece

Topping:

- ✓ 2 tablespoon tomato paste (can)
- ✓ ½ pieces zucchini

- ✓ ½ pieces eggplant
- ✓ 2 pieces tomato
- ✓ 2 tablespoon olive oil (mild)
- ✓ 1 tablespoon balsamic vinegar

Directions:

- ☞ Preheat the oven to 190 ° C and line a baking sheet with parchment paper. Cut the vegetables into thin slices. Mix the tapioca flour with salt, Italian herbs, and coconut flour in a large bowl.
- ☞ Pour in olive oil and warm water and stir well.
- ☞ Then add the egg and stir until you get an even dough. If the dough is too shrill, add 1 tablespoon of coconut flour at a time until it is the desired thickness. Always wait a few minutes before adding more coconut flour, as it will take some time to absorb the moisture. The intent is to get a soft, sticky dough.

- ☞ Split the dough into two parts and spread them in flat circles on the baking sheet (or make 1 large sheet of pizza as shown in the picture). Bake in the oven for about 10 minutes.
- ☞ Brush the pizza with tomato paste and spread the aubergines, zucchini, and tomato overlapping on the pizza.
- ☞ Drizzle the pizza with olive oil and bake in the oven for another 10-15 minutes.
- ☞ Drizzle balsamic vinegar over the pizza before serving.

Nutrition: Calories: 229 Cal Fat: 103 g Carbs: 32 g Protein: 24 g Fiber: 31 g

48. Fried Chicken and Broccolini

Preparation Time: 10 minutes **Cooking Time:** 15 minutes **Servings:** 5

Ingredients:

- ✓ 2 tablespoon coconut oil
- ✓ 400 g chicken breast

- ✓ Bacon cubes 150 g
- ✓ Broccolini 250 g

Directions:

- ☞ Cut the chicken into cubes.
- ☞ Melt the coconut oil in a pan over medium heat and brown the chicken with the bacon cubes and cook through.

- ☞ Season with chili flakes, salt, and pepper.
- ☞ Add broccolini and fry.
- ☞ Stack on a plate and enjoy!

Nutrition: Calories: 198 Cal Fat: 64.2 g Carbs: 0 g Protein: 83.4 g Fiber: 0 g

49. Braised Leek with Pine Nuts

Preparation Time: 15 minutes   **Cooking Time:** 15 minutes   **Servings:** 4

Ingredients:

- ✓ 20 g ghee
- ✓ 2 teaspoon olive oil
- ✓ 2 pieces leek
- ✓ 150 ml vegetable broth
- ✓ Fresh parsley
- ✓ 1 tablespoon fresh oregano
- ✓ 1 tablespoon Pine nuts (roasted)

Directions:

- ☞ Cut the leek into thin rings and finely chop the herbs. Roast the pine nuts in a dry pan over medium heat.
- ☞ Melt the ghee together with the olive oil in a large pan.
- ☞ Cook the leek until golden brown for 5 minutes, stirring constantly. Add the vegetable broth and cook for another 10 minutes until the leek is tender.
- ☞ Stir in the herbs and sprinkle the pine nuts on the dish just before serving.

Nutrition: Calories: 189 Cal Fat: 9.67 g Carbs: 25.21 g Protein: 2.7 g Fiber: 3.2 g

50. Sweet and Sour Pan with Cashew Nuts

Preparation Time: 15 minutes   **Cooking Time:** 20 minutes   **Servings:** 4

Ingredients:

- ✓ 2 tablespoon coconut oil
- ✓ 2 pieces red onion
- ✓ 2 pieces yellow bell pepper
- ✓ 250 g white cabbage
- ✓ 150 g Pak choi
- ✓ 50 g Mung bean sprouts
- ✓ 4 pieces pineapple slices
- ✓ 50 g cashew nuts

For the sweet and sour sauce:

- ✓ 60 ml apple cider vinegar
- ✓ 4 tablespoon coconut blossom sugar
- ✓ 1 ½ tablespoon tomato paste
- ✓ 1 teaspoon coconut-Aminos
- ✓ 2 teaspoon arrowroot powder
- ✓ 75 ml water

Directions:

- ☞ Roughly cut the vegetables.
- ☞ Mix the arrowroot with five tablespoons of cold water into a paste.
- ☞ Then mix in all the other ingredients for the sauce in a saucepan and add the arrowroot paste for binding.
- ☞ Melt the coconut oil in a pan and fry the onion.
- ☞ Add the bell pepper, cabbage, Pak choi, and bean sprouts and stir-fry until the vegetables become a little softer.
- ☞ Add the pineapple and cashew nuts and stir a few more times.
- ☞ Pour a little sauce over the wok dish and serve.

Nutrition: Calories: 114 Cal Fat: 55.62 g Carbs: 55.3 g Protein: 30.49 g Fiber: 24.1 g

51. Butternut Pumpkin with Buckwheat

Preparation Time: 5 minutes

Cooking Time: 50 minutes

Servings: 4

Ingredients:

- ✓ Three cloves of garlic, finely chopped
- ✓ Two small chilies, finely chopped
- ✓ One tablespoon cumin
- ✓ One cinnamon stick
- ✓ Two tablespoons turmeric
- ✓ 800g chopped canned tomatoes
- ✓ 300ml vegetable broth
- ✓ 100g dates, seeded and chopped
- ✓ one 400g tin of chickpeas, drained
- ✓ 500g butter squash, peeled, seeded, and cut into pieces
- ✓ 200g buckwheat
- ✓ 5g coriander, chopped
- ✓ 10g parsley, chopped
- ✓ One tablespoon of extra virgin olive oil
- ✓ One red onion, finely chopped
- ✓ One tablespoon fresh ginger, finely chopped

Directions:

- ☞ Preheat the oven to 400 °.
- ☞ Heat the olive oil in a frying pan and sauté the onion, ginger, garlic, and Thai chili. After two minutes, add cumin, cinnamon, and turmeric and cook for another two minutes while stirring.
- ☞ Add the tomatoes, dates, stock, and chickpeas, stir well and cook over low heat for 45 to 60 minutes. Add some water as required. In the meantime, mix the pumpkin pieces with olive oil. Bake in the oven for about 30 minutes until soft.
- ☞ Cook the buckwheat according to the directions and add the remaining turmeric. When everything is cooked, add the pumpkin to the other ingredients in the roaster and serve with the buckwheat. Sprinkle with coriander and parsley.

Nutrition: Calories per serving 248.1 Total Fat .8.7g Saturated fat per serving 2.6g Monounsaturated fat per serving 1.5g Polyunsaturated fat per serving 4.0g Protein per serving 8.5g

52. Pasta with Kale And Black Olive

Preparation Time: 10 minutes

Cooking Time: 40 minutes

Servings: 3

Ingredients:

- ✓ 60 g of buckwheat pasta
- ✓ 180 gr of pasta
- ✓ Six leaves of washed curly kale

- ✓ 20 black olives
- ✓ Two tablespoons of oil
- ✓ ½ chili pepper

Directions:

☞ Cut the curly kale leaves into strips about 4 cm wide; cook them in salted boiling water for 5 minutes. Also, add the pasta to the pan. While the pasta is cooking, in a non-stick pan, towards the oil and olives.

☞ Drain the pasta and cabbage (keeping some cooking water aside) and add them to the olives.

☞ Mix well, adding, if needed, a little cooking water. Add the chili pepper and keep everything well.

Nutrition: Calories per serving 372.7 g Total Fat .28.0g Saturated fat per serving 2.7g Monounsaturated fat per serving 10.0g Polyunsaturated fat per serving 2.1g Protein per serving 3.6g

53. Butter Bean and Miso Dip with Celery Sticks and Oatcakes

Preparation Time: 5 minutes

Cooking Time: 55 minutes

Servings: 4

Ingredients:

- ✓ 2 x 14-ounce cans (400g each) of butter beans, drained and rinsed
- ✓ Three tablespoons extra virgin olive oil
- ✓ Two tablespoons brown miso paste
- ✓ Juice and grated zest of 1/2 unwaxed lemon
- ✓ Four medium scallions, trimmed and finely chopped
- ✓ One garlic clove, crushed
- ✓ 1/4 Thai chili, finely chopped celery sticks, to serve
- ✓ Oatcakes, to serve

Directions:

☞ Simply mash the first seven ingredients together with a potato masher until you have a coarse mixture.

☞ Serve as a dip with celery sticks and oatcakes.

Nutrition: Calories 143. Total fat 3 g .saturated fat Trace. Trans fat 0 g. Monounsaturated fat 2 g. Cholesterol Trace.

54. Spiced Scrambled Eggs

Preparation Time: 5 minutes

Cooking Time: 15 minutes

Servings: 4

Ingredients:

- ✓ One teaspoon extra virgin olive oil
- ✓ 1/8 cup (20g) red onion, finely chopped
- ✓ 1/2 Thai chili, finely chopped
- ✓ Three medium eggs
- ✓ 1/4 cup (50ml) milk
- ✓ One teaspoon ground turmeric
- ✓ Two tablespoons (5g) parsley, finely chopped

Directions:

- ☞ Heat the oil in a frying pan and fry the red onion and chili until soft but not browned.
- ☞ Whisk together the eggs, milk, turmeric, and parsley. Add to the hot pan and continue cooking over low to medium heat, continually moving the egg mixture around the pan to scramble it and stop it from sticking/burning.
- ☞ When you have achieved your desired consistency, serve.

Nutrition: Calories 218.2. Total fat 15.3 g. Saturated fat 6.3 g. Fat 0 g. Monounsaturated fat 5.5 g. Cholesterol 386.9 mg

55. Shitake Soup with Tofu

Preparation Time: 5 minutes

Cooking Time: 15 minutes

Servings: 4

Ingredients:

- ✓ 10g dried Wakame algae (instant)
- ✓ 1-liter vegetable stock
- ✓ 200g shitake mushrooms, sliced
- ✓ 120g miso paste
- ✓ 400g natural tofu, cut into cubes
- ✓ Two spring onions
- ✓ One red chili, chopped

Directions:

- ☞ Bring the stock to boil, add the mushrooms, and cook for 2 minutes. In the meantime, dissolve the miso paste in a bowl with some warm stock, put it back into the pot together with the tofu, do not let it boil anymore.
- ☞ Soak the Wakame as needed (on the packet), add the spring onions and Tai Chi, and stir again and serve.

56. Chicken Curry with Potatoes and Kale

Preparation Time: 5 minutes

Cooking Time: 45 minutes

Servings: 4

Ingredients:

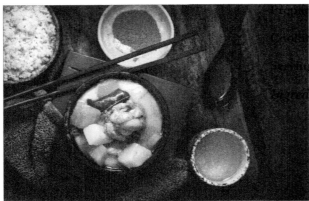

- ✓ Three cloves of garlic, finely chopped
- ✓ One tablespoon freshly chopped ginger
- ✓ One tablespoon curry powder
- ✓ One tin of small tomatoes (400ml)
- ✓ 500ml chicken broth
- ✓ 200ml coconut milk
- ✓ Two pieces cardamom
- ✓ One cinnamon stick
- ✓ 600g chicken breast, cut into pieces
- ✓ 600g potatoes (mainly waxy)
- ✓ Four tablespoons of extra virgin olive oil
- ✓ 10g parsley, chopped
- ✓ Three tablespoons turmeric
- ✓ 175g kale, chopped
- ✓ Two red onions, sliced
- ✓ 5g coriander, chopped
- ✓ Two red chilies, finely chopped

Directions:

- ☞ Marinate the chicken in a teaspoon of olive oil and a tablespoon of turmeric for about 30 minutes. Then fry in a high frying pan at high heat for about 4 minutes. Remove from the pan and set aside.
- ☞ Heat a tablespoon of oil in a pan with chili, garlic, onion, and ginger. Boil everything over medium heat and then add the curry powder and a tablespoon of turmeric and cook for another two minutes, stirring occasionally. Add tomatoes, cook for another two minutes until finally chicken stock, coconut milk, cardamom, and cinnamon stick are added. Cook for about 45 to 60 minutes and add some broth if necessary.
- ☞ In the meantime, preheat the oven to 425°. Peel and chop the potatoes. Bring water to the boil, add the vegetables with turmeric, and cook for 5 minutes. Then pour off the water and let it evaporate for about 10 minutes. Spread olive oil with the potatoes on a baking tray and bake in the oven for 30 minutes.
- ☞ When the potatoes and curry are almost ready, add the coriander, kale, and chicken and cook for five minutes until the chicken is hot. Add parsley to the potatoes and serve with the chicken curry.

Nutrition: Calories 894 Carbs 162g Fat 22g Protein 25g Fiber 26g Carbs 136g Sodium 2447mg Cholesterol 0mg

57. Buckwheat Noodles with Salmon and Rocket

Preparation Time: 5 minutes

Cooking Time: 45 minutes

Servings: 4

Ingredients:

- ✓ Two tablespoons of extra virgin olive oil
- ✓ One red onion, finely chopped
- ✓ Two cloves of garlic, finely chopped
- ✓ Two red chilies, finely chopped
- ✓ 150g cherry tomatoes halved
- ✓ 100ml white wine
- ✓ 300g buckwheat noodles
- ✓ 250g smoked salmon
- ✓ Two tablespoons of capers
- ✓ Juice of half a lemon
- ✓ 60g rocket salad
- ✓ 10g parsley, chopped

Directions:

- ☞ Heat 1 teaspoon of the oil in a coated pan, add onions, garlic, and chili at medium temperature, and fry briefly. Then add the tomatoes and the white wine to the pan and allow the wine to reduce. Cook the pasta according to the directions.
- ☞ In the meantime, cut the salmon into strips, and when the pasta is ready, add it to the pan together with the capers, lemon juice, capers rocket, remaining olive oil, and parsley, and mix.

Nutrition: Calories 320.1 Carbs. 25.2 Fat 13.0 g Protein 27.0 g

58. Tofu with Cauliflower

Preparation Time: 5 Minutes

Cooking Time: 45 Minutes

Servings: 2

Ingredients:

- ✓ ¼ cup red pepper, seeded
- ✓ 1 Thai chili, cut in two halves, seeded
- ✓ 2 cloves of garlic
- ✓ 1 tsp of olive oil
- ✓ 1 pinch of cumin
- ✓ 1 pinch of coriander
- ✓ Juice of a half lemon
- ✓ 8oz tofu
- ✓ 8oz cauliflower, roughly chopped
- ✓ 1 ½oz red onions, finely chopped
- ✓ 1 tsp finely chopped ginger
- ✓ 2 teaspoons turmeric
- ✓ 1oz dried tomatoes, finely chopped
- ✓ 1oz parsley, chopped

Directions:

1. Preheat oven to 400 °F. Slice the peppers and put them in an ovenproof dish with chili and garlic.
2. Pour some olive oil over it, add the dried herbs and put it in the oven until the peppers are soft about 20 minutes).
3. Let it cool down, put the peppers together with the lemon juice in a blender and work it into a soft mass.
4. Cut the tofu in half and divide the halves into triangles.
5. Place the tofu in a small casserole dish, cover with the paprika mixture and place in the oven for about 20 minutes. Chop the

61

cauliflower until the pieces are smaller than a grain of rice.

6. Then, in a small saucepan, heat the garlic, onions, chili and ginger with olive oil until

they become transparent. Add turmeric and cauliflower mix well and heat again.

7. Remove from heat and add parsley and tomatoes mix well. Serve with the tofu in the sauce.

Nutrition: Calories 298kcal, Fat 5 g, Carbohydrate 55 g, Protein 27.5g

59. Lemongrass and Ginger Mackerel

Preparation Time: 10 minutes　　**Cooking Time:** 25 minutes　　**Servings:** 4

Ingredients:
- ✓ 4 mackerel fillets, skinless and boneless
- ✓ 2 tbsp. olive oil
- ✓ 1 tbsp. ginger, grated
- ✓ 2 lemongrass sticks, chopped
- ✓ 2 red chilies, chopped
- ✓ Juice of 1 lime
- ✓ A handful parsley, chopped

Directions:
1. In a roasting pan, combine the mackerel with the oil, ginger and the other ingredients, toss and bake at 390° F for 25 minutes. Divide between plates and serve.

Nutrition: Calories 251kcal, Fat 3.7 g, Carbohydrate 14 g, Protein 30g

60. Serrano Ham & Rocket Arugula

Preparation Time: 5 Minutes　　**Cooking Time:** 60 Minutes　　**Servings:** 2

Ingredients:
- ✓ 6oz Serrano ham
- ✓ 4oz rocket arugula leaves
- ✓ 2 tbsp. olive oil
- ✓ 1 tbsp. orange juice

Directions:
1. Pour the oil and juice into a bowl and toss the rocket arugula in the mixture. Serve the rocket onto plates and top it off with the ham.

Nutrition: Calories 220kcal, Fat 7 g, Carbohydrate 7 g, Protein 33.5g

61. Buckwheat with Mushrooms and Green Onions

Preparation Time: 10 minutes　　**Cooking Time:** 40 minutes　　**Servings:** 2

Ingredients:
- ✓ 1 cup buckwheat groats
- ✓ 2 cups vegetable or chicken broth
- ✓ 3 green onions, thinly sliced
- ✓ 1 cup mushrooms, sliced
- ✓ Salt and pepper to taste
- ✓ 2 tsp oil

Directions:
1. Combine all ingredients in a pot and cook on low heat for about 35-40min until the broth is completely absorbed.
2. Divide in two plates and serve immediately.

Nutrition: Calories 340kcal, Fat 10 g, Carbohydrate 51 g, Protein 11g

62. Sweet and Sour Pan with Cashew Nuts:

Preparation Time: 30 minutes　　**Cooking Time:** 0 minutes　　**Servings:** 2

Ingredients:
- ✓ 2 tbsp. Coconut oil
- ✓ 2 pieces Red onion
- ✓ 2 pieces yellow bell pepper
- ✓ 12oz White cabbage
- ✓ 6oz Pak choi
- ✓ 1 ½oz Mung bean sprouts
- ✓ 4 Pineapple slices
- ✓ 1 ½oz Cashew nuts
- ✓ ¼ cup Apple cider vinegar
- ✓ 4 tbsp. Coconut blossom sugar
- ✓ 1½ tbsp. Tomato paste
- ✓ 1 tsp Coconut-Aminos
- ✓ 2 tsp Arrowroot powder

✓ ¼ cup Water

Directions:

1. Roughly cut the vegetables. Mix the arrow root with five tbsp. of cold water into a paste.
2. Then put all the other ingredients for the sauce in a saucepan and add the arrowroot paste for binding. Melt the coconut oil in a pan and fry the onion. Add the bell pepper, cabbage, pak choi and bean sprouts and stir-fry until the vegetables become a little softer.
3. Add the pineapple and cashew nuts and stir a few more times. Pour a little sauce over the wok dish and serve.

Nutrition: Calories: 573 kcal Fat: 27.81 g Carbohydrates: 77.91 g Protein: 15.25 g

63. Casserole with Spinach and Eggplant

Preparation Time: 1 hour   **Cooking Time:** 40 minutes   **Servings:** 2

Ingredients:

✓ 1 medium Eggplant
✓ 2 medium Onion
✓ 3 tbsp. Olive oil
✓ 3 cups Spinach, fresh
✓ 4 pieces Tomatoes
✓ 2 Eggs
✓ ¼ cup Almond milk, unsweetened
✓ 2 tsp Lemon juice
✓ 4 tbsp. Parmesan

Directions:

1. Preheat the oven to 400 ° F. Cut the eggplants, onions and tomatoes into slices and sprinkle salt on the eggplant slices. Brush the eggplants and onions with olive oil and fry them in a grill pan. Cook spinach in a large saucepan over moderate heat and drain in a sieve. Put the vegetables in layers in a greased baking dish: first the eggplant, then the spinach and then the onion and the tomato.
2. Repeat this again. Whisk eggs with almond milk, lemon juice, salt and pepper and pour over the vegetables.
3. Sprinkle parmesan over the dish and bake in the oven for about 30 to 40 minutes.

Nutrition: Calories: 446 kcal Fat: 31.82 g Carbohydrates: 30.5 g Protein: 13.95 g

64. Vegetarian Curry

Preparation Time: 15 minutes   **Cooking Time:** 1 hour   **Servings:** 2

Ingredients:

✓ 4 medium Carrots
✓ 2 medium Sweet potatoes
✓ 1 large Onion
✓ 3 cloves Garlic
✓ 4 tbsp. Curry powder
✓ ½ tsp caraway, ground
✓ ½ tsp Chili powder
✓ Sea salt to taste
✓ 1 pinch Cinnamon
✓ ½ cup Vegetable broth
✓ 1 can Tomato cubes
✓ 8oz Sweet peas
✓ 2 tbsp. Tapioca flour

Directions:

1. Roughly chop carrots, sweet potatoes onions potatoes and garlic and put them all in a pot.
2. Mix tapioca flour with curry powder, cumin, chili powder, salt and cinnamon and sprinkle this mixture on the vegetables.
3. Add tomato cubes. Pour the vegetable broth over it. Close the pot with a lid, bring to a boil and let it simmer for 60 minutes on a low heat. Stir in snap peas after 30min. Cauliflower rice is a great addition to this dish.

Nutrition: Calories: 397 kcal Fat: 6.07 g Carbohydrates: 81.55 g Protein: 9.35 g

65. Fried Cauliflower Rice:

Preparation Time: 55 minutes   **Cooking Time:** 10 minutes   **Servings:** 2

Ingredients:

✓ 1 medium Cauliflower
✓ 2 tbsp. Coconut oil
✓ 1 medium Red onion
✓ 4 cloves Garlic
✓ ¼ cup Vegetable broth
✓ 2-inch fresh ginger

- ✓ 1 tsp Chili flakes
- ✓ 1/2 Carrot
- ✓ 1/2 Red bell pepper
- ✓ 1/2 Lemon, juiced
- ✓ 2 tbsp. Pumpkin seeds
- ✓ 2 tbsp. fresh coriander

Directions:

1. Cut the cauliflower into small rice grains using a food processor.
2. Finely chop the onion, garlic and ginger, cut the carrot into thin strips, dice the bell pepper and finely chop the herbs. Melt 1 tbsp. of coconut oil in a pan and add half of the onion and garlic to the pan and fry briefly until translucent. Add cauliflower rice and season with salt. Pour in the broth and stir everything until it evaporates, and the cauliflower rice is tender.
3. Take the rice out of the pan and set it aside. Melt the rest of the coconut oil in the pan and add the remaining onions, garlic, ginger, carrots and peppers.
4. Fry for a few minutes until the vegetables are tender. Season them with a little salt.
5. Add the cauliflower rice again, heat the whole dish and add the lemon juice.
6. Garnish with pumpkin seeds and coriander before serving.

Nutrition: Calories: 230 kcal Fat: 17.81 g Carbohydrates: 17.25 g, Protein: 5.13 g

66. Buckwheat with Onions

Preparation Time: 10 minutes   **Cooking Time**: 40 minutes   **Servings**: 4

Ingredients:

- ✓ 3 cups of buckwheat, rinsed
- ✓ 4 medium red onions, chopped
- ✓ 1 big white onion, chopped
- ✓ 5 oz. extra-virgin olive oil
- ✓ 3 cups of water
- ✓ Salt and pepper, to taste

Direction:

1. Soak the buckwheat in the warm water for around 10 minutes. Then add in the buckwheat to your pot. Add in the water, salt and pepper to your pot and stir well.
2. Close the lid and cook for about 30-35 minutes until the buckwheat is ready. In the meantime, in a skillet, heat the extra-virgin olive oil and fry the chopped onions for 15 minutes until clear and caramelized.
3. Add some salt and pepper and mix well. Portion the buckwheat into four bowls or mugs. Then dollop each bowl with the onions. Remember that this dish should be served warm.

Nutrition: Calories: 132; Fat: 32g; Carbohydrates: 64g; Protein: 22g

67. Baked Salmon Salad With Creamy Mint Dressing

Preparation Time: 20 minutes   **Cooking Time**: 25 minutes   **Servings**: 1

Ingredients:

- ✓ 1 salmon fillet
- ✓ 1 cup mixed salad leaves
- ✓ 1 cup lettuce leaves
- ✓ Two radishes, thinly sliced
- ✓ 1/2 cucumber, sliced
- ✓ 2 spring onions, trimmed and chopped
- ✓ 1/2 oz. parsley, roughly sliced
- ✓ For the dressing:
- ✓ 1 tsp low-carb mayonnaise
- ✓ 1 tbsp. natural yogurt
- ✓ 1 tbsp. rice vinegar
- ✓ 2 stalks mint, finely chopped

Directions:

1. Put the salmon fillet onto a baking tray and bake for 16--18 minutes until cooked
2. In a bowl, blend together the mayonnaise, yogurt, rice vinegar, mint leaves and salt and set aside 5 minutes to the flavors to mix well.
3. Arrange the salad leaves and lettuce onto a serving plate and top with all the radishes, cucumber, lettuce, celery, spring onions and parsley.
4. Drizzle the dressing.

Nutrition: Calories: 433 Fat: 9g Carbohydrate: 32g Protein: 18g

CHAPTER 4: DINNER

68. Tofu Thai Curry

Preparation Time: 5 minutes

Cooking Time: 65 minutes

Servings: 2

Ingredients:

- ✓ 200g (7oz) sugar snaps peas
- ✓ 5cm (2 inches) chunk fresh ginger root, peeled and finely chopped
- ✓ 2 red onions, chopped
- ✓ 2 cloves of garlic, crushed
- ✓ 400g (14oz) tofu, diced
- ✓ 2 bird's eye chilies
- ✓ 2 tablespoons tomato puree
- ✓ 1 stalk of lemongrass, inner stalks only
- ✓ 1 tablespoon fresh coriander (cilantro), chopped
- ✓ 1 teaspoon cumin
- ✓ 300mls (½ pint) coconut milk
- ✓ 200mls (7fl oz) vegetable stock (broth)
- ✓ 1 tablespoon virgin olive oil
- ✓ Juice of 1 lime

Directions:

☞ Heat the oil in a frying pan, add the onion and cook for 4 minutes. Add in the chilies, cumin, ginger, and garlic, and cook for 2 minutes.

☞ Add the tomato puree, lemongrass, sugar-snap peas, lime juice, and tofu and cook for 2 minutes. Pour in the stock (broth), coconut milk, and coriander (cilantro) and simmer for 5 minutes.

☞ Serve with brown rice or buckwheat and a handful of rockets (arugula) leaves on the side.

Nutrition: Calories 346.3. Total fat 26.4 g. Saturated fat Trace 2.0 g. Trans fat 0 g. Monounsaturated fat 5.4 g.

69. Beans & Kale Soup

Preparation Time: 15 minutes

Cooking Time: 30 minutes

Servings: 6

Ingredients:

- ✓ 2 tablespoons olive oil
- ✓ 2 onions, chopped
- ✓ 4 garlic cloves, minced
- ✓ 1-pound kale, tough ribs removed and chopped
- ✓ 2 (14-ounce) cans cannellini beans, rinsed and drained
- ✓ 6 cups of water

✓ Salt and ground black pepper, as required

Directions:

☞ In a large pan, heat the oil over medium heat and sauté the onion and garlic for about 4-5 minutes.

☞ Add the kale and cook for about 1-2 minutes.

☞ Add beans, water, salt, and black pepper and bring to a boil.

☞ Cook partially covered for about 15-20 minutes. Serve hot.

Nutrition: Calories 270.4. Total fat 4.7 g. Saturated fat Trace 0.6 g. Trans fat 0 g. Monounsaturated fat 2.6 g. Cholesterol Trace. 0.0 mg

70. Lentils & Greens Soup

Preparation Time: 15 minutes

Cooking Time: 55 minutes

Servings: 6

Ingredients:

✓ 3 garlic cloves, minced

✓ 1½ teaspoon ground cumin

✓ 1 teaspoon ground turmeric

✓ ¼ teaspoon red pepper flakes

✓ 1 (14½-ounce) can diced tomatoes

✓ 1 cup red lentils, rinsed

✓ 5½ cups water

✓ 2 cups fresh mustard greens, chopped

✓ Salt and ground black pepper, as required

✓ 2 tablespoons fresh lemon juice

✓ 1 tablespoon olive oil

✓ 2 carrots, peeled and chopped

✓ 2 celery stalks, chopped

✓ 1 medium red onion, chopped

Directions:

☞ Heat olive oil in a large pan over medium heat and sauté the carrots, celery, and onion for about 5-6 minutes. Add the garlic and spices and sauté for about 1 minute.

☞ Add the tomatoes and cook for about 2-3 minutes.

☞ Stir in the lentils and water and bring to a boil.

☞ Now, reduce the heat to low and simmer, covered for about 35 minutes.

☞ Stir in greens and cook for about 5 minutes.

☞ Stir in salt, black pepper, and lemon juice and remove from the heat. Serve hot.

Nutrition: Calories 167.4 Total fat 5.5 g. Saturated fat 1.2 g Monounsaturated fat 4.3 g. Cholesterol. 3.3 mg

71. Asian Slaw

Preparation Time: 5 minutes
Cooking Time: 25 minutes
Servings: 2

Ingredients:

- ✓ Peanuts, chopped - .5 cup
- ✓ Sriracha – 2 teaspoons
- ✓ Rice wine vinegar - .25 cup
- ✓ Sesame seed oil - .5 teaspoon
- ✓ Sea salt – 1 teaspoon
- ✓ Garlic, minced – 1 clove
- ✓ Peanut butter, natural – 2 tablespoons
- ✓ Extra virgin olive oil – 2 tablespoons
- ✓ Tamari sauce – 2 tablespoons
- ✓ Ginger, peeled and grated – 2 teaspoons
- ✓ Honey – 2 teaspoons
- ✓ Black pepper, ground - .25 teaspoon

- ✓ Red cabbage, shredded – 2 cups
- ✓ Broccoli florets, chopped – 2 cups
- ✓ Carrots, shredded – 1 cup
- ✓ Red onion, finely sliced – 1
- ✓ Red bell pepper, finely sliced - .5
- ✓ Cilantro, chopped - .5 cup
- ✓ Sesame seeds – 1 tablespoon

Directions:

- ☞ In a large salad bowl, toss together the vegetables, cilantro, and peanuts.
- ☞ In a smaller bowl, whisk together the remaining ingredients until emulsified. Pour this dressing over the vegetables and toss together until fully coated.
- ☞ Chill the slaw for at least ten minutes so that the flavors meld. Refrigerate the Asian slaw for up to a day in advance for deeper feelings.

Nutrition: Calories 179 Total fat 11.8 g. Saturated fat: 2.9 g. Trans fat 0 g. Monounsaturated fat 4.3 g. Chol: 3.3mg

72. Egg Fried Buckwheat

Preparation Time: 5 minutes
Cooking Time: 45 minutes
Servings: 2

Ingredients:

- ✓ Eggs, beaten – 2
- ✓ Extra virgin olive oil – 2 tablespoons, divided
- ✓ Onion, diced – 1
- ✓ Peas, frozen - .5 cup
- ✓ Carrots, finely diced – 2
- ✓ Garlic, minced – 2 cloves
- ✓ Ginger, grated – 1 teaspoon
- ✓ Green onions, thinly sliced – 2
- ✓ Tamari sauce – 2 tablespoons
- ✓ Sriracha sauce – 2 teaspoons
- ✓ Cooked buckwheat groats, cold – 3 cups

Directions:

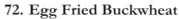

- Add half of the olive oil to a large skillet or wok set to medium heat and add in the egg, constantly stirring until it is fully cooked. Remove the egg and transfer it to another dish.
- Add the remaining olive oil to your wok along with the peas, carrots, and onion. Cook until the carrots and onions are softened, about four minutes. Add in the grated ginger and minced garlic, cooking for an additional minute until fragrant.
- Add the sriracha sauce, tamari sauce, and cooked buckwheat groats to the wok. Continue to cook the buckwheat groats and stir the mixture until the buckwheat is warmed all the way through and the flavors have melded about two minutes.
- Add the cooked eggs and green onions to the wok, giving it a good toss to combine and serve warm.

Nutrition: Protein 5.68 g Fat 1.04 g Carb: 33.5 g Fiber 4.5 g; 148 mg of potassium. 118 mg of phosphorus. 86 mg of magnesium. 12 mg of calcium.

73. Aromatic Ginger Turmeric Buckwheat

Preparation Time: 5 minutes

Cooking Time: 65 minutes

Servings: 2

Ingredients:

- ✓ Buckwheat groats rinsed and drained – 1 cup
- ✓ Water – 1.75 cup
- ✓ Extra virgin olive oil – 1 tablespoon
- ✓ Ginger, grated – 1 tablespoon
- ✓ Garlic, minced – 3 cloves
- ✓ Turmeric root, grated – 1 teaspoon
- ✓ Lemon juice – 1 tablespoon
- ✓ Sea salt – 1 teaspoon
- ✓ Cranberries, dried - .5 cup
- ✓ Parsley, chopped - .33 cup
- ✓ Pine nuts, toasted - .25 cup (optional)

Directions:

- Into a medium saucepan, add the buckwheat groats, water, olive oil, ginger, garlic, turmeric, lemon juice, and sea salt. Bring the water in the pot to a boil and then cover the mixture with a lid. Allow it to simmer over medium-low until all of the liquid is absorbed, about twenty minutes.
- About fifteen minutes into the cooking time of the buckwheat sir, the dried cranberries into the buckwheat allow them to plump up the last few minutes of the cooking time.
- Top the buckwheat with the pine nuts and parsley before serving.

Nutrition : Calories 37 Protein 23g Fats 3g Carbs 7gf

74. Kale and Corn Succotash

Preparation Time: 5 minutes

Cooking Time: 55 minutes

Servings: 2

Ingredients:

- ✓ Kale, chopped – 2 cups
- ✓ Red onion, finely diced – 1
- ✓ Garlic, minced – 2 cloves
- ✓ Grape tomatoes, sliced in half lengthwise – 1 cup
- ✓ Sea salt – 1 teaspoon
- ✓ Parsley, chopped – 2 tablespoons

- ✓ Corn kernels – 2 cups
- ✓ Black pepper, ground - .5 teaspoon
- ✓ Extra virgin olive oil – 1 tablespoon

Directions:

- ☞ Into a large skillet pour the olive oil, red onion, and the corn kernels, sauteing until hot and tender, about four minutes. Add the sea salt, garlic, kale, and black pepper to the skillet, cooking until the kale has wilted, about three to five minutes.
- ☞ Remove the large skillet from the stove and toss in the parsley and fresh grape tomatoes. Serve warm.

Nutrition: Calories 137.4. Total fat 6.7 g. Saturated fat 1.0 g. Trans fat 0 g. Monounsaturated fat 1.8 g.

---

75. Cheesy Baked Eggs

Preparation Time: 5 minutes   **Cooking Time:** 15 minutes   **Servings:** 4

Ingredients:

- ✓ 4 large eggs
- ✓ 75g (3oz) cheese, grated
- ✓ 25g (1oz) fresh rocket (arugula) leaves, finely chopped
- ✓ 1 tablespoon parsley
- ✓ ½ teaspoon ground turmeric
- ✓ 1 tablespoon olive oil

Directions:

- ☞ Grease each ramekin dish with a little olive oil. Divide the rocket (arugula) between the ramekin dishes then break an egg into each one.
- ☞ Sprinkle a little parsley and turmeric on top then sprinkle on the cheese. Place the ramekins in a preheated oven at 220C/425F for 15 minutes, until the eggs are set and the cheese is bubbling.

Nutrition: Calories 198 Fat 9g Fiber 3g Carbs 2g Protein 13g

76. Green Egg Scramble

Preparation Time: 10 minutes   **Cooking Time:** 5 minutes   **Servings:** 1

Ingredients:

- ✓ 2 eggs, whisked
- ✓ 25g (1oz) rocket (arugula) leaves
- ✓ 1 teaspoon chives, chopped
- ✓ 1 teaspoon fresh basil, chopped
- ✓ 1 teaspoon fresh parsley, chopped
- ✓ 1 tablespoon olive oil

Directions:

- ☞ Mix the eggs together with the rocket (arugula) and herbs. Heat the oil in a frying pan and pour it into the egg mixture.
- ☞ Gently stir until it's lightly scrambled. Season and serve.

Nutrition: Calories 250 Fat 5g Fiber 7g Carbs 8g Protein 11g

---

77. Spiced Scramble

Preparation Time: 10 minutes   **Cooking Time:** 5 minutes   **Servings:** 1

Ingredients:

- ✓ 25g (1oz) kale, finely chopped
- ✓ 2 eggs
- ✓ 1 spring onion (scallion) finely chopped
- ✓ 1 teaspoon turmeric
- ✓ 1 tablespoon olive oil
- ✓ Sea salt
- ✓ Freshly ground black pepper

Directions:

- ☞ Crack the eggs into a bowl. Add the turmeric and whisk them. Season with salt and pepper. Heat the oil in a frying pan, add the kale and spring onions (scallions) and cook until it has wilted.
- ☞ Pour in the beaten eggs and stir until eggs have scrambled together with the kale.

Nutrition: Calories 259 Fat 3g Fiber 4g Carbs 3 Protein 9g

---

78. Bulgur Appetizer Salad

Preparation Time: 30 minutes

Cooking Time: 0 minutes

Servings: 4

Ingredients:

- ✓ 1 cup bulgur
- ✓ 2 cups hot water
- ✓ Black pepper to the taste
- ✓ 2 cups corn
- ✓ 1 cucumber, chopped
- ✓ 2 tablespoons lemon juice
- ✓ 2 tablespoons balsamic vinegar
- ✓ ¼ cup olive oil

Directions:

☞ In a bowl, mix bulgur with the water, cover, leave aside for 30 minutes, fluff with a fork, and transfer to a salad bowl.

☞ Add corn, cucumber, oil with lemon juice, vinegar, and pepper, toss, divide into small cups and serve.

Nutrition: Calories 130 Fat 2 Fiber 2 Carbs 7 Protein 6

79. Cocoa Bars

Preparation Time: 2 hours   **Cooking Time:** 0 minutes   **Servings:** 12

Ingredients:

- ✓ 1 cup unsweetened cocoa chips
- ✓ 2 cups rolled oats
- ✓ 1 cup low-fat peanut butter
- ✓ ½ cup chia seeds
- ✓ ½ cup raisins
- ✓ ¼ cup coconut sugar
- ✓ ½ cup coconut milk

Directions:

☞ Put 1 and ½ cups oats in your blender, pulse well, transfer this to a bowl, add the rest of the oats, cocoa chips, chia seeds, raisins, sugar, and milk, stir really well, spread this into a square pan, press well, keep in the fridge for 2 hours, slice into 12 bars and serve.

Nutrition: Calories 198 Fat 5g Fiber 4g Carbs 10g Protein 89g

80. Greek Party Dip

Preparation Time: 10 minutes   **Cooking Time:** 0 minutes   **Servings:** 4

Ingredients:

- ✓ ½ cup coconut cream
- ✓ 1 cup fat-free Greek yogurt
- ✓ 2 teaspoons dill, dried
- ✓ 2 teaspoons thyme, dried
- ✓ 1 teaspoon sweet paprika
- ✓ 2 teaspoons no-salt-added sun-dried tomatoes, chopped
- ✓ 2 teaspoons parsley, chopped
- ✓ 2 teaspoons chives, chopped
- ✓ Black pepper to the taste

Directions:

☞ In a bowl, mix cream with yogurt, dill with thyme, paprika, tomatoes, parsley, chives, and pepper, stir well, divide into smaller bowls and serve as a dip.

Nutrition: Calories 100 Fat 1g Fiber 4g Carbs 8g Protein 3g

81. Spicy Pumpkin Seeds Bowls

Preparation Time: 10 minutes   **Cooking Time:** 20 minutes   **Servings:** 6

Ingredients:

- ✓ ½ tablespoon chili powder
- ✓ ½ teaspoon cayenne pepper
- ✓ 2 cups pumpkin seeds
- ✓ 2 teaspoons lime juice

Directions:

☞ Spread pumpkin seeds on a lined baking sheet, add lime juice, cayenne, and chili powder, toss well, introduce in the oven, roast at 275 degrees F for 20 minutes, divide into small bowls and serve as a snack.

Nutrition: Calories 170 Fat 2g Fiber 7g Carbs 12g Protein 6g

82. Apple and Pecans Bowls

Preparation Time: 10 minutes   **Cooking Time:** 0 minutes   **Servings:** 4

Ingredients:

- ✓ 4 big apples, cored, peeled, and cubed
- ✓ 2 teaspoons lemon juice
- ✓ ¼ cup pecans, chopped

Directions:

- ☞ In a bowl, mix apples with lemon juice and pecans, toss, divide into small bowls, and serve as a snack.

Nutrition: Calories 120 Fat 4g Fiber 3g Carbs 12g Protein 3g

83. Shrimp Muffins

Preparation Time: 10 minutes   **Cooking Time:** 45 minutes   **Servings:** 6

Ingredients:

- ✓ 1 spaghetti squash, peeled and halved
- ✓ 2 tablespoons avocado mayonnaise
- ✓ 1 cup low-fat mozzarella cheese, shredded
- ✓ 8 ounces' shrimp, peeled, cooked, and chopped
- ✓ 1 and ½ cups almond flour
- ✓ 1 teaspoon parsley, dried
- ✓ 1 garlic clove, minced
- ✓ Black pepper to the taste
- ✓ Cooking spray

Directions:

- ☞ Arrange the squash on a lined baking sheet, introduce in the oven at 375 degrees F, bake for 30 minutes, scrape flesh into a bowl, add pepper, parsley flakes, flour, shrimp, mayo, and mozzarella and stir well.
- ☞ Divide this mix into a muffin tray greased with cooking spray, bake in the oven at 375 degrees F for 15 minutes and serve them cold as a snack.

Nutrition: Calories 140 Fat 2g Fiber 4g Carbs 14g Protein 12g

84. Zucchini Bowls

Preparation Time: 10 minutes   **Cooking Time:** 20 minutes   **Servings:** 12

Ingredients:

- ✓ Cooking spray
- ✓ ½ cup dill, chopped
- ✓ 1 egg
- ✓ ½ cup whole wheat flour
- ✓ Black pepper to the taste
- ✓ 1 yellow onion, chopped
- ✓ 2 garlic cloves, minced
- ✓ 3 zucchinis, grated

Directions:

- ☞ In a bowl, mix zucchinis with garlic, onion, flour, pepper, egg, and dill, stir well, shape small bowls out of this mix, arrange them on a lined baking sheet, grease them with some cooking spray.
- ☞ Bake at 400 degrees F for 20 minutes, flipping them halfway, divide them into bowls and serve as a snack.

Nutrition: Calories 120 Fat 1g Fiber 4g Carbs 12g Protein 6g

85. Cheesy Mushrooms Caps

Preparation Time: 10 minutes   **Cooking Time:** 30 minutes   **Servings:** 20

Ingredients:

- ✓ 20 white mushroom caps
- ✓ 1 garlic clove, minced
- ✓ 3 tablespoons parsley, chopped
- ✓ 2 yellow onions, chopped
- ✓ Black pepper to the taste
- ✓ ½ cup low-fat parmesan, grated
- ✓ ¼ cup low-fat mozzarella, grated
- ✓ A drizzle of olive oil
- ✓ 2 tablespoons non-fat yogurt

Directions:

- ☞ Heat up a pan with some oil over medium heat, add garlic and onion, stir, cook for 10 minutes and transfer to a bowl.
- ☞ Add black pepper, garlic, parsley, mozzarella, parmesan, and yogurt, stir well, stuff the mushroom caps with this mix, arrange them on a lined baking sheet, bake in the oven at 400 degrees F for 20 minutes and serve them as an appetizer.

Nutrition: Calories 120 Fat 1g Fiber 3g Carbs 11g Protein 7g

---

86. Mozzarella Cauliflower Bars

Preparation Time: 10 minutes   **Cooking Time:** 40 minutes   **Servings:** 12

Ingredients:

- ✓ 1 big cauliflower head, riced
- ✓ ½ cup low-fat mozzarella cheese, shredded
- ✓ ¼ cup egg whites
- ✓ 1 teaspoon Italian seasoning
- ✓ Black pepper to the taste

Directions:

- ☞ Spread the cauliflower rice on a lined baking sheet, cook in the oven at 375 degrees F for 20 minutes, transfer to a bowl, add black pepper, cheese, seasoning, and egg whites, stir well, spread into a rectangle pan, and press well on the bottom.
- ☞ Introduce in the oven at 375 degrees F, bake for 20 minutes, cut into 12 bars, and serve as a snack.

Nutrition: Calories 140 Fat 1g Fiber 3g Carbs 6g Protein 6g

---

87. Shrimp and Pineapple Salsa

Preparation Time: 10 minutes   **Cooking Time:** 40 minutes   **Servings:** 4

Ingredients:

- ✓ 1-pound large shrimp, peeled and deveined
- ✓ 20 ounces canned pineapple chunks
- ✓ 1 tablespoon garlic powder
- ✓ 1 cup red bell peppers, chopped
- ✓ Black pepper to the taste

Directions:

- ☞ Place shrimp in a baking dish, add pineapple, garlic, bell peppers, and black pepper, toss a bit, introduce in the oven.

☞ Bake at 375 degrees F for 40 minutes, divide into small bowls and serve cold.

Nutrition: Calories 170 Fat 5g Fiber 4g Carbs 15g Protein 11g

88. Strawberry Buckwheat Pancakes

Preparation Time: 20 minutes   **Cooking Time:** 5 minutes   **Servings:** 4

Ingredients:

- ✓ 100g (3½oz) strawberries, chopped
- ✓ 100g (3½ oz.) buckwheat flour
- ✓ 1 egg
- ✓ 250mls (8fl oz.) milk
- ✓ 1 teaspoon olive oil
- ✓ 1 teaspoon olive oil for frying
- ✓ Freshly squeezed juice of 1 orange
- ✓ 175 calories per serving

Directions:

☞ Pour the milk into a bowl and mix in the egg and a teaspoon of olive oil. Sift in the flour to the liquid mixture until smooth and creamy.

☞ Allow it to rest for 15 minutes. Heat a little oil in a pan and pour in a quarter of the mixture (or to the size you prefer.) Sprinkle in a quarter of the strawberries into the batter. Cook for around 2 minutes on each side. Serve hot with a drizzle of orange juice. You could try experimenting with other berries such as blueberries and blackberries

Nutrition: Calories 323 Fat 4g Fiber 12g Carbs 10g Protein 22g

89. Strawberry & Nut Granola

Preparation Time: 10 minutes   **Cooking Time:** 50 minutes   **Servings:** 12

Ingredients:

- ✓ 200g (7oz) oats
- ✓ 250g (9oz) buckwheat flakes
- ✓ 100g (3½ oz.) walnuts, chopped
- ✓ 100g (3½ oz.) almonds, chopped
- ✓ 100g (3½ oz.) dried strawberries
- ✓ 1½ teaspoons ground ginger
- ✓ 1½ teaspoons ground cinnamon
- ✓ 120mls (4fl oz.) olive oil
- ✓ 2 tablespoon honey

Directions:

☞ Combine the oats, buckwheat flakes, nuts, ginger, and cinnamon. In a saucepan, warm the oil and honey. Stir until the honey has melted.

☞ Pour the warm oil into the dry ingredients and mix well. Spread the mixture out on a large baking tray (or two) and bake in the oven at 150C (300F) for around 50 minutes until the granola is golden.

☞ Allow it to cool. Add in the dried berries. Store in an airtight container until ready to use. Can be served with yogurt, milk or even dry as a handy snack.

Nutrition: Calories 391 Fat 0g Fiber 6g Carbs 3g Protein 8g

90.   Chilled Strawberry & Walnut Porridge

Preparation Time: 10 minutes

Cooking Time: 0 minutes

Servings: 1

Ingredients:

- 100g (3½ oz.) strawberries
- 50g (2oz) rolled oats
- walnut halves, chopped
- teaspoon chia seeds
- 200mls (7fl oz.) unsweetened soya milk
- 100ml (3½ FL oz.) water

Directions:

- Place the strawberries, oats, soya milk, and water into a blender and process until smooth. Stir in the chia seeds and mix well.
- Chill in the fridge overnight and serve in the morning with a sprinkling of chopped walnuts. It's simple and delicious.

Nutrition: Calories 384 Fat 2 Fiber 5 Carbs 3 Protein7

91. Fruit & Nut Yogurt Crunch

Preparation Time: 5 minutes

Cooking Time: 0 minutes

Servings: 1

Ingredients:

- 100g (3½ oz.) plain Greek yogurt
- 50g (2oz) strawberries, chopped
- 6 walnut halves, chopped
- Sprinkling of cocoa powder

Directions:

- Stir half of the chopped strawberries into the yogurt.
- Using a glass, place a layer of yogurt with a sprinkling of strawberries and walnuts, followed by another layer of the same until you reach the top of the glass.
- Garnish with walnuts pieces and a dusting of cocoa powder.

Nutrition: Calories 296 Fat 4g Fiber 2g Carbs 5g Protein 9g

92. Tuna, Egg & Caper Salad

Preparation Time: 5 Minutes   **Cooking Time**: 20 Minutes   **Servings**: 2

Ingredients:
- ✓ 3½ oz. red chicory
- ✓ 5oz tinned tuna, drained
- ✓ 3 ½ oz. cucumbers
- ✓ 1oz rocket arugula
- ✓ 6 black olives, pitted

- ✓ 2 hard-boiled eggs, quartered
- ✓ 2 tomatoes, chopped
- ✓ 2 tbsp. fresh parsley, chopped
- ✓ 1 red onion, chopped

- ✓ 1 stalk of celery
- ✓ 1 tbsp. capers
- ✓ 2 tbsp. extra virgin olive oil
- ✓ 1 tbsp. white vinegar
- ✓ 1 clove garlic, crushed

Directions:
1. Place the tuna, cucumber, olives, tomatoes, onion, chicory, celery, and parsley and rocket arugula into a bowl. Combine olive oil, vinegar, garlic and a pinch of salt in a vinaigrette dressing.

2. Pour in the vinaigrette and toss the salad in the dressing. Serve onto plates and scatter the eggs and capers on top.

Nutrition: Calories: 309 kcal, Fat: 12.23 g, Carbohydrates: 25.76 g, Protein: 26.72 g

93. Dahl with Kale, Red Onions and Buckwheat

Preparation Time: 5 Minutes   **Cooking Time**: 20 Minutes   **Servings**: 2

Ingredients:
- ✓ 1 tsp. of extra virgin olive oil
- ✓ 1 tsp. of mustard seeds
- ✓ 1 ½ oz. red onions, finely chopped
- ✓ 1 clove of garlic, very finely chopped

- ✓ 1 tsp very finely chopped ginger
- ✓ 1 Thai chili, very finely chopped
- ✓ 1 tsp. curry powder
- ✓ 2 tsp. turmeric
- ✓ 10 fl. oz. vegetable broth

- ✓ 1 ½ oz. red lentils
- ✓ 1 ⅝ oz. kale, chopped
- ✓ fl. oz. coconut milk
- ✓ 1 ⅝ oz. buckwheat

Directions:
1. Heat oil in a pan at medium temperature and add mustard seeds. When they crack, add onion, garlic, ginger and chili. Heat until everything is soft.
2. Add the curry powder and turmeric, mix well. Add the vegetable stock, bring to the boil.

3. Add the lentils and cook them for 25 to 30 minutes until they are ready. Then add the kale and coconut milk and simmer for 5 minutes.
4. The dahl is ready. While the lentils are cooking, prepare the buckwheat. Serve buckwheat with the dahl.

Nutrition Facts: Calories: 273 kcal Fat: 2.41 g Carbohydrates: 24.83 g Protein: 7.67 g

94. Miso Caramelized Tofu

Preparation Time: 55 minutes   **Cooking Time**: 15 minutes   **Servings**: 2

Ingredients:
- ✓ 1 tbsp. mirin
- ✓ ¾ oz. miso paste
- ✓ 5 ¼ oz. firm tofu
- ✓ 1 ½ oz. celery, trimmed
- ✓ 1 ¼ oz. red onion
- ✓ 4 ¼ oz. zucchini
- ✓ 1 bird's eye chili

- ✓ 1 garlic clove, finely chopped
- ✓ 1 tsp. fresh ginger, finely chopped
- ✓ ⅝ oz. kale, chopped
- ✓ 2 tsp. sesame seeds
- ✓ 1 ¼ oz. buckwheat

- ✓ 1 tsp. ground turmeric
- ✓ 2 tsp. extra virgin olive oil
- ✓ 1 tsp. tamari (or soy sauce)

Directions
1. Pre-heat your over to 400°F. Cover a tray with parchment paper. Combine the mirin

and miso together. Dice the tofu and let it marinate it in the mirin-miso mixture. Chop

76

the vegetables (except for the kale) at a diagonal angle to produce long slices.
2. Using a steamer, cook for the kale for 5 minutes and set aside. Disperse the tofu across the lined tray and garnish with sesame seeds. Roast for 20 minutes, or until caramelized. Rinse the buckwheat using running water and a sieve.

3. Add to a pan of boiling water alongside turmeric and cook the buckwheat according to the packet instructions.
4. Heat the oil in a skillet over high heat. Toss in the vegetables, herbs and spices then fry for 2-3 minutes. Reduce to a medium heat and fry for a further 5 minutes or until cooked but still crunchy.

Nutrition: Calories: 101 kcal Fat: 4.7 g Carbohydrates: 12.38 g Protein: 4.22 g

95. Sirtfood Cauliflower Couscous & Turkey Steak

Preparation Time: 45 minutes   **Cooking Time**: 10 minutes   **Servings**: 2

Ingredients:
- ✓ 5 ¼ oz. cauliflower, roughly chopped
- ✓ 1 garlic clove, finely chopped
- ✓ 1 ½ oz. red onion, finely chopped
- ✓ 1 bird's eye chili, finely chopped
- ✓ 1 tsp. fresh ginger, finely chopped
- ✓ 2 tbsp. extra virgin olive oil
- ✓ 2 tsp. ground turmeric
- ✓ 1 oz. sun dried tomatoes, finely chopped
- ✓ ⅜ oz. parsley
- ✓ 5 ¼ oz. turkey steaks
- ✓ 1 tsp. dried sage
- ✓ ½ lemon, juiced
- ✓ 1 tbsp. capers

Directions:
1. Put the cauliflower using in the food processor and blend it in 1-2 pulses until it has a breadcrumb-like consistency.
2. In a skillet, fry garlic, chili, ginger and red onion in 1 tsp. olive oil for 2-3 minutes. Throw in the turmeric and cauliflower then cook for another 1-2 minutes. Remove from

heat and add tomatoes and parsley. Marinate the turkey steak with sage, capers, lemon juice and olive oil for 10 minutes..
3. In a skillet, over medium heat, fry the turkey steak, turning occasionally. Serve with the couscous.

Nutrition: Calories: 462 kcal Fat: 39.86 g Carbohydrates: 9.94 g Protein: 16.81 g

96. Mushroom & Tofu Scramble

Preparation Time: 30 minutes   **Cooking Time**: 15 minutes   **Servings**: 1

Ingredients:
- ✓ 3 ½ oz. tofu, extra firm
- ✓ 1 tsp. ground turmeric
- ✓ 1 tsp. mild curry powder
- ✓ ¾ oz. kale, roughly chopped
- ✓ 1 tsp. extra virgin olive oil
- ✓ ¾ oz. red onion, thinly sliced
- ✓ 1 ⅝ oz. mushrooms, thinly sliced
- ✓ A few parsley leaves, finely chopped

Directions:
1. Place 2 sheets of kitchen towel under and on-top of the tofu, then rest a considerable weight such as saucepan onto the tofu, to ensure it drains off the liquid. Combine the curry powder, turmeric and 1-2 tsp. of water to form a paste. Using a steamer, cook kale for 3-4 minutes. In a skillet, warm oil over a medium heat. Add the chili, mushrooms and onion, cooking for several minutes or until

brown and tender. Break the tofu in to small pieces and toss in the skillet. Coat with the spice paste and stir, ensuring everything becomes evenly coated.
2. Cook for up to 5 minutes, or until the tofu has browned then add the kale and fry for 2 more minutes. Garnish with parsley before serving.

Nutrition: Calories: 333 kcal Fat: 22.89 g Carbohydrates: 18.8 g Protein: 20.9 g

97. Prawn & Chili Pak Choi

Preparation Time: 30 minutes   **Cooking Time**: 15 minutes   **Servings**: 1

Ingredients:

- ✓ 2 ¼ oz. brown rice
- ✓ 1 pak choi
- ✓ 2 fl. oz. chicken stock
- ✓ 1 tbsp. extra virgin olive oil
- ✓ 1 garlic clove, finely chopped
- ✓ 1 ⅝ oz. red onion, finely chopped
- ✓ ½ bird's eye chili, finely chopped
- ✓ 1 tsp. freshly grated ginger
- ✓ 4 ¼ oz. raw king prawns
- ✓ 1 tbsp. soy sauce
- ✓ 1 tsp. five-spice
- ✓ 1 tbsp. freshly chopped flat-leaf parsley

Directions:

1. Bring a medium sized saucepan of water to the boil and cook the brown rice for 25-30 minutes, or until softened.
2. Tear the pak choi into pieces. Warm the chicken stock in a skillet over medium heat and toss in the pak choi, cooking until the pak choi has slightly wilted.
3. In another skillet, warm olive oil over high heat. Toss in the ginger, chili, red onions and garlic frying for 2-3 minutes. Put in the prawns, five-spice and soy sauce and cook for 6-8 minutes, or until the cooked.
4. Drain the brown rice and add to the skillet, stirring and cooking for 2-3 minutes. Add the pak choi, garnish with parsley and serve.

Nutrition: Calories 403 kcal Fat: 15.28 g Carbohydrates: 50.87 g Protein: 16.15 g

98. Tomato & Goat's Cheese Pizza

Preparation Time: 5 Minutes   **Cooking Time**: 50 Minutes   **Servings**: 2

Ingredients:

- ✓ 8oz buckwheat flour
- ✓ 2 tsp. dried yeast
- ✓ Pinch of salt
- ✓ 5fl oz. slightly water
- ✓ 1 tsp. olive oil
- ✓ 3oz feta cheese, crumbled
- ✓ 3oz passata or tomato paste
- ✓ 1 tomato, sliced
- ✓ 1 medium red onion, finely chopped
- ✓ 1oz rocket leaves, chopped

Directions:

1. In a bowl, combine all the ingredients for the pizza dough then allow it to stand for at least two hours until it has doubled in size. Roll the dough out to a size to suit you. Spoon the passata onto the base and add the rest of the toppings. Bake in the oven at 400F for 15-20 minutes or until browned at the edges and crispy and serve.

Nutrition: Calories: 417kcal Fat: 16g Carbohydrate: 50g Protein: 16g

99. Green Beans With Crispy Chickpeas

Preparation Time: 30 minutes   **Cooking Time**: 10 minutes   **Servings**: 4

Ingredients:

- ✓ 1 can chickpeas, rinsed
- ✓ 1 tsp. whole coriander
- ✓ 1 lb. green beans, trimmed
- ✓ 2 tbsp. olive oil, divided
- ✓ Kosher salt and freshly ground black pepper
- ✓ 1 tsp. cumin seeds
- ✓ Grilled lemons, for serving

Directions

1. Heat grill to medium. Gather chickpeas, coriander, cumin, and 1 tbsp. oil in a medium cast-iron skillet. Put skillet on grill and cook chickpeas, mixing occasionally, until golden brown and coriander begins to pop, 5 to 6 minutes. Season with salt and pepper.
2. Transfer to a bowl. Add green beans and remaining tbsp. olive oil to the skillet. Add salt and pepper. Cook, turning once, until charred and barely tender, 3 to 4 minutes.
3. Toss green beans with chickpea mixture and serve with grilled lemons alongside.

Nutrition: Calories: 460 Fat: 15g Carbs: 57g Protein: 16g

CHAPTER 5: SIDES

100. Tofu Guacamole

Preparation Time: 10 minutes

Cooking Time: 30 minutes

Servings: 1

Ingredients:

- ✓ 8oz silken tofu
- ✓ 3 avocados
- ✓ 2 tablespoons fresh coriander (cilantro) chopped
- ✓ 1 bird's-eye chili
- ✓ Juice of 1 lime

Directions:

- ☞ Place all of the ingredients into a food processor and blend a soft chunky consistency.
- ☞ Serve with crudités.

Nutrition: Calories: 178 Sodium: 31 mg Dietary Fiber: 1.2 g Total Fat: 4.1 g Carbs: 16.6 g Protein: 1.4 g

101. Ganache Squares

Preparation Time: 25 minutes   **Cooking Time:** 15 minutes   **Servings:** 10

Ingredients:

- ✓ 250 ml coconut milk (can)
- ✓ 1 ½ tablespoon coconut oil
- ✓ 100 g honey
- ✓ ½ teaspoon vanilla extract
- ✓ 350 g pure chocolate (> 70% cocoa)
- ✓ 1 pinch salt
- ✓ 2 hands pecans

Directions:

- ☞ Put the coconut milk in a saucepan and heat for 5 minutes over medium heat. Add the vanilla extract, coconut oil, and honey and cook for 15 minutes. Add a pinch of salt and stir well.
- ☞ Break the chocolate into a bowl and pour the hot coconut milk over it. Continuously stir until all of the chocolate has dissolved in the coconut milk.
- ☞ In the meantime, roughly chop the pecans. Heat a pan without oil and roast the pecans.
- ☞ Stir the pecans through the ganache.
- ☞ Let the ganache cool to room temperature. (You may be able to speed this up by placing the bowl in a bowl of cold water.). Line a baking tin with a sheet of parchment paper. Pour the cooled ganache into it.
- ☞ Place the ganache in the refrigerator for 2 hours to allow it to harden.
- ☞ When the ganache has hardened, you can take it out of the mold and cut it into the desired shape.

Nutrition: Calories: 141 Cal Fat: 17.56 g Carbs: 31 g Protein: 7.65 g Fiber: 9.3 g

102. Date Candy

Preparation Time: 25 minutes   **Cooking Time:** 10 minutes   **Servings:** 10

Ingredients:

- ✓ 10 pieces Medjoul dates
- ✓ 1 hand Almonds
- ✓ 100 g Pure chocolate (> 70% cocoa)
- ✓ 2 ½ tablespoon Grated coconut

Directions:

- ☞ Melt chocolate in a water bath.
- ☞ Roughly chop the almonds.
- ☞ In the meantime, cut the dates lengthways and take out the core.
- ☞ Fill the resulting cavity with the roughly chopped almonds and close the dates again.
- ☞ Place the dates on a sheet of parchment paper and pour the melted chocolate over each date.
- ☞ Sprinkle the grated coconut over the chocolate dates.
- ☞ Place the dates in the fridge so the chocolate can harden.

Nutrition: Calories: 292 Cal Fat: 2.07 g Carbs: 39 g Protein: 4.31 g Fiber: 8.8 g

103. Paleo Bars with Dates And Nuts

Preparation Time: 25 minutes   **Cooking Time:** 15 minutes   **Servings:** 15

Ingredients:

- ✓ 180 g dates
- ✓ 60 g almonds
- ✓ 60 g walnuts
- ✓ 50 g grated coconut
- ✓ 1 teaspoon cinnamon

Directions:

- ☞ Roughly cut the dates and soak them in warm water for 15 minutes.
- ☞ In the meantime, roughly chop the almonds and walnuts.
- ☞ Drain the dates.
- ☞ Place the dates with the nuts, coconut, and cinnamon in the food processor and mix to an even mass. (But not too long, crispy pieces or nuts make it particularly tasty)
- ☞ Roll out the mass on 2 baking trays to form an approx. 1 cm thick rectangle.
- ☞ Cut the rectangle into bars and keep each bar in a piece of parchment paper.

Nutrition: Calories: 126 Cal Fat: 69.92 g Carbs: 160 g Protein: 26.7 g Fiber: 27.9 g

104. Banana Strawberry Milkshake

Preparation Time: 15 minutes   **Cooking Time:** 5 minutes   **Servings:** 2

Ingredients:

- ✓ 2 pieces banana (frozen)
- ✓ 1 hand strawberries (frozen)
- ✓ 250 ml coconut milk (can)

Directions:

- ☞ Skin the bananas, slice them, and place them in a bag or on a tray. Put them in the freezer the night before.

☞ Put all ingredients in the blender and mix to an even milkshake.
☞ Spread on the glasses.

Nutrition: Calories: 4 Cal Fat: 0.04 g Carbs: 0.92 g Protein: 0.08 g Fiber: 0.2 g

---

105.   Buns With Chicken And Cucumber

Preparation Time: 25 minutes   **Cooking Time:** 20 minutes   **Servings:** 12

Ingredients:

- ✓ 12 slices chicken breast (spread)
- ✓ 1 piece cucumber
- ✓ 1 piece red pepper
- ✓ 50 g fresh basil
- ✓ 3 tablespoons olive oil
- ✓ 3 tablespoons pine nuts
- ✓ Garlic 1 clove

Directions:

☞ Wash the cucumber and cut into thin strips, then cut the peppers into thin strips.
☞ Put the basil, olive oil, pine nuts, and garlic in a food processor. Stir to an even pesto.
☞ Season the pesto and season with salt and pepper if necessary.

☞ Place a slice of chicken fillet on a plate, brush with 1 teaspoon of pesto and top the strips with cucumber and peppers. Carefully roll up the chicken fillet to create a nice roll.
☞ If necessary, secure the rolls with a cocktail skewer.

Nutrition: Calories: 240 Cal Fat: 36 g Carbs: 10.69 g Protein: 72 g Fiber: 3 g

---

106.   Hazelnut Balls

Preparation Time: 15 minutes   **Cooking Time:** 10 minutes   **Servings:** 15 balls

Ingredients:

- ✓ 130 g dates
- ✓ 140 g hazelnuts
- ✓ 2 tablespoon cocoa powder
- ✓ ½ teaspoon vanilla extract
- ✓ 1 teaspoon honey

Directions:

☞ Place the hazelnuts in a food processor and grind them until you get hazelnut flour (of course you can also use ready-made hazelnut flour).
☞ Put the hazelnut flour in a bowl and set it aside.
☞ Put the dates in the food processor and grind them until you get a ball.

☞ Add the hazelnut flour, vanilla extract, cocoa, and honey and pulse until you get a nice and even mix.
☞ Remove the mixture from the food processor and turn it into beautiful balls.
☞ Store the balls in the fridge.

Nutrition: Calories: 130 Cal Fat: 86.97 g Carbs: 133 g Protein: 26.09 g Fiber: 27.2 g

107.   Stuffed Eggplants

Preparation Time: 20 minutes   **Cooking Time:** 35 minutes   **Servings:** 4

Ingredients:

- ✓ 4 pieces eggplant
- ✓ 3 tablespoons coconut oil
- ✓ 1 piece onion
- ✓ 250 g ground beef
- ✓ 2 cloves garlic
- ✓ 3 pieces tomatoes
- ✓ 1 tablespoon tomato paste
- ✓ 1 hand capers
- ✓ 1 hand fresh basil

Directions:

- ☞ Finely chop the onion and garlic. Cut the tomatoes into cubes and shred the basil leaves.
- ☞ Bring a large pot of water to a boil, add the eggplants and let it cook for about 5 minutes.
- ☞ Drain, let cool slightly and remove the pulp with a spoon (leave a rim about 1 cm thick around the skin). Cut the pulp finely and set it aside. Put the eggplants in a baking dish.
- ☞ Preheat the oven to 175 ° C.
- ☞ Heat 3 tablespoons of coconut oil in a pan on a low flame and glaze the onion.
- ☞ Add the minced meat and garlic and fry until the beef is loose. Add the finely chopped eggplants, tomato pieces, capers, basil, and tomato paste, and fry them on the pan with the lid for 10 minutes. Season with salt and pepper.
- ☞ Fill the eggplant with the beef mixture and bake in the oven for about 20 minutes.

Nutrition: Calories: 151 Cal Fat: 72.89 g Carbs: 147.52 g Protein: 91.16 g Fiber: 69.2 g

108.   Chicken Teriyaki with Cauliflower Rice

Preparation Time: 45 minutes   **Cooking Time:** 4 hours   **Servings:** 8

Ingredients:

- ✓ 500 g chicken breast
- ✓ 90 ml coconut amino
- ✓ 2 tablespoons coconut blossom sugar
- ✓ 1 tablespoon olive oil
- ✓ 1 teaspoon sesame oil
- ✓ 50 g fresh ginger
- ✓ 2 cloves garlic
- ✓ 250 g Chinese cabbage
- ✓ 1 piece leek
- ✓ 2 pieces red peppers
- ✓ 1 piece cauliflower (rice)
- ✓ 1 piece onion
- ✓ 1 teaspoon ghee
- ✓ 50 g fresh coriander
- ✓ 1 piece lime

Directions:

- ☞ Cut the chicken into cubes. Mix coconut amino, coconut blossom sugar, olive oil, and sesame oil in a small bowl. Finely chop the ginger and garlic and add to the marinade. Put the chicken in the marinade in the fridge overnight.
- ☞ Roughly cut Chinese cabbage, leek, garlic, and paprika and add to the slow cooker. Finally, add the marinated chicken and let it cook for about 2 to 4 hours. When the chicken is almost ready, you can cut the cauliflower into small florets. Then put the florets in a food processor and pulse briefly to prepare rice.
- ☞ Finely chop an onion, heat a pan with a teaspoon of ghee, and fry the onion. Then add the cauliflower rice and fry briefly. Spread the chicken and cauliflower rice on the plates and garnish with a little chopped coriander and a wedge of lime.

Nutrition: Calories: 280 Cal Fat: 105 g Carbs: 75 g Protein: 25 g Fiber: 21 g

109. Curry Chicken with Pumpkin Spaghetti

Preparation Time: 45 minutes   **Cooking Time:** 4 hours   **Servings:** 8

Ingredients:

- ✓ 500 g chicken breast
- ✓ 2 teaspoons chili powder
- ✓ 1 piece onion
- ✓ 1 clove garlic
- ✓ 2 teaspoons ghee
- ✓ 3 tablespoon curry powder
- ✓ 500 ml coconut milk (can)
- ✓ 200 g pineapple
- ✓ 200 g mango
- ✓ 1 piece red pepper
- ✓ 1 piece butternut squash
- ✓ 25 g spring onion
- ✓ 25 g fresh coriander

Directions:

- ☞ Cut the chicken into strips and season with pepper, salt, and chili powder. Then put the chicken in the slow cooker. Finely chop the onion and garlic and lightly fry with 2 teaspoons of ghee. Then add the curry powder.
- ☞ Deglaze with the coconut milk after a minute. Add the sauce to the slow cooker along with the pineapple, mango cubes, and chopped peppers and let it cook for 2 to 4 hours.
- ☞ Cut the pumpkin into long pieces and make spaghetti out of it with a spiralizer (that's not easy, it works better with a carrot). Briefly fry the pumpkin spaghetti in the pan and spread the chicken curry on top.
- ☞ Garnish with thinly sliced spring onions and chopped coriander.

Nutrition: Calories: 328 Cal Fat: 51 g Carbs: 92 g Protein: 113 g Fiber: 20.3 g

110. French Style Chicken Thighs

Preparation Time: 45 minutes   **Cooking Time:** 4 hours   **Servings:** 8

Ingredients:

- ✓ 700 g chicken leg
- ✓ 1 tablespoon olive oil
- ✓ 2 pieces onion
- ✓
- ✓ 4 pieces carrot
- ✓ 2 cloves garlic
- ✓ 8 stems celery
- ✓ 25 g fresh rosemary
- ✓ 25 g fresh thyme
- ✓ 25 g fresh parsley

Directions:

- ☞ Season the chicken with olive oil, pepper, and salt and rub it into the meat.
- ☞ Roughly cut onions, carrots, garlic, and celery and add to the slow cooker. Place the chicken on top and finally sprinkle a few sprigs of rosemary, thyme, and parsley on top. Let it cook for at least four hours.
- ☞ Serve with a delicious salad, enjoy your meal!

Nutrition: Calories: 122 Cal. Fat: 45.96 g Carbs: 58.78 g Protein: 142 g Fiber: 18.5 g

111. Spicy Ribs with Grilled Vegetables

Preparation Time: 20 minutes   **Cooking Time:** 20 minutes   **Servings:** 5

Ingredients:

- ✓ 400 g spareribs
- ✓ 4 tablespoons coconut-aminos
- ✓ 2 tablespoons honey
- ✓ 1 tablespoon olive oil
- ✓ 50 g spring onions
- ✓ Garlic 2 cloves
- ✓ 1-piece green chili peppers
- ✓ 1 piece onion

- ✓ 1-piece red pepper
- ✓ Pumpkin 1 piece
- ✓ Paprika powder 1 tsp.

For the roasted pumpkin:

- ✓ Coconut oil 1 tablespoon

Directions:

- ☞ Marinate the ribs the day before. Cut the ribs into pieces with four ribs each. Place the coconut amino, honey, and olive oil in a mixing bowl and mix. Chop the spring onions, garlic, and green peppers and add them. Spread the ribs on plastic containers and pour the marinade over them. Leave them in the fridge overnight.
- ☞ Cut the onions, peppers, and peppers into pieces and put them in the slow cooker.

- Spread the ribs, including the marinade, and let them cook for at least 4 hours.
- ☞ Preheat the oven to 200 ° C for the pumpkin.
- ☞ Cut the pumpkin into moons and place it on a baking sheet lined with parchment paper.
- ☞ Spread a tablespoon of coconut oil on the baking sheet and season with paprika, pepper, and salt. Roast the pumpkin in the oven for about 20 minutes and serve with the spareribs.

Nutrition: Calories: 151 Cal Fat: 105 g Carbs: 68.85 g Protein: 80.34 g Fiber: 6 g

112.   Apple Pastry

Preparation Time: 5 minutes   **Cooking Time:** 25 minutes   **Servings:** 1

Ingredients:

- ✓ Three tablespoons all-purpose flour
- ✓ Dash salt
- ✓ Two teaspoons margarine
- ✓ One tablespoon plain low-fat yogurt

- ✓ One small apple
- ✓ Dash each ground nutmeg and ground cinnamon
- ✓ Two teaspoons reduced-calorie apricot spread

Directions:

- ☞ Combine everything.
- ☞ Preheat oven to 350°F.
- ☞ Core, pare, and thinly slice apple; arrange slices decoratively over the dough and sprinkle with nutmeg and cinnamon. Bake until crust is golden, 20 to 30 minutes.

Nutrition: Calories: 238 calories Fat: 8 g Carbs: 38 g Protein: 4 g Fiber: 0 g

113.   Baked Maple Apple

Preparation Time: 5 minutes   **Cooking Time:** 25 minutes   **Servings:** 2

Ingredients:

- ✓ Two small apples
- ✓ Two teaspoons reduced-calorie apricot
- ✓ Spread

- ✓ One teaspoon reduced-calorie maple-flavored syrup

Directions:

- ☞ Remove the core from each apple to 1/2 inch from the bottom.
- ☞ Remove a thin strip of peel from around the center of each apple (this helps keep skin from bursting).

- ☞ Fill each apple with one teaspoon apricot spread and 1/2 teaspoon maple syrup. Place each apple upright in an individual baking dish; cover dishes with foil and bake at 400°F until apples are tender 25 to 30 minutes.

Nutrition: Calories: 75 Cal Fat: 1 g Carbs: 19 g Protein: 0.2 g Fiber: 0 g

114.   Apple-Raisin Cake

Preparation Time: 5 minutes

Cooking Time: 25 minutes

Servings: 12

Ingredients:

- ✓ One teaspoon baking soda
- ✓ 1/2 cups applesauce
- ✓ Two small golden delicious apples, cored, pared, and shredded
- ✓ 1 cup less 2 tablespoons raisins
- ✓ 2/4 cups self-rising flour
- ✓ 1 teaspoon ground cinnamon
- ✓ 1/2 teaspoon ground cloves 1/3 cup plus 2 teaspoons unsalted margarine
- ✓ 1/4 cup granulated sugar

Directions:

- ☞ Spray an 8 x 8 x 2-inch baking pan with nonstick cooking spray and set aside. Into a medium bowl sift together flour, cinnamon, and cloves; set aside.
- ☞ Preheat oven to 350°F. In a medium mixing bowl, using an electric mixer, cream margarine, add sugar and stir to combine. Stir baking soda into applesauce, then add to margarine mixture and stir to combine; add sifted ingredients and, using an electric mixer on medium speed, beat until thoroughly combined. Fold in apples and raisins; pour batter into the sprayed pan and bake for 45 to 50 minutes (until cake is browned and a cake tester or toothpick, inserted in center, comes out dry).

Nutrition: Calories: 151 Cal Fat: 4 g Carbs: 28 g Protein: 2 g Sodium: 96 g Cholesterol: 0 mg

115.   Cinnamon-Apricot Bananas

Preparation Time: 10 minutes   **Cooking Time:** 25 minutes   **Servings:** 2

Ingredients:

- ✓ 4 graham crackers 2x2-inch 1 medium banana, peeled and cut in squares), made into crumbs half lengthwise
- ✓ 2 teaspoons shredded coconut
- ✓ 1/4 teaspoon ground cinnamon
- ✓ 1 tablespoon plus 1 teaspoon reduced-calorie apricot spread

Directions:

- ☞ Combine crumbs, coconut, and cinnamon, and toast lightly, being careful not to burn; transfer to a sheet of wax paper or a paper plate and set aside.

☞ In the same skillet heat apricot spread until melted; remove from heat. Roll each banana half in a spread, then quickly roll in crumb mixture, pressing crumbs so that they adhere to the banana; place coated halves on a plate, cover lightly, and refrigerate until chilled.

Nutrition: Calories: 130 Cal Fat: 2 g Carbs: 29 g Protein: 2 g Sodium: 95 g Cholesterol: 0 mg

116.   Meringue Crepes with Blueberry Custard Filling

Preparation Time: 5 minutes   **Cooking Time:** 35 minutes   **Servings:** 4

Ingredients:

- ✓ 2 cups blueberries (reserve 8 berries for garnish)
- ✓ 8 crepes
- ✓ 1 cup evaporated skimmed milk
- ✓ 2 large eggs, separated
- ✓ 1 tablespoon plus 1 teaspoon
- ✓ Granulated sugar, divided
- ✓ 2 teaspoons each cornstarch
- ✓ Lemon juice

Directions:

☞ Combine milk, egg yolks, and one tablespoon sugar; cook over low heat, continually stirring, until slightly thickened and bubbles form around sides of the mixture. In a cup or small bowl dissolve cornstarch in lemon juice; gradually stir into milk mixture and cook, constantly stirring, until thick. Remove from heat and fold in blueberries; let cool.

☞ Fill the pastry bag with egg whites and pipe an equal amount over each crepe (if pastry bag is not available, spoon egg whites over crepes); top each with a reserved blueberry and broil until meringue is lightly browned, 10 to 15 seconds. Serve immediately.

Nutrition: Calories: 300 Cal Fat: 6 g Carbs: 45 g Protein: 16 g Sodium: 180 mg Cholesterol: 278 mg

117.   Chilled Cherry Soup

Preparation Time: 5 minutes   **Cooking Time:** 25 minutes   **Servings:** 2

Ingredients:

- ✓ 20 large frozen pitted cherries
- ✓ 1/2 cup water
- ✓ 1/2 teaspoons granulated sugar
- ✓ 2-inch cinnamon stick
- ✓ 1 strip lemon peel
- ✓ 2 tablespoons rose wine
- ✓ 1 teaspoon cornstarch
- ✓ 1/4 cup plain low-fat yogurt

Directions:

☞ In a small saucepan, combine cherries, water, sugar, cinnamon stick, and lemon peel; bring to a boil. Reduce heat, cover, and let simmer for 20 minutes.

☞ In a heatproof bowl, stir yogurt until smooth; add cherry mixture and stir to combine. Cover with plastic wrap and refrigerate until well chilled.

Nutrition: Calories: 98 Ca Fat: 1 g Carbs: 19 g Protein: 2 g Sodium: 21 g Cholesterol: 2 mg

118.   Iced Orange Punch

Preparation Time: 5 minutes   **Cooking Time:** 15 minutes   **Servings:** 8

Ingredients:

- ✓ Ice mold
- ✓ Club soda
- ✓ 1 lemon, sliced
- ✓ 1 lime, sliced
- ✓ Punch
- ✓ 1 quart each chilled orange juice (no sugar added), club soda, and diet ginger ale)

Directions:

To prepare ice mold:

- ☞ Pour enough club soda into a 10- or 12-cup ring mold to fill mold; add lemon and lime slices, arranging them in an alternating pattern. Cover the mold and carefully transfer to freezer; freeze until solid.

To prepare punch:

- ☞ In a large punch bowl, combine juice and sodas. Remove ice mold from ring mold and float ice mold in a punch.

Nutrition: Calories: 56 Cal Fat: 0.1 g Carbs: 14 g Protein: 1 g Sodium: 35 mg Cholesterol: 0 mg

119.   Meatless Borscht

Preparation Time: 5 minutes   **Cooking Time:** 25 minutes   **Servings:** 2

Ingredients:

- ✓ 1 teaspoon margarine
- ✓ 1 cup shredded green cabbage
- ✓ 1/4 cup chopped onion
- ✓ 1/4 cup sliced carrot
- ✓ 1 cup coarsely shredded pared
- ✓ 2 tablespoons tomato paste beets
- ✓ 1 tablespoon lemon juice
- ✓ 2 cups of water
- ✓ 1/2 teaspoon granulated sugar
- ✓ 2 packets instant beef broth and 1 teaspoon pepper
- ✓ Seasoning mix
- ✓ 1/4 cup plain low-fat yogurt
- ✓ 1/2 bay leaf

Directions:

- ☞ Heat margarine until bubbly and hot; add onion and sauté until softened. Add beets and toss to combine; add water, broth mix, and bay leaf and bring to a boil.
- ☞ Cover pan and cook over medium heat for 10 minutes; stir in remaining ingredients except

for yogurt, cover, and let simmer until vegetables are tender about 25 minutes.
- ☞ Pour borscht into 2 soup bowls and top each portion with 2 tablespoons yogurt.

Nutrition: Calories: 120 Cal Fat: 3 g Carbs: 21 g Protein: 5 g Sodium: 98 g Cholesterol: 2 mg

120.   Sauteed Sweet 'n' Sour Beets

Preparation Time: 5 minutes   **Cooking Time:** 25 minutes   **Servings:** 2

Ingredients:

- ✓ 2 teaspoons margarine
- ✓ 1 tablespoon diced onion
- ✓ 1 cup drained canned small whole beets, cut into quarters
- ✓ 1 tablespoon each lemon juice and water
- ✓ 1 teaspoon each salt and pepper
- ✓ Dash granulated sugar substitute

Directions:

- ☞ In small nonstick skillet heat margarine over medium-high heat until bubbly and hot; add onion and sauté until softened, 1 to 2 minutes.
- ☞ Reduce heat to low and add remaining ingredients; cover pan and cook, stirring once, for 5 minutes longer.

Nutrition: Calories: 70 Cal Fat: 4 g Carbs: 9 g Protein: 1 g Sodium: 96 g Cholesterol: 0 mg

---

121.   Orange Beets

Preparation Time: 5 minutes   **Cooking Time:** 25 minutes   **Servings:** 2

Ingredients:

- ✓ 1/2 teaspoons lemon juice
- ✓ 1 teaspoon cornstarch Dash salt
- ✓ 1 teaspoon orange marmalade
- ✓ 1 cup peeled and sliced cooked beets
- ✓ 2 teaspoons margarine
- ✓ 1 teaspoon firmly packed brown
- ✓ Sugar 1/4 cup orange juice

Directions:

- ☞ Combine beets, margarine, and sugar; cook over low heat, continually stirring until margarine and sugar are melted.
- ☞ Combine juices, cornstarch, and salt, stirring to dissolve cornstarch; pour over beet mixture and, constantly stirring, bring to a boil. Continue cooking and stirring
- ☞ Reduce heat, add marmalade, and stir until combined. Serve.

Nutrition: Calories: 99 Cal Fat: 4 g Carbs: 16 g Protein: 2 g Sodium: 146 g Cholesterol: 0 mg

---

122.   Cabbage 'n' Potato Soup

Preparation Time: 5 minutes   **Cooking Time:** 35 minutes   **Servings:** 4

Ingredients:

- ✓ 2 teaspoons vegetable oil
- ✓ 4 cups shredded green cabbage
- ✓ 1 cup sliced onions
- ✓ 1 garlic clove, minced
- ✓ 3 cups of water
- ✓ 6 ounces peeled potato, sliced
- ✓ 1 cup each sliced carrot and tomato puree
- ✓ 4 packets instant beef broth and seasoning mix
- ✓ 1 each bay leaf and whole clove

Directions:

- ☞ Heat oil, add cabbage, onions, and garlic, and saute over medium heat, frequently stirring, until cabbage is soft.
- ☞ Reduce heat to low and add remaining ingredients; cook until vegetables are tender. Serve.

Nutrition: Calories: 119 Cal Fat: 3 g Carbs: 22 g Protein: 4 g Sodium: 900 mg Cholesterol: 0 mg

---

123.   Eggplant Pesto

Preparation Time: 5 minutes   **Cooking Time:** 45 minutes   **Servings:** 2

Ingredients:

- ✓ Serve hot or chilled.
- ✓ 1 medium eggplant
- ✓ Dash salt
- ✓ 2 tablespoons each chopped
- ✓ Fresh basil and grated Parmesan cheese
- ✓ 1 tablespoon olive oil
- ✓ 1 small garlic clove, mashed
- ✓ Dash freshly ground pepper

Directions:

- ☞ In a small bowl, combine all ingredients except for the medium eggplant.
- ☞ Spread an equal amount of mixture over each eggplant slice. Transfer slices to I1/2-quart casserole, return to oven, and bake until heated, about 10 minutes longer.

Nutrition: Calories: 144 Cal Fat: 9 g Carbs: 14 g Protein: 5 g Sodium: 163 mg Cholesterol: 4 mg

124.   Ratatouille

Preparation Time: 5 minutes   **Cooking Time:** 50 minutes   **Servings:** 4

Ingredients:

- ✓ 1 tablespoon plus 1 teaspoon olive oil
- ✓ 1 cup each sliced onions and red or green bell peppers
- ✓ 3 garlic cloves, chopped
- ✓ 4 cups cubed eggplant
- ✓ 1/2 cups canned tomatoes,
- ✓ Chopped 1 cup sliced zucchini
- ✓ 3 tablespoons chopped fresh basil
- ✓ 2 teaspoons dried
- ✓ 1 teaspoon salt
- ✓ Ground pepper

Directions:

- ☞ In a 12-inch skillet heat oil over medium heat; add onions, bell peppers, and garlic and sauté until vegetables are tender-crisp.
- ☞ Add remaining ingredients and stir to combine. Reduce heat, cover, and let simmer until vegetables are tender.

Nutrition: Calories: 237 Cal Fat: 15 g Carbs: 18 g Protein: 11 g Sodium: 842 mg Cholesterol: 30 mg

125.   Chilled Eggplant Relish

Preparation Time: 15 minutes
Cooking Time: 25 minutes
Servings: 4
Ingredients:

- ✓ 3 cups eggplant
- ✓ 1 teaspoon salt

- ✓ 1 tablespoon plus
- ✓ 1 teaspoon olive oil
- ✓ 1 cup thinly sliced onions
- ✓ 2 garlic cloves
- ✓ 1 cup each diced celery and chopped tomatoes
- ✓ 2 teaspoons wine vinegar
- ✓ 1 teaspoon granulated sugar
- ✓ 8 black olives
- ✓ 1 tablespoon capers

Directions:

- ☞ Heat oil over medium heat; add onions and garlic and saute until onions are translucent, 3 to 5 minutes. Add eggplant and cook, occasionally stirring, until eggplant begins to soften, about 5 minutes; stir in celery and tomatoes, cover pan, and let simmer until celery is tender.
- ☞ Stir in vinegar and sugar and cook, uncovered, for 5 minutes longer. Remove from heat and add olives and capers, tossing to combine; transfer to a glass, plastic, or stainless-steel container, cover, and refrigerate until chilled.

Nutrition: Calories: 113 Cal Fat: 7 g Carbs: 13 g Protein: 3 g Sodium: 429 mg Cholesterol: 0 mg

126. Endive-Tomato Salad with Sesame Dressing

Preparation Time: 5 minutes   **Cooking Time:** 25 minutes   **Servings:** 2

Ingredients:

- ☞ 5 medium Belgian endives
- ☞ 2 cup chopped watercress leaves
- ☞ 6 cherry tomatoes, cut into quarters

Dressing:

- ☞ 1 teaspoon each sesame seed, toasted, lemon juice, rice vinegar, and water
- ☞ 2 garlic clove, mashed
- ☞ Dash salt

Directions:

To prepare salad:

- ☞ Separate each endive into individual leaves. Line a clear 1-quart salad bowl with endive leaves with tips facing the rim of bowl-like flower petals. Fill center of the bowl with chopped watercress; top watercress with cherry tomato quarters, arranged in a circular pattern. Refrigerate for at least 30 minutes.

To prepare dressing: Using a mortar and pestle, mash sesame seed. In a small bowl or cup, combine mashed grain with lemon juice, vinegar, water, garlic, and salt; mix well. Refrigerate for at least 30 minutes.

Nutrition: Calories: 50Cal Fat: 1 g Carbs: 9 g Protein: 3 g Sodium: 86 mg Cholesterol: 0 mg

CHAPTER 6: SOUPS

127. Bouillabaise

Preparation Time: 20 minutes

Cooking Time: 2 hours and 30 minutes

Servings: 6

Ingredients:

- ✓ 1 ½ lb clams (cleaned, rinsed)
- ✓ 1 ½ lbs grouper
- ✓ ½ lb octopus
- ✓ 1 tablespoon
- ✓ Parsley (fresh)
- ✓ 3 teaspoons olive oil
- ✓ 2 garlic cloves
- ✓ Black pepper (to taste)
- ✓ Salt (to taste)
- ✓ 1 red bell pepper (chopped)
- ✓ 1 green bell pepper (chopped)
- ✓ 2 jalapeno peppers (minced)
- ✓ 10 ounces tomatoes (canned)
- ✓ ½ teaspoon dill weed (dried)
- ✓ ½ teaspoon lemon rind (freshly grated is better)
- ✓ 1 teaspoon rosemary (dried)
- ✓ ½ teaspoon basil (dried)
- ✓ 3 cups water

Directions:

- ☞ Grab your sous vide water bath and preheat it to 140 degrees F. You could use your ping pong balls to regulate the temperature even better. Season your clams to your taste with salt and pepper.
- ☞ Put the clams, garlic, parsley, and a teaspoon of olive oil into a Ziploc bag. Seal the bag nice and tight.
- ☞ Submerge the Ziploc bag into your sous vide water bath, making sure it's below the ping pong balls. Allow this to cook for 10 minutes, then you can take it out.
- ☞ Now, preheat your water bath to 149 degrees F. Leave the ping pong balls if you've got them in there!
- ☞ Now, you're going to season your octopus with pepper and salt to taste.
- ☞ After seasoning the octopus, put it in a Ziploc bag. Add a teaspoon of olive oil to the bag, and then seal it nice and tight. Put it in the sous vide water bath and allow it to cook for an hour and fifty minutes. Take it out when the time elapses. Now, preheat your sous vide water bath to 137 degrees F.
- ☞ Grab another Ziploc bag, and then add in the rest of the olive oil, as well as the peppers, grouper, tomatoes, and seasonings. Submerge the Ziploc bag into your sous vide water bath and all it to cook for just 20 minutes.
- ☞ Once done, take all the ingredients out of their Ziploc bags, and then move them to a stockpot on medium-high heat.
- ☞ Add in three cups of water, and then allow your stew to simmer, until it's all nicely heated up.
- ☞ Ladle this glorious stew into your serving bowls.
- ☞ Enjoy!

Nutrition: Calories 27 Protein: 45.1g Fat: 5.1g Carbs: 9.3g Sugars: 2.7g

128.   Coconut Cod Stew

Preparation Time: 30 minutes   **Cooking Time:** 30 minutes   **Servings:** 6

Ingredients:

- 2 lbs. fresh cod (cut into fillets
- Salt and freshly ground black pepper, to taste
- 1 can (15 ounces coconut milk, divided)
- 1 tablespoon olive oil
- 1 sweet onion (julienned)
- 1 red bell pepper (julienned)
- 4 garlic cloves (minced)
- 1 can (15 ounces) crushed tomatoes
- 1 teaspoon fish sauce
- 1 teaspoon lime juice
- Sriracha hot sauce, to taste
- 2 tablespoon chopped fresh cilantro leaves

Directions:

- ☞ Preheat water to 130°F in a sous vide cooker or with an immersion circulator.
- ☞ Season cod fillets with salt and pepper and vacuum-seal with 1/4 cup coconut milk in a sous vide bag (or use a plastic zip-top freezer bag, removing as much air as possible from the bag before sealing). Submerge bag in water and cook for 30 minutes.
- ☞ Immediately begin preparing the sauce. Heat olive oil in a nonstick skillet over medium-high heat and sauté onion and bell pepper until softened, 3 to 4 minutes, stirring frequently. Add garlic and sauté about 1 minute more, stirring constantly. Add undrained tomatoes, fish sauce, lime juice, sriracha sauce, and remaining coconut milk and stir until thoroughly combined. Season sauce to taste with salt and pepper, reduce heat to low, and simmer until the end of the cooking time for the cod, stirring occasionally.
- ☞ Remove cod from the cooking bag, add to sauce and turn gently to coat with sauce. Let stew stand for about 5 minutes. Garnish the stew with cilantro leaves to serve. Enjoy!

Nutrition: Calories: 400 Total Fat: 18g Saturated Fat: 13g Protein: 40g Carbs: 23g Fiber: 5g Sugar: 2g

129.   Cornish Hen Stew

Preparation Time: 20 minutes   **Cooking Time:** 4 hours   **Servings:** 4

Ingredients:

- 2 tablespoons coconut oil
- 4 medium shallots, smashed and peeled
- 3 cloves garlic, smashed and peeled
- 2 lemongrass stalks, roughly chopped
- Piece fresh ginger, thinly sliced
- 5 dried red Thai chilies
- 2 teaspoons dried green peppercorns, coarsely ground
- 1 teaspoon ground turmeric cups water
- 2 whole Cornish game hens
- 1/2 cup chopped cilantro
- 2 scallions, coarsely chopped
- 2 tablespoons Asian fish sauce
- 1 teaspoon finely grated lime zest
- Kosher salt and freshly ground black pepper

Directions:

- ☞ Set your sous to vide machine to 150°F.
- ☞ In a large skillet, melt the coconut oil over medium heat. When hot, add the shallots, garlic, lemongrass, ginger, chilies, peppercorns, and turmeric. Cook, stirring

94

occasionally until shallots begin to soften, about 5 minutes.

☞ Add the water to the skillet and stir, making sure to scrape the bottom of the pan. Carefully transfer to a large ziplock or vacuum-seal bag. Add the game hens to the bag and then seal using the water displacement method. Place the bag in the water bath and set the timer for 4 hours.

☞ When ready, remove the bag from the water bath and take out the hens. Let the hen rest until cool enough to handle. Separate the legs, wings, and breast meat.

☞ Add the cooking liquid to a large pot and bring it to a simmer over medium-high heat. Stir in the cilantro, scallions, fish sauce, lime juice, and game hen meat. Season to taste with salt and pepper.

Nutrition: Calories: 82 Total Fat: 7g Total Carbs: 5.4g Fiber: 0.8g Sugars: 0.3 Protein: 0.9g

130. Spicy Asian Noodle Soup

Preparation Time: 10 minutes   **Cooking Time:** 30 minutes   **Servings:** 2

Ingredients:

✓ One packet of buckwheat noodles, prepared as directed on the package

✓ One small red onion

✓ 2 Celery stalks washed and chopped

✓ One piece of ginger, diced

✓ One garlic clove, chopped

✓ 1 cup arugula

✓ ¼ cup basil leaves, clean, dry, then chop

✓ ¼ cup walnuts

✓ 1 A teaspoon of sesame seeds

✓ 2 Tablespoons of black currant

✓ ½ chili

✓ 5 cups chicken or vegetable broth

✓ ½ lime juice

✓ One teaspoon extra virgin olive oil

✓ One tablespoon soya sauce

Directions:

☞ Cook the pasta according to the instructions and set aside. Sauté all the vegetables, ginger, garlic, chili, and nuts in a pan over deficient heat for about 10 minutes, add the broth and simmer for another 5 minutes. Cut the pasta (roughly) so that it is small enough to be eaten comfortably in a soup.

☞ Add this to the broth, add the sesame seeds and lime juice, and remove from the heat. Refrigerate and serve.

Nutrition: Carbs 12 g Sugar 2 g Fat 2 g Fiber 0g Protein 0 g

131. Vegetarian Parmesan Risotto

Preparation Time: 65 minutes

Cooking Time: 50 minutes

Servings: 5

Ingredients:

✓ 2 cups Arborio rice

✓ ½ cup plain white rice

✓ 1 cup veggie stock

✓ 1 cup water

✓ 6-8 ounces Parmesan cheese, grated

✓ 1 onion, chopped

✓ 1 tbsp. butter

✓ Salt and black pepper to taste

Directions:

☞ Prepare a water bath and place Sous Vide in it. Set to 185 F. Melt the butter in a saucepan over medium heat.

☞ Add onions, rice, and spices, and cook for a few minutes. Transfer to a vacuum-sealable bag. Release air by the water displacement method, seal and submerge the bag in a water bath. Set the timer for 50 minutes.

☞ Once the timer has stopped, remove the bag and stir in the Parmesan cheese.

Nutrition: Calories: 433 Total Fat: 10.5g Cholesterol: 30mg Total Carbs: 68.1g Fiber: 2.6g Sugars: 1.3g Protein: 16.6g

132. Green Soup

Preparation Time: 55 minutes   **Cooking Time:** 40 minutes   **Servings:** 3

Ingredients:

✓ 4 cups vegetable stock
✓ 1 tbsp. olive oil
✓ 1 clove garlic, crushed
✓ 1-inch ginger, sliced
✓ 1 tsp. coriander powder
✓ 1 large zucchini, diced
✓ 3 cups kale
✓ 2 cups broccoli, cut into florets
✓ 1 lime, juiced, and zested

Directions:

☞ Make a water bath, place Sous Vide in it, and set to 185 F. Place the broccoli, zucchini, kale, and parsley in a vacuum-sealable bag. Release air by the water displacement method, seal, and submerge the bag in the water bath. Set the timer for 30 minutes.

☞ Once the timer has stopped, remove, and unseal the bag. Add the steamed ingredients to a blender with garlic and ginger—puree to smooth.

☞ Pour the green puree into a pot and add the remaining listed ingredients. Put the pot over medium heat and simmer for 10 minutes. Serve as a light dish.

Nutrition: Calories: 129 Total Fat: 5.3g Cholesterol: 0mg Total Carbs: 18.9g Fiber: 5.2g Sugars: 4.2g Protein: 5.8g

133. Chicken, Kale and Lentil Soup

Cooking Time: 20 minutes
Servings: 2

Preparation Time: 20 minutes

Ingredients:

✓ 5 cups chicken or vegetable broth
✓ One minced chicken breast (good use for remaining chicken broths from other recipes!
✓ One small red onion
✓ 2 Cups of finely chopped kale
✓ 1 cup chopped spinach
✓ 1 cup lentils
✓ One celery stalk, chopped
✓ One carrot, chopped
✓ One little pepper or a pinch of cayenne pepper
✓ A pinch of salt
✓ One teaspoon extra virgin olive oil

Directions:

- ☞ Cook the lentils according to the package but take them out only a few minutes before they are cooked. Put aside.
- ☞ Put the vegetables in a large saucepan and sauté in a little oil over medium heat. Stir until the vegetables are softer but not well cooked.
- Add the chicken (pre-cooked skinless chicken), add the reserved lentils, and cook for another 3 to 5 minutes. Add a pinch of salt.
- ☞ Add the broth, simmer and simmer for 20 minutes. Stay away from heat. Serve as fresh.

Nutrition: Calories: 467kcal Carb: 61g Protein: 43g Fat: 7g Fat: 2g Cholesterol: 56mg Sodium: 848mg Fiber: 12g Sugar:4g

---

134. Fall Squash Cream Soup

Preparation Time: 20 minutes   **Cooking Time:** 2 hours   **Servings:** 6

Ingredients:

- ✓ ¾ cup heavy cream
- ✓ 1 winter squash, chopped
- ✓ 1 large pear
- ✓ ½ yellow onion, diced
- ✓ 3 fresh thyme sprigs
- ✓ 1 garlic clove, chopped
- ✓ 1 tsp. ground cumin
- ✓ Salt and black pepper to taste
- ✓ 4 tbsp. crème fraîche

Directions:

- ☞ Prepare a water bath and place the Sous Vide in it. Set to 186 F.
- ☞ Combine the squash, pear, onion, thyme, garlic, cumin, and salt. Place it in a vacuum-sealable bag. Release air by the water displacement seal and submerge the bag in the water bath—Cook for 2 hours.
- ☞ Once the timer has stopped, remove the bag and transfer all the contents into a blender. Puree until smooth. Add the cream and stir well. Season with salt and pepper. Transfer the mix into serving bowls and top with some créme Fraiche. Garnish with pear chunks.

Nutrition: Calories: 101 Total Fat: 5.8g Cholesterol: 21mg Carbs: 12.9g Fiber: 2.3g Sugars: 2.7g Protein: 1.2g

135.   Cream of Corn Soup

Preparation Time: 10 minutes   **Cooking Time:** 40 minutes   **Servings:** 4

Ingredients:

- ✓ Kernels of 4 corn ears
- ✓ 6 cups still water
- ✓ 1 cup heavy cream
- ✓ 1 tbsp. olive oil
- ✓ Salt and pepper to taste

Directions:

- ☞ Set your cooking device to 183 degrees F.
- ☞ Place the kernels, salt, pepper, and olive oil into the plastic bag and seal it, removing the air. Set the cooking time for 25 minutes.
- ☞ Transfer the cooked kernels with the liquid to a pot. Add the cream and still water (if needed
- and simmer on medium heat for about 10 minutes.
- ☞ Blend the soup with an immersion blender, and salt and pepper if needed, and serve with chopped parsley.

Nutrition: Calories: 105 Protein: 4 g Fats: 3 g Carbs: 18 g

136.   Cold Pea & Yogurt Soup

Preparation Time: 10 minutes   **Cooking Time:** 1 hour   **Servings:** 4

Ingredients:

- ✓ 1 onion, chopped
- ✓ 2 garlic cloves, minced
- ✓ 1 carrot, peeled and grated
- ✓ 1 1/2 cups frozen peas
- ✓ 2 cups vegetable stock
- ✓ Salt and pepper to taste
- ✓ Greek yogurt for serving
- ✓ Chopped dill or cilantro for serving

Directions:

- ☞ Set your cooking device to 183 degrees F.
- ☞ Place the onion, garlic, and carrot into the vacuum bag and seal it, removing the air.
- ☞ Set the cooking time for 50 minutes.
- ☞ Blend the cooked vegetable with the stock using an immersion blender, and salt and pepper to taste.
- ☞ Serve refrigerated with yogurt and chopped dill or cilantro.

Nutrition: Calories: 135 Protein: 7 g Fats: 1 g Carbs: 27 g

137.   Potato & Curry Soup

Preparation Time: 10 minutes   **Cooking Time:** 1 hour   **Servings:** 4

Ingredients:

- ✓ 1 onion, chopped
- ✓ 2 garlic cloves, minced
- ✓ 1 carrot, peeled and grated
- ✓ 1 1/2 cup potato, peeled and cubed
- ✓ 2 cups vegetable stock
- ✓ Salt and pepper to taste
- ✓ 2 tbsp. curry powder
- ✓ Chopped cilantro for serving

Directions:

- ☞ Preheat the cooking device to 183 degrees F. Put the vegetables and curry powder into the

98

- vacuum bag, and seal it, removing the air. Set the cooking time for 50 minutes.
- Transfer the cooked vegetables to a pot, add the vegetable stock, and blend everything using an immersion blender.
- Bring the soup to a boil and simmer for 2-3 minutes.
- Add salt and pepper to taste.
- Serve with yogurt and chopped dill or cilantro.

Nutrition: Calories: 355 Protein: 11 g Fats: 17 g Carbs: 42 g

138.   Carrot & Celery Soup

Preparation Time: 10 minutes   **Cooking Time:** 2 h 30 minutes   **Servings:** 4

Ingredients:

- ✓ 2 medium carrots, peeled and chopped
- ✓ 1 celery stalk, chopped
- ✓ 1 yellow onion, peeled and chopped
- ✓ 2 garlic cloves, minced
- ✓ 1 tsp. dried rosemary
- ✓ 2 bay leaves
- ✓ 6 cups vegetable stock
- ✓ Salt and pepper to taste

Directions:

- Preheat the cooking device to 183 degrees F.
- Put the ingredients into the vacuum bag, and seal it, removing the air. Set the cooking time for 2 hours, 10 minutes. Transfer the cooked vegetables with the liquid into a pot.
- Add the vegetable stock, bring to boil, and simmer for ten more minutes.
- Blend everything using an immersion blender.
- Serve with yogurt and chopped dill or cilantro.

Nutrition: Calories: 80 Protein: 5 g Fats: 1g Carbs: 16 g

139.   Warm Beef Soup with Ginger

Preparation Time: 15 minutes   **Cooking Time:** 4 hours   **Servings:** 8

Ingredients:

- ✓ 2 lbs. chopped beef
- ✓ ¼ cup chopped onion
- ✓ ½ cup chopped celery
- ✓ ¼ tsp. pepper
- ✓ ½ tsp. nutmeg
- ✓ ½ tsp. ginger
- ✓ 2 quarts water

Directions:

- Preheat an oven to 450°F or 232°, then line a baking sheet with parchment paper. Set aside.
- Place the beef in a bowl together with chopped onion, celery, pepper, nutmeg, and ginger. Mix well. Place all on the prepared baking sheet and bake for about 10 minutes. Meanwhile, set the Sous Vide machine to 145°F or 63°C and wait until it reaches the
- targeted temperature. Next, remove the beef from the oven and transfer it all to a big Sous Vide plastic bag.
- Pour water into the bag, then seal it properly and cook for 4 hours.
- Once it is done, transfer to a serving bowl and enjoy immediately.

Nutrition: Calories 214 Protein 35g Fiber 2g Sugars 3g Fat 1g

140. Kale Soup with Roasted Chickpeas

Preparation Time: 5 minutes **Cooking Time:** 30 minutes **Servings:** 4

Ingredients:

- ✓ 1 cup chickpeas
- ✓ 1 tbsp. olive oil
- ✓ 1 tsp. paprika
- ✓ 1 tsp. cayenne powder
- ✓ 2 cups chopped kale
- ✓ 1 tsp. minced garlic
- ✓ 2 tbsp. lemon juice
- ✓ 1 cup low sodium vegetable broth
- ✓ 1 cup chopped onion
- ✓ 1 tsp. vegetable oil

Directions:

- ☞ Preheat an oven to 400 °F or 204° then line a baking sheet with aluminum foil. Set aside.
- ☞ Pour olive oil into a bowl then add chickpeas to it. Sprinkle paprika and cayenne over the chickpeas and mix well. Transfer the chickpeas to the prepared baking sheet and spread evenly in a single layer.
- ☞ Bake until the chickpeas are completely golden and crispy. Remove from the oven and set aside. Next, set the Sous Vide machine to 183°F or 84° then wait until the Sous Vide machine achieves the targeted temperature.
- ☞ Place the chopped kale in a Sous Vide plastic bag then add minced garlic and lemon juice to it.

- ☞ Vacuum seal the plastic bag properly then places it in the water bath. Sous Vide cook for 30 minutes then removes from the Sous Vide machine. Cut the plastic bag then transfer the kale to a blender along with the cooking liquid.
- ☞ Preheat a saucepan over medium heat then pour vegetable oil in it. Once the oil is hot, stir in chopped onion, then sauté until wilted and aromatic. Transfer the onion to the blender then blend all together until smooth.
- ☞ Pour the kale soup into a soup bowl then sprinkle roasted chickpeas on top.
- ☞ Serve and enjoy immediately.

Nutrition: Calories 260 Protein 12g Fiber 12g Sugars 1g Fat 9g

CHAPTER 7: SALADS

141.   Tuna Salad

Preparation Time: 10 minutes

Cooking Time: 0 minute

Servings: 2

Ingredients:

- ✓ 100g red chicory
- ✓ 150g tuna flakes in brine, drained
- ✓ 100g cucumber
- ✓ 25g rocket
- ✓ 6 kalamata olives, pitted
- ✓ 2 hard-boiled eggs, peeled and quartered

- ✓ 2 tomatoes, chopped
- ✓ 2 tbsp. fresh parsley, chopped
- ✓ 1 red onion, chopped
- ✓ 1 celery stalk

- ✓ 1 tbsp. capers
- ✓ 2 tbsp. garlic vinaigrette

Directions:

☞ Combine all ingredients in a bowl and serve.

Nutrition: Calories 251 Fat: 13 g Protein: 2 g Fiber: 1 g

142.   Kale & Feta Salad

Preparation Time: 10 minutes   **Cooking Time:** 0 minute   **Servings:** 1

Ingredients:

- ✓ 250g kale, finely chopped
- ✓ 50g walnuts, chopped
- ✓ 75g feta cheese, broken
- ✓ 1 apple, peeled, cored & diced

- ✓ 4 Medjool dates, chopped
- ✓ 75g cranberries
- ✓ ½ red onion, chopped
- ✓ 3 tbsp. olive oil

- ✓ 3 tbsp. water
- ✓ 2 tsp. honey, 1 tbsp. red wine vinegar
- ✓ A pinch of salt

Directions:

☞ In a bowl, throw together the kale, walnuts, feta cheese, apple, and dates, and then stir.

☞ In a food processor, add cranberries, red onion, olive oil, water, honey, red wine vinegar, and a pinch of salt. Process until smooth and fluid, adding water if necessary. Pour the cranberry dressing over the salad and serve.

Nutrition: Calories: 186 Fiber: 2.5 g Fat: 13 g Protein: 2 g

143.　　Pasta Salad

Preparation Time: 10 minutes　　**Cooking Time:** 10 minutes　　**Servings:** 1

Ingredients:

- ✓ 50g buckwheat pasta
- ✓ Rockets
- ✓ Basil leaves
- ✓ 8 cherry tomatoes, halved
- ✓ 1/2 avocado, diced
- ✓ 10 olives
- ✓ 1 tbsp. additional virgin olive oil
- ✓ 20g pine nuts

Directions:

- ☞ Delicately join every one of the ingredients aside from the pine nuts and orchestrate on a plate or in a bowl.
- ☞ Then dissipate the pine nuts over the top.

Nutrition: Calories 247 Fat: 13 g Carbohydrates: 28 g Protein: 2 g Fiber: 1 g

144.　　Sirt Fruit Salad

Preparation Time: 15 minutes　　**Cooking Time:** 25 minutes　　**Servings**: 1

Ingredients:

- ✓ ½ cup crisply made green tea
- ✓ 1 tsp. nectar
- ✓ 1 orange, divided
- ✓ 1 apple, cored and generally slashed
- ✓ 10 red seedless grapes
- ✓ 10 blueberries

Directions:

- ☞ Stir the nectar into a large portion of some green tea. When broken down, including the juice of a large portion of the orange. Leave to cool.
- ☞ Chop the other portion of the orange and spot it in a bowl together with the cleaved apple, grapes, and blueberries. Pour over the cooled tea and leave to soak for a couple of moments before serving.

Nutrition: Calories 234 kcal Fat: 13 g Carbohydrates: 28 g Protein: 2 g Fiber: 1 g

145.　　Chicken Salad

Preparation Time: 5 minutes　　**Cooking Time:** 10 minutes　　**Servings:** 1

Ingredients:

- ✓ 75 g natural yogurt
- ✓ Juice of 1/4 of a lemon
- ✓ 1 tsp. Coriander, cleaved
- ✓ 1 tsp. Ground turmeric
- ✓ 1/2 tsp. Mild curry powder
- ✓ 100 g cooked chicken bosom, cut into scaled-down pieces
- ✓ 6 walnut parts, finely slashed
- ✓ 1 Medjool date, finely slashed
- ✓ 20 g red onion, diced
- ✓ 1 bird's eye bean stew
- ✓ 40 g rocket, to serve

Directions:

- ☞ Blend the yogurt, lemon juice, coriander, and flavors together in a bowl.
- ☞ Include all the rest of the ingredients and serve on a bed of the rocket.

Nutrition: Calories 314 Fat: 13 g Carbohydrates: 28 g Protein: 2 g Fiber: 1 g

146. Sirt Super Salad

Preparation Time: 15 minutes **Cooking Time:** 15 minutes **Servings:** 1

Ingredients:

- ✓ 1 ¾ ounce (50g) arugula
- ✓ 1 ¾ ounce (50g) endive leaves
- ✓ 3 ½ ounces (100g) smoked salmon cuts
- ✓ ½ cup (80g) avocado, stripped, stoned, and cut
- ✓ 1/2 cup (50g) celery including leaves, cut
- ✓ 1/8 cup (20g) red onion, cut

- ✓ 1/8 cups (15g) pecans, slashed
- ✓ 1 tablespoon escapades
- ✓ 1 enormous Medjool date, hollowed and slashed
- ✓ 1 tablespoon additional virgin olive oil
- ✓ Juice of ¼ lemon
- ✓ ¼ cup (10g) parsley, slashed

Directions:

- ☞ Spot, the serving of mixed greens, leaves on a plate or in an enormous bowl.
- ☞ Combine all the rest of the ingredients and serve over the leaves.

Nutrition: Calories 236 Fat: 13 g Carbohydrates: 28 g Protein: 2 g

147. Buckwheat Porridge

Preparation Time: 10 minutes **Cooking Time:** 15 minutes **Servings:** 2

Ingredients:

- ✓ 1 cup buckwheat, rinsed
- ✓ 1 cup unsweetened almond milk

- ✓ 1 cup water
- ✓ ½ teaspoon ground cinnamon

- ✓ ½ teaspoon vanilla extract
- ✓ 1–2 tablespoons raw honey
- ✓ ¼ cup fresh blueberries

Directions:

- ☞ In a pan, add all the ingredients (except honey and blueberries) over medium-high heat and bring to a boil.
- ☞ Now, reduce the heat to low and simmer, covered for about 10 minutes. Stir in the honey and remove from the heat. Set aside, covered, for about 5 minutes. With a fork, fluff the mixture, and transfer it into serving bowls. Top with blueberries and serve.

Nutrition: Calories 358 kcal Total Fat 4.7 g Carbs 3.7 g Sodium 95 mg Fiber 9.8 g Protein 12 g

148. Walnuts Avocado Salad

Preparation Time: 8 minutes **Cooking Time:** 0 minutes **Servings:** 1

Ingredients:

- ✓ ¼ cup of chopped parsley
- ✓ ¼ lemon juice
- ✓ 1 tbsp. of extra virgin olive oil
- ✓ 1 large Medjool date, pitted and chopped
- ✓ 1 tbsp. of capers
- ✓ 1/8 cups of chopped walnuts

- ✓ 1/8 cup of sliced red onion
- ✓ ½ cup of celery including leaves, sliced
- ✓ ½ cup of avocado, peeled, stoned, and sliced
- ✓ 100 grams of smoked salmon slices (3 ½ oz.)
- ✓ 50 grams of endive leaves (1 ¾ oz.)
- ✓ 50 grams of arugula (1 ¾ oz.)

Directions:

☞ Place the endive leaves, parsley, celery leaves, and arugula in a large bowl or plate.

☞ Mix together the remaining ingredients and serve over the leaves.

Nutrition: Calories 89 Sugar 2g Carbohydrate 33g Vitamin K and C

---

149. Poached Pear Salad with Dijon Vinegar Dressing

Preparation Time: 15 minutes

Cooking Time: 0 minutes

Servings: 1

Ingredients:

✓ Freshly ground pepper to taste

✓ Salt to taste

✓ 200 grams of Gorgonzola cheese, slice finely

✓ Few rocket leaves

✓ 100 grams of Walnuts

✓ 2 Ripe pears (peeled and core) cut into quarters

✓ 2 Bay leaves

✓ Small bunch of thyme

✓ 40 grams of caster sugar

✓ 180 ml of red wine

✓ **For the Dressing**

✓ 75 ml olive oil

✓ 75 ml walnut oil

✓ 1 tbsp. of red wine vinegar

✓ 1 tbsp. of Dijon mustard

Directions:

☞ Boil the wine in a saucepan. Along with the bay leaves, sugar, and thyme. simmer over medium-low heat.

☞ Add the pear into the simmering liquid and poach for 10 minutes. Remove pan from heat and set aside to cool pears in poaching liquid.

☞ In a bowl, whisk together the mustard, salt, vinegar, and pepper until well whisk; slowly steam in the oil and whisk as you add.

☞ Arrange salad ingredients on a serving plate and drizzle with the dressing.

Nutrition: Calories 88 Sugar 4g Carbohydrate 24g

---

150. Steak Arugula Strawberry Salad

Preparation Time: 10 minutes   **Cooking Time:** 15 minutes   **Servings:** 4

Ingredients:

✓ **Steak:**

✓ 1/2 tbsp. extra virgin olive oil

✓ Montreal steak seasoning

✓ 2 Beef tenderloin steaks

✓ **Salad:**

✓ 1/8 cup of slivered walnuts

✓ 1/4 cup of crumbled feta cheese

✓ 1/2 cup of sliced strawberries

- ✓ 1/2 cup blueberries
- ✓ 1/2 cup of raspberries
- ✓ 3 cups of arugula
- ✓ Balsamic Vinaigrette
- ✓ Salt and pepper
- ✓ 1/4 tsp. of Dijon mustard
- ✓ 1 1/2 tsp. of sugar
- ✓ 1/8 cup of olive oil
- ✓ 1/8 cup of balsamic vinegar

Directions:

Steak:

- ☞ Run the Montreal steak seasoning all over the steak and let sit for 5-10 minutes.
- ☞ Heat oil over medium-high heat in a cast-iron skillet. Once it's simmering, add in the steak and cook about 5-7 minutes; flip and cook the other side for 3-4 minutes or until it's cooked the way you like your meat.
- ☞ Set steak aside on a plate and let cool for 5 minutes before slicing into strips.

Salad:

- ☞ Combine together the salad ingredients in a large bowl.
- ☞ In a small shaker, add together the all vinaigrette ingredients and shake until well mixed. Pour dressing over salad and toss to evenly coat.

To serve:

- ☞ Divide the salad between 2 bowls, and top with steak.
- ☞ Notes:
- ☞ You can keep the dressing for up to one week in the fridge.

Nutrition: Kcal: 506 Net carbs: 17g Fat: 37g Fiber: 5g Protein: 23 g

151.   Super Fruit Salad

Preparation Time: 10 minutes   **Cooking Time:** 0 minutes   **Servings:** 1

Ingredients:

- ✓ 10 blueberries
- ✓ 10 red seedless grapes
- ✓ 1 apple, cored and chopped roughly
- ✓ 1 orange, halved
- ✓ 1 tsp. of honey
- ✓ ½ cup of freshly made matcha green tea

Directions:

- ☞ Combine 1/2 cup green tea with the honey and stir until dissolved, Squeeze in half of the orange into the green tea mix. Leave to cool.
- ☞ Chop the second orange half into pieces and transfer into a bowl. Add in the blueberries, chopped apple, and grapes. Pour the cooled tea on top of the salad mix and allow to soak a little before serving.

Nutrition: Kcal: 200 Net carbs: 40g Fat: 1g Fiber: 5g Protein: 2 g

152.   Sirtfood Salmon Lentils Salad

Preparation Time: 10 minutes   **Cooking Time:** 0 minutes   **Servings:** 1

Ingredients:

- ✓ 20 grams of sliced red onion
- ✓ 40 grams of sliced celery
- ✓ 10 grams of chopped lovage
- ✓ 10 grams of chopped parsley
- ✓ Juice of 1/4 of a lemon
- ✓ 1 tbsp. of extra virgin olive oil
- ✓ 1 large Medjool date, remove pit and chopped
- ✓ 1 tbsp. of capers
- ✓ 15 grams of chopped walnuts
- ✓ 80 grams of avocado, peeled, pitted, and sliced
- ✓ 100g tinned green lentils or cooked Puy lentils
- ✓ 50 grams of chicory leaves
- ✓ 50 grams of rocket

Directions:

- ☞ On a large plate, add the salad leaves.
- ☞ Mix together the remaining ingredients and spread the mixture over leaves to serve.

Nutrition: Kcal: 400 Net carbs: 20g Fat: 25g Fiber: 14g Protein: 10 g

---

153.   Blueberry Kale Salad with Ginger-Lime Dressing

Preparation Time: 10 minutes   **Cooking Time:** 60 minutes   **Servings:** 4

Ingredients:

- ✓ 3 tbsps. of white wine vinegar
- ✓ 1 tbsp. of honey
- ✓ 2 tbsps. of finely chopped ginger, crystallized
- ✓ 3 tbsps. of lime juice
- ✓ Salt and pepper to tast

Salad:

- ✓ 1/4 cup of slivered walnuts toasted
- ✓ 1/2-3/4 cup of fresh blueberries
- ✓ 1/3 thinly sliced red onion
- ✓ 8 cups of kale, de-stemmed and chopped into pieces

Directions:

- ☞ Combine together the entire dressing ingredients in a medium bowl until well mixed.
- ☞ Add sliced onion chopped kale, toss to coat. Leave to marinate for about 1-4 hours, depending on how much time you have, tossing periodically. This is an important step to remove the bitterness from the kale.
- ☞ Add toasted walnuts and blueberries. Toss to coat.

Nutrition: Kcal: 91 Net carbs: 10g Fat: 3.69g Fiber: 3g Protein: 3g

---

154.   Fancy Chicken Salad

Preparation Time: 1 minute   **Cooking Time:** 10 minutes   **Servings:** 1

Ingredients:

- ✓ 1 bird's eye chili
- ✓ 20 grams of diced red onion
- ✓ 1 finely chopped Medjool date
- ✓ 6 finely chopped Walnut halves
- ✓ 100 grams of cooked chicken breast, chopped into bite-sized chunks
- ✓ 1/2 tsp. of mild curry powder
- ✓ 1 tsp. of ground turmeric
- ✓ 1 tsp. of chopped Coriander
- ✓ Juice of 1/4 of a lemon
- ✓ 75 grams of natural yoghurt
- ✓ 40 grams of rocket

Directions:

- ☞ In a bowl, mix together the lemon juice, yoghurt, spices, and coriander. Mix in the other ingredients until well blended.
- ☞ Serve over the bed of rocket.

Nutrition: Kcal: 340 Net carbs: 22g Fat: 13g Fiber: 5g Protein: 36g

---

155. Olive, Tomato, Yellow Pepper, Red Onion, Cucumber Slices, and Feta Skewers

Preparation Time: 5 minutes   **Cooking Time:** 0 minutes   **Servings:** 2

Ingredients:

- ✓ 100 grams of feta, cut into 8 cubes
- ✓ 100 grams of cucumber, cut in quarters and halved
- ✓ Half red onion, cut in half, and sliced into 8 pieces
- ✓ 1 yellow pepper (or any color you like) cut into 8 squares
- ✓ 8 cherry tomatoes
- ✓ 8 large black olives
- ✓ 2 wooden skewers, soaked for 30 minutes in water before use

- ✓ **For the dressing:**
- ✓ ½ crushed clove garlic
- ✓ 1 tsp. of balsamic vinegar
- ✓ ½ lemon Juice
- ✓ Few finely chopped basil leaves (or ½ tsp. of dried mixed herbs)
- ✓ 1 tbsp. of extra virgin olive oil
- ✓ Few leaves finely chopped oregano (Skip this if using dried mixed herbs)
- ✓ Freshly ground black pepper
- ✓ Salt to taste

Directions:

- ☞ Pierce each skewer through the olive, tomato, yellow pepper, red onion, cucumber slices, and feta. Repeat a second time.
- ☞ Combine the dressing ingredients in a sealable container and mix thoroughly. Pour dressing over the skewers.

Nutrition: Kcal: 228 Net carbs: 13g Fat: 15g Fiber: 3g Protein: 8.7g

---

156. Sesame Soy Chicken Salad

Preparation Time: 10 minutes

Cooking Time: 0 minutes

Servings: 2

Ingredients:

- ✓ 150 grams of cooked chicken, shredded
- ✓ Large handful of chopped parsley (20g)
- ✓ ½ finely sliced red onion

- ✓ 60 grams of Pak choi, very finely shredded
- ✓ 100 grams of roughly chopped baby kale
- ✓ 1 peeled cucumber, slice in half lengthwise, remove the seed, and cut into slices
- ✓ 1 tbsp. of sesame seeds

For the dressing:

- ✓ 2 tsp. of soy sauce

107

- ✓ 1 tsp. of clear honey
- ✓ Juice of 1 lime

Directions:

- ☞ Clean your frying pan well and make sure it's dry, toast the sesame seeds for 2 minutes in the pan until fragrant and lightly browned. Set aside on a plate to cool.

To make the dressing

- ☞ Mix together the lime juice, soy sauce, olive oil, sesame oil, and honey in a small bowl.

Nutrition: Kcal: 304 Fat 6g Protein 33g Carbs 35g

- ✓ 1 tsp. of sesame oil
- ✓ 1 tbsp. of extra virgin olive oil

- ☞ Place the kale, cucumber, parsley, red onion, and Pak choi in a large bowl and mix gently. Pour dressing over salad and mix together.
- ☞ Serve the salad on two different plates and add shredded chicken on top. Just before serving, sprinkle with sesame seeds.

157.   Salmon Chicory Rocket Super Salad

Preparation Time: 10 minutes   **Cooking Time:** 0 minutes   **Servings:** 1

Ingredients:

- ✓ 10 grams of chopped lovage or celery leaves
- ✓ 10 grams of chopped parsley
- ✓ Juice ¼ lemon
- ✓ 1 tbsp. of extra-virgin olive oil
- ✓ 1 large Medjool date, pitted and chopped
- ✓ 1 tbsp. of capers
- ✓ 15 grams of chopped walnuts

- ✓ 20 grams of sliced red onion
- ✓ 40 grams of sliced celery
- ✓ 80 grams of avocado, peeled, sliced
- ✓ 100 grams of smoked salmon slices of cooked chicken breast
- ✓ 50 grams of chicory leaves
- ✓ 50 grams of rocket

Directions:

- ☞ On a large plate, place the salad leaves.
- ☞ Mix together the remaining ingredients and spread the mixture over leaves to serve.

Nutrition: Kcal: 300 Net carbs: 30g Fat: 21g Fiber: 10g Protein: 20g

158.   Fresh Chopped Salad with Vinegar

Preparation Time: 20 minutes   **Cooking Time:** 20 minutes   **Servings:** 8

Ingredients:

- ✓ 1/2 cup of fresh parsley, coarsely chopped
- ✓ 1/2 cup of Kalamata olives, pitted and chopped coarsely
- ✓ Freshly ground pepper
- ✓ 4 medium seeded and diced tomatoes

- ✓ 2 tablespoon of white wine vinegar
- ✓ 1/2 cup of chopped scallions
- ✓ 1/2 teaspoon salt
- ✓ 2 cups of diced seedless cucumber
- ✓ 4 tablespoons of extra-virgin olive oil

Directions:

- ☞ Combine all the entire ingredients in a medium bowl; carefully toss to combine finely.

- ☞ Serve within an hour.

Nutrition: Kcal: 113 Net carbs: 5g Fat: 10g Protein: 1g

159.   King Prawns Prawn Parcels

Preparation Time: 15 minutes   **Cooking Time:** 10-15 minutes   **Servings:** 2

Ingredients:

- ✓ 2 lemon slices
- ✓ 50 ml of vegetable stock
- ✓ 1 tsp. of garlic crushed

- ✓ 300 grams of king prawns raw or cooked
- ✓ 2 thinly sliced broccoli florets

- ✓ 1 stick celery
- ✓ 1 courgette
- ✓ 1 carrot, peeled
- ✓ (Optional) fresh dill

Directions:

- ☞ Preheat your oven to 180°C or 160°C fans
- ☞ Shave the carrot, courgette, and celery into ribbons with a veggie peeler and set aside.
- ☞ Arrange two pieces of tin foil, (large enough to hold your vegetables) add a smaller piece of greaseproof paper on top of each tin foil. Curl up edges so the filling can hold.

- ☞ Add half of the veggies over each piece of paper; add the prawns and a slice of lemon.
- ☞ Mix vegetable stock with garlic and add on top the veggies. Sprinkle top with dill if using. Seal the foil and transfer to the baking sheet.
- ☞ Place baking sheet in the oven and bake until vegetables are soft, about 10-15 minutes. Remove foil and serve.

Nutrition: Kcal: 204 Net carbs: 4g Fat: 3g Fiber: 10g Protein: 36g

CHAPTET 8: SNACKS

160.   Herbed Mixed Nuts

Preparation Time: 10 minutes   **Cooking Time:** 25 minutes   **Servings:** 12

Ingredients:

- ✓ 1 tbsp. butter, melted
- ✓ 1 tbsp. Worcestershire sauce
- ✓ 2 tsp. dried basil and/or oregano, crushed
- ✓ ½ tsp. garlic salt
- ✓ 3 cups walnuts, soy nuts, and/or almonds
- ✓ 2 tbsps. grated Parmesan cheese

Directions:

- ☞ Set an oven to preheat to 325 degrees F.
- ☞ Mix together the garlic salt, herb, Worcestershire sauce, and melted butter in a bowl, then add nuts and mix until coated.
- ☞ Use foil to line a 15x10x1-inch baking pan, then spread the nuts in the pan. Put parmesan on top, then stir until coated.
- ☞ Let it bake for 15 minutes, mixing two times. Allow it to cool. Tightly cover and store up to a maximum of one week.

Nutrition: Calories: 221 Carbohydrates: 16g Protein: 2g Fat: 2g Sugar: 0.4g Sodium: 120mg Fiber: 0.7g

161.   Cinnamon Graham Popcorn

Preparation Time: 10 minutes   **Cooking Time:** 30 minutes   **Servings:** 3

Ingredients:

- ✓ 2-1/2 quarts popped popcorn
- ✓ 2 cups Golden Grahams
- ✓ 1-1/2 cups golden raisins
- ✓ 1 cup chopped dates
- ✓ 1 cup miniature marshmallows
- ✓ 1/3 cup butter, melted
- ✓ 1/4 cup packed brown sugar
- ✓ 2 tsps. ground cinnamon
- ✓ 1/2 tsp. ground ginger
- ✓ 1/2 tsp. ground nutmeg

Directions:

- ☞ Mix marshmallows, dates, raisins, cereal, and popcorn together in a big bowl.
- ☞ Mix the rest of the ingredients together. Put on the popcorn mixture and mix to blend.
- ☞ Put in two oiled 15x0x1-in. baking pans.
- ☞ Bake without a cover at 250°, tossing 1 time, about 20 minutes. Preserve in an airtight container.

Nutrition: Calories: 243 Carbohydrates: 20gmProtein: 1g Fat: 3g; Sugar: 2g Sodium: 34mg Fiber: 1g

162.   Cheesy Ranch Chex

Preparation Time: 15 minutes   **Cooking Time:** 15 minutes   **Servings:** 26

Ingredients:

- ✓ 9 cups Corn Chex®, Rice Chex® or Wheat Chex® cereal (or a combination)
- ✓ 2 cups bite-size pretzel twists
- ✓ 2 cups bite-size cheese crackers
- ✓ 3 tbsps. butter or margarine, melted

- ✓ 1 (1 oz.) package ranch dressing and seasoning mix

Directions:

- ☞ Microwave butter in a big microwave-safe bowl without a cover on a high setting until butter is melted, about a half minute.
- ☞ Stir in crackers, pretzels, and cereal until well-coated. Stir in cheese and dressing mix until coated evenly.

- ✓ 1/2 cup grated Parmesan cheese

- ☞ Microwave on high setting without cover for 3 minutes while stirring every minute. Scatter cereal mixture on foil or waxed paper to let it cool, for 15 minutes.
- ☞ Keep in an airtight container.

Nutrition: Calories: 119 Carbohydrates: 23g Protein: 3g Fat: 2g Sugar: 1g Sodium: 16mg Fiber: 4g

163. Almonds with Rosemary and Cayenne

Preparation Time: 10 minutes **Cooking Time:** 15 minutes **Servings:** 16

Ingredients:

- ✓ 8 oz. unblanched almonds or pecan halves (about 2 cups)

- ✓ 1½ tsps. margarine or butter
- ✓ 1 tbsp. finely snipped fresh rosemary

- ✓ 1½ tsps. brown sugar
- ✓ ¼ to ½ tsp. salt
- ✓ ¼ tsp. ground red pepper

Directions:

- ☞ Set an oven to preheat to 350 degrees F. Spread the almonds or pecans on the baking tray in a single layer. Let it bake for around 10 minutes or until it becomes aromatic and a bit toasted.
- ☞ In the meantime, melt the margarine or butter in a medium saucepan on medium heat until it

sizzles. Take it out of the heat. Stir in red pepper, salt, sugar, and rosemary.
- ☞ Add the nuts to the butter mixture and toss until coated.
- ☞ Allow it to cool a bit before serving.

Nutrition: Calories: 80 Carbohydrates: 13g Protein: 2g Fat: 2g Sugar: 2.1g Sodium: 59mg Fiber: 1g

164. Plum & Pistachio Snack

Preparation Time: 5 minutes **Cooking Time:** 5 minutes **Servings:** 1

Ingredients:

- ✓ ¼ cup unsalted dry-roasted pistachios (measured in a shell)

- ✓ 1 plum

Directions:

- ☞ Hull and serve pistachios together with plum.

Nutrition: Calories: 275 Carbohydrates: 23g; Protein: 3.5g; Fat: 1g; Sugar: 1g; Sodium: 308mg; Fiber: 3g

165. Peanut Butter & Pretzel Truffles

Preparation Time: 20 minutes **Cooking Time:** 2 hours **Servings:** 20

Ingredients:
- ✓ ½ cup crunchy natural peanut butter
- ✓ ¼ cup finely chopped salted pretzels
- ✓ ½ cup milk chocolate chips, melted

Directions:
- ☞ In a small bowl, mix pretzels and peanut butter. Cool in the freezer for about 15 minutes until firm.
- ☞ Roll peanut butter mixture into 20 balls (of about 1 tsp. each).
- ☞ Transfer to a baking sheet that is lined with wax paper or parchment and then freeze for about 1 hour until very firm. Roll the frozen balls in the melted chocolate. Place in a fridge for about 30 minutes until chocolate is set.

Nutrition: Calories: 110 Carbohydrates: 43g Protein: 12g Fat: 1g Sugar: 1.9g Sodium: 21mg Fiber: 3g

166.   Chocolate Bark

Preparation Time: 30 minutes **Cooking Time:** 3 hours **Servings:** 2

Ingredients:
- ✓ 1 thin peel orange
- ✓ ¾ cup pistachio nuts, roasted, chilled, and chopped into large pieces
- ✓ ¼ cup hazelnuts, toasted, chilled, peeled and chopped into large pieces
- ✓ ¼ cup pumpkin seeds, toasted and chilled
- ✓ 1 tablespoon chia seeds
- ✓ 1 tablespoon sesame seeds, toasted and cooled
- ✓ 1 teaspoon grated orange peel
- ✓ 1 cardamom pod, finely crushed and sieved
- ✓ 12 ounces (340 g) tempered, dairy-free dark chocolate (85% cocoa content)
- ✓ 2 teaspoons flaky sea salt
- ✓ Candy or candy thermometer

Directions:
- ☞ Preheat the oven to 100-150°F (66 ° C). Line a baking sheet with parchment paper.
- ☞ Finely slice the orange crosswise and place it on the prepared baking sheet. Bake for 2 to 3 hours until dry but slightly sticky. Remove it from the oven and let it cool. When they cool enough to handle them, cut the orange slices into fragments; set them aside.
- ☞ In a large bowl, mix the nuts, seeds, and grated orange peel until completely combined. Place the mixture in a single layer on a baking sheet lined with kitchen parchment. Set it aside.
- ☞ Melt the chocolate in a water bath until it reaches 88 to 90°F (32 to 33°C) and pours it over the nut mixture to cover it completely.
- ☞ When the chocolate is semi-cold but still sticky, sprinkle the surface with sea salt and pieces of orange. Place the mixture in a cold area of your kitchen or refrigerate until the crust cools completely and cut it into bite-sized pieces.

Nutrition: Protein: 20.7 g **C**alories: 523 kcal Fat: 40.76 g Carbohydrates: 26.65 g

167.   Mini Bagel Pizzas

Preparation Time: 10 minutes **Cooking Time:** 20 minutes **Servings:** 4

Ingredients:

- ✓ 8 mini bagels, split
- ✓ 1/4 cup pizza sauce
- ✓ 1/3 cup shredded pizza cheese blend
- ✓ 16 slices turkey pepperoni (such as Hormel®)

Directions:

- ☞ Set the oven to 220°C or 425°F. Use aluminum foil to line a baking sheet.
- ☞ On a prepared baking sheet, add bagels, with cut sides up. Scoop over each bagel half with a thin payer of pizza sauce, then sprinkle with pizza cheese. Put on each bagel with 2 pepperoni slices.
- ☞ In the preheated oven, bake for 6 minutes, until pepperoni is browned a little bit and cheese is melted.

Nutrition: Calories: 38 Total Carbohydrate: 30.3 g Cholesterol: 33 mg Total Fat: 5.8 g Protein: 13.9 g Sodium: 788 mg

168. Candy Wraps

Preparation Time: 5 minutes

Cooking Time: 3 hours 5 minutes

Servings: 4

Ingredients:

- ✓ 1 (10 inches) whole wheat tortilla
- ✓ 1 tsp. orange marmalade
- ✓ 1 tsp. pure maple syrup

Directions:

- ☞ On a clean surface or dinner plate, lay out the tortilla. Spread orange marmalade on one half while the other with maple syrup. Roll up the tortilla tightly, beginning at the end with the syrup and finishing with marmalade.
- ☞ Hold it together with toothpicks, if necessary, or use plastic wrap to wrap. Chill for a couple of hours then cut into 1" pieces to serve.

Nutrition: Calories: 90 Total Carbohydrate: 24.4 g Total Fat: 0.5 g Protein: 3 g Sodium: 173 mg

169. Spicy Almonds

Preparation Time: 10 minutes

Cooking Time: 25 minutes

Servings: 4

Ingredients:

- ✓ 1 tbsp. sugar
- ✓ 1-1/2 tsp. kosher salt
- ✓ 1 tsp. paprika
- ✓ 1/2 tsp. ground cinnamon
- ✓ 1/2 tsp. ground cumin
- ✓ 1/2 tsp. ground coriander
- ✓ 1/4 tsp. cayenne pepper
- ✓ 2-1/2 cups unblanched almonds
- ✓ 1 tbsp. canola oi

Directions:

- ☞ Mix the initial 7 ingredients in a small bowl. Mix oil and almonds in a separate small bowl.
- ☞ Drizzle with spice mixture; coat by tossing.
- ☞ In a 15x10x1-inch foil-lined baking pan sprayed with cooking spray, put the mixture. Bake till lightly browned for 15 to 20 minutes at 325°, mixing two times. Cool completely. Keep in an airtight container.

Nutrition: Calories: 230 Total Carbohydrate: 9 g Fat: 20 g Fiber: 4 g Protein: 8 g Sodium: 293 mg

170. Rosemary Walnuts

Preparation Time: 10 minutes   **Cooking Time:** 20 minutes   **Servings:** 8

Ingredients:

- ✓ 2 cups walnuts
- ✓ 2 cloves garlic, minced
- ✓ 1 tbsp. honey
- ✓ 1 tbsp. extra-virgin olive oil
- ✓ 1 tbsp. minced fresh rosemary
- ✓ 1 tsp. salt

Directions:

☞ Preheat your oven to 350°F (175°C). Prepare your baking pan and line it with parchment paper. In a clean bowl, combine honey, rosemary, salt, garlic, walnuts, and olive oil. Mix until the walnuts are completely coated and transfer them into the prepared baking pan.Bake the walnuts in the preheated oven for about 10 minutes or until lightly brown in color

Nutrition: Calories: 188 Total Carbohydrate: 5.9 g Total Fat: 18 g Protein: 3.9 g Sodium: 291 mg

171. Gluten-free Snack Mix

Preparation Time: 10 minutes   **Cooking Time:** 25 minutes   **Servings:** 8

Ingredients:

- ✓ 8 cups popped popcorn
- ✓ 2 cups Koala Crisp cereal
- ✓ 1 package (5 oz.) dried cherries
- ✓ 1/3 cup butter, cubed
- ✓ 1/3 cup honey
- ✓ 1/2 tsp. ground cinnamon

Directions:

☞ Mix together cherries, cereal, and popcorn in a big ungreased roasting pan. Melt butter in a small saucepan. Put in cinnamon and honey, then cook and stir until heated through. Drizzle over popcorn mixture and toss to coat well.

☞ Bake at 325 degrees for about 15 minutes while stirring after every 5 minutes. Allow cooling thoroughly. Store in airtight containers.

Nutrition: Calories: 110 Carbohydrate: 16 g Cholesterol: 8 mg Fat: 5 g Fiber: 1 g Protein: 1g Sodium: 89 mg

172. Cranberry Pretzels

Preparation Time: 15 minutes   **Cooking Time:** 15 minutes   **Servings:** 15

Ingredients:

- ✓ 3/4 cup dried cranberries
- ✓ 1/3 cup unsweetened applesauce
- ✓ 2 tbsps. sugar, divided
- ✓ 1 package (1/4 oz.) active dry yeast
- ✓ 1 cup warm milk (110° to 115°)
- ✓ 3 tbsps. canola oil
- ✓ 1-1/2 tsps. salt
- ✓ 3-1/2 to 4 cups all-purpose flour
- ✓ 2 quarts water
- ✓ Topping:
- ✓ 1 egg white, beaten
- ✓ 1/2 tsp. ground cinnamon
- ✓ 1 tbsp. sugar
- ✓ Honey or cream cheese, optional

Directions:

☞ In a blender or food processor, put 1 tbsp. sugar, applesauce, and dried cranberries. Put a cover on and blend until chopped finely; set aside. Dissolve yeast with warm milk in a bowl. Put in the remaining sugar and allow to stand for about 5 minutes. Put in salt, oil, sufficient flour, and cranberry mixture to make a soft dough. Transfer to a surface coated lightly with flour, then knead the dough for 6 to 8 minutes, until elastic and smooth. Put in a bowl coated with cooking spray and turn one time to coat the top. Cover and allow to rise on a warm area for 1 1/2 hours, until doubled in size.

☞ Punch dough down then transfer onto a floured surface. Split the dough into 15 balls, rolling each ball into a 14-in. rope, and form into a pretzel shape.Bring water in a big saucepan to a boil, then drop in pretzels, one at a time. Boil about 10 seconds on each side; take out of the water, using a slotted spoon. Transfer to paper towels to drain.

☞ On baking sheets coated with cooking spray, place pretzels. Put a cover on and allow to rise in a warm area for 25 minutes, until puffy. Coat the surface with egg white. Mix sugar and cinnamon in, then sprinkle over tops of pretzels. Bake at 375° until turning golden brown, about 12 to 14 minutes. Serve with cream cheese or honey, if wanted.

Nutrition: Calories: 170 Total Carbohydrate: 31 g Cholesterol: 1 mg Total Fat: 3 g Fiber: 1 g Protein: 4 g Sodium: 248 mg

---

173. Pumpkin Custard

Preparation Time: 30 minutes   **Cooking Time:** 35 minutes   **Servings:** 8

Ingredients:

- ✓ Custard
- ✓ 8 egg yolks
- ✓ 1¾ cups (1 15-ounce can) pure pumpkin puree

Topping

- ✓ 1 cup crushed gingersnap cookies
- ✓ 1 tablespoon melted butter
- ✓ Whipped Cream
- ✓ 1 cup heavy whipping cream

- ✓ 1¾ cups heavy whipping cream
- ✓ ½ cup sugar
- ✓ 1½ teaspoons pumpkin pie spice
- ✓ 1 teaspoon vanilla

- ✓ 1 tablespoon superfine sugar (or regular sugar if you have no caster sugar)
- ✓ ½ teaspoon pumpkin pie spice

Garnish:

- ✓ 8 whole gingersnap cookies

Directions:

- Preheat the oven to 350°F. Separate the yolks from 8 eggs and whisk them together in a large mixing bowl until they are well blended and creamy.
- Add the pumpkin, sugar, vanilla, heavy cream, and pumpkin pie spice and whisk to combine.
- Cook the custard mixture in a double boiler, stirring until it has thickened enough that it coats a spoon. Pour the mixture into individual custard cups or an 8×8-inch baking pan and bake for about 20 minutes if using individual cups or 30–35 minutes for the baking pan, until it is set, and a knife inserted comes out clean.
- While the custard is baking, make the topping by combining the crushed gingersnaps and melted butter. After the custard has been in the oven for 15 minutes, sprinkle the gingersnap mixture over the top. When the custard has passed the clean knife test, remove it from the oven and let it cool to room temperature.
- Whisk the heavy cream and pumpkin pie spice together with the caster sugar and beat just until it thickens.
- Serve the custard with the whipped cream and garnish each serving with a gingersnap.

Nutrition: Calories: 255 Fat: 35 g Carbs: 25 g Protein: 76 g Sodium: 877 mg

174. Baked Apple Dumplings

Preparation Time: 20 minutes
Cooking Time: 40 minutes
Servings: 2 to 4

Ingredients:

- 1 (17½ ounce) package frozen puff pastry, thawed
- 1 cup sugar
- 6 tablespoons dry breadcrumbs
- 2 teaspoons ground cinnamon
- 1 pinch ground nutmeg
- 1 egg, beaten
- 4 Granny Smith apples, peeled, cored, and halved
- Vanilla ice cream for serving
- Icing
- 1 cup confectioners' sugar
- 1 teaspoon vanilla extract
- 3 tablespoons milk
- Pecan Streusel
- 2/3 cup chopped toasted pecans
- 2/3 cup packed brown sugar
- 2/3 cup all-purpose flour
- 5 tablespoons melted butter

Directions:

- Preheat the oven to 425°F. When the puff pastry has completely thawed, roll out each sheet to measure 12 inches by 12 inches. Cut the sheets into quarters.
- Combine the sugar, breadcrumbs, cinnamon, and nutmeg together in a small bowl.
- Brush one of the pastry squares with some of the beaten egg. Add about 1 tablespoon of the breadcrumb mixture on top, then add half an apple, core side down, over the crumbs. Add another tablespoon of the breadcrumb mixture.
- Seal the dumpling by pulling up the corners and pinching the pastry together until the seams are totally sealed. Repeat this process with the remaining squares. Assemble the ingredients for the pecan streusel in a small bowl.
- Grease a baking sheet, or line it with parchment paper. Place the dumplings on the sheet and brush them with a bit more of the beaten egg. Top with the pecan streusel.
- Bake for 15 minutes, then reduce heat to 350°F and bake for 25 minutes more or until lightly browned.
- Make the icing by combining the confectioners' sugar, vanilla, and milk until you reach the proper consistency.
- When the dumplings are done, let them cool to room temperature and drizzle them with icing before serving

Nutrition: Calories: 145 Fat: 57 g Carbs: 87 g Protein: 66.9 g Sodium: 529 mg

175. Peach Cobbler

Preparation Time: 10 minutes · **Cooking Time:** 45 minutes · **Servings:** 4

Ingredients:

- ✓ 1¼ cups Bisques
- ✓ 1 cup milk
- ✓ ½ cup melted butter
- ✓ ¼ teaspoon nutmeg
- ✓ ½ teaspoon cinnamon
- ✓ Vanilla ice cream, for serving
- ✓ Filling
- ✓ 1 (30-ounce) can peach in syrup, drained
- ✓ ¼ cup sugar
- ✓ Topping
- ✓ ½ cup brown sugar
- ✓ ¼ cup almond slices
- ✓ ½ teaspoon cinnamon
- ✓ 1 tablespoon melted butter

Directions:

- ☞ Preheat the oven to 375°F. Grease the bottom and sides of an 8×8-inch pan.
- ☞ Whisk together the Bisques, milk, butter, nutmeg, and cinnamon in a large mixing bowl. When thoroughly combined, pour into the greased baking pan.
- ☞ Mix together the peaches and sugar in another mixing bowl. Put the filling on top of the batter in the pan. Bake for about 45 minutes. In another bowl, mix together the brown sugar, almonds, cinnamon, and melted butter. After the cobbler has cooked for 45 minutes, cover evenly with the topping and bake for an additional 10 minutes. Serve with a scoop of vanilla ice cream.

Nutrition: Calories: 168 Fat: 76 g Carbs: 15 g Protein: 78.9 g Sodium: 436 mg

176. Maple Walnut Cupcakes with Matcha Green Tea Icing

Preparation Time: 20 minutes

Cooking Time: 25 minutes

Servings: 4

Ingredients:

- ✓ **For the Cupcakes:**
- ✓ 2 cups of All-Purpose flour
- ✓ ½ cup buckwheat flour
- ✓ 2 ½ teaspoons baking powder
- ✓ ½ teaspoon salt
- ✓ 1 cup cocoa butter
- ✓ 1 cup white sugar
- ✓ 1 tablespoon pure maple syrup
- ✓ 3 eggs
- ✓ 1 teaspoon maple extract
- ✓ 2/3 cup milk
- ✓ ¼ cup walnuts, chopped
- ✓ **For the Icing:**
- ✓ 3 tablespoons coconut oil, thick at room temperature
- ✓ 3 tablespoons icing sugar
- ✓ 1 tablespoon Matcha green tea powder
- ✓ ½ teaspoon vanilla bean paste
- ✓ 3 tablespoons cream cheese, softened

Directions:

- ☞ Preheat oven to 350 degrees F.
- ☞ Place paper baking cups into muffin tins for 24 regular-sized muffins. In a medium bowl, mix flours, baking powder, and salt.

117

- In a separate large bowl, cream the sugar, butter, syrup, and eggs with a hand or stand mixer.
- Pause to stir in maple extract.
- At a low speed, alternate blending in dry mixture and milk. Fold in nuts.

To make the icing:

- Add the coconut oil and icing sugar to a bowl and use a hand-mixer to cream until it's pale and smooth.
- Fold in the matcha powder and vanilla.

- Pour batter into muffin cup until 2/3 full.
- Bake for 20-25 minutes or until an inserted toothpick comes out clean.
- Cool completely before icing.

- Finally, add the cream cheese and beat until smooth.
- Pipe or spread over the cupcakes once they're cool.

Nutrition: Calories 224 Fat 14.5g Fiber 5.2g Carbs 12.7g Protein 5.3g

177. Chocolate Maple Walnuts

Preparation Time: 15 minutes

Cooking Time: 30 minutes

Servings: 4

Ingredients:

- ½ cup pure maple syrup, divided
- 2 cups raw, whole walnuts

- ✓ 5 squares of dark chocolate, at least 85%
- ✓ 1 ½ tablespoons coconut oil, melted
- ✓ 1 tablespoonful of water
- ✓ Sifted icing sugar
- ✓ 1 teaspoonful of vanilla extract

Directions:

- Line a large baking sheet with parchment paper. In a medium to a large skillet, combine the walnuts and ¼ cup of maple syrup and cook over medium heat, stirring continuously, until walnuts are completely covered with syrup and golden in color, about 3 – 5 minutes.
- Pour the walnuts onto the parchment paper and separate them into individual pieces with a fork. Allow cooling completely, at least 15 minutes.
- In the meantime, melt the chocolate in a double boiler with the coconut oil. Add the

remaining maple syrup and stir until thoroughly combined.
- When walnuts are cooled, transfer them to a glass bowl and pour the melted chocolate syrup over top. Use a silicone spatula to gently mix until walnuts are completely covered.
- Transfer back to the parchment paper-lined baking sheet and, once again, separate each of the nuts with a fork.
- Place the nuts in the fridge for 10 minutes or the freezer for 3 – 5 minutes, until chocolate has completely set. Store in an airtight bag in your fridge.

178.   Matcha and Chocolate Dipped Strawberries

Preparation Time: 5 minutes

Cooking Time: 10 minutes

Servings: 4

Ingredients:

- ✓ 4 tablespoons cocoa butter
- ✓ 4 squares of dark chocolate, at least 85%
- ✓ ¼ cup coconut oil
- ✓ 1 teaspoon Matcha green tea powder
- ✓ 20 – 25 large whole strawberries, stems on

Directions:

- ☞ Melt cocoa butter, dark chocolate, coconut oil, and Matcha in a double boiler until nearly smooth.
- ☞ Remove from heat and continue stirring until chocolate is completely melted.
- ☞ Pour into a large glass bowl and stir constantly until the chocolate thickens and starts to lose its sheen, about 2 - 5 minutes.
- ☞ Working one at a time, hold the strawberries by stems and dip into chocolate matcha mixture to coat. Let excess drip back into the bowl.
- ☞ Place on a parchment-lined baking sheet and chill dipped berries in the fridge until the shell is set, 20–25 minutes.
- ☞ You may need to reheat the matcha mixture if it starts to set before you have dipped all the berries.

Nutrition: Calories 261, Fat 7.6g Fiber 2.2g Carbs 22.8g Protein 12.5g

179. Vegan Rice Pudding

Preparation Time: 10 minutes

Cooking Time: 20 minutes

Servings: 3

Ingredients:

- ✓ ½ tsp. ground cinnamon
- ✓ 1 c. rinsed basmati
- ✓ 1/8 tsp. ground cardamom
- ✓ ¼ c. sugar
- ✓ 1-quart vanilla non-dairy milk
- ✓ 1 tsp. pure vanilla extract
- ✓ 1/8 tsp. pure almond extract

Directions:

- Measure all of the ingredients into a saucepan and stir well to combine. Bring to a boil over medium-high heat.
- Once boiling, reduce heat to low and simmer, stirring very frequently, about 15–20 minutes.
- Remove from heat and cool. Serve sprinkled with additional ground cinnamon if desired

Nutrition: Calories: 148, Fat:2 g, Carbs:26 g, Protein:4 g, Sugars:35 g, Sodium:150 mg

180. Cinnamon-Scented Quinoa

Preparation Time: 5 minutes

Cooking Time: 10 minutes

Servings: 4

Ingredients:

- ✓ Chopped walnuts
- ✓ 1 ½ c. water
- ✓ Maple syrup
- ✓ 2 cinnamon sticks
- ✓ 1 c. quinoa

Directions:

- Add the quinoa to a bowl and wash it in several changes of water until the water is clear. When washing quinoa, rub grains and allow them to settle before you pour off the water.
- Use a large fine-mesh sieve to drain the quinoa. Prepare your pressure cooker with a trivet and steaming basket. Place the quinoa and the cinnamon sticks in the basket and pour the water.
- Close and lock the lid. Cook at high pressure for 6 minutes. When the cooking time is up, release the pressure using the quick release directions.
- Fluff the quinoa with a fork and remove the cinnamon sticks. Divide the cooked quinoa among serving bowls and top with maple syrup and chopped walnuts.

Nutrition: Calories: 160, Fat:3 g, Carbs:28 g, Protein:6 g, Sugars:19 g, Sodium:40 mg

181. Green Vegetable Smoothie

Preparation Time: 5 minutes

Cooking Time: 20 minutes

Servings: 4

Ingredients:

- ✓ 1 c. cold water
- ✓ ½ c. strawberries
- ✓ 2 oz. baby spinach
- ✓ 1 lemon juice
- ✓ 1 tbsp. fresh mint
- ✓ 1 banana
- ✓ ½ c. blueberries

Directions:

☞ Put all the ingredients in a juicer or blender and puree.

Nutrition: Calories: 52, Fat:2 g, Carbs:12 g, Protein:1 g, Sugars:18 g, Sodium:36 mg

182. Garlic Lovers Hummus

Preparation Time: 5 minutes

Cooking Time: 10 minutes

Servings: 4

Ingredients:

- ✓ 3 tbsps. Freshly squeezed lemon juice
- ✓ All-purpose salt-free seasoning
- ✓ 3 tbsps. Sesame tahini
- ✓ 4 garlic cloves
- ✓ 15 oz. no-salt-added garbanzo beans
- ✓ 2 tbsps. Olive oil

Directions:

☞ Drain garbanzo beans and rinse well. Place all the ingredients in a food processor and pulse until smooth.

☞ Serve immediately or cover and refrigerate until serving.

Nutrition: Calories: 103, Fat:5 g, Carbs:11 g, Protein:4 g, Sugars:2 g, Sodium:88 mg

183. Endive Leaves with Citrus Cream

Preparation Time: 15 minutes

Cooking Time: 30+ minutes

Servings: 4

Ingredients:

- ✓ 4-6 heads Red endive
- ✓ 8 ounces cream cheese
- ✓ 1 tablespoon shallot, finely chopped
- ✓ ¼ cup sour cream
- ✓ ¼ cup Vegannaise or mayonnaise
- ✓ Zest from one small lemon
- ✓ 1 tablespoon lemon juice
- ✓ 2 tablespoons fresh tarragon, chopped
- ✓ 2 tablespoons fresh dill, chopped, plus extra for garnish if desired
- ✓ 2 tablespoons parsley, chopped
- ✓ 1 tablespoon green onions, finely chopped
- ✓ Anchovies paste (optional), to taste
- ✓ Salt and pepper, to taste

Directions:

☞ In a medium bowl, whisk all ingredients together, except the endive leaves, until smooth. Refrigerate until needed. When well chilled, place filling into a piping bag with a French tip.

☞ Trim the stem end of the endive leaves and carefully peel the leaves off of the base of the head so you have individual leaves.

☞ Place the leaves in a single layer on a platter and fill with the cream from the piping bag.

Alternatively, spoon the filling into a small bowl or ramekin and serve the endive leaves and crackers around it for guests to help themselves.

Nutrition: Calories 304 Fat 13.2g Fiber 6.5g Carbs 19.1g Protein 15.4g

184.   Greek Stuffed Mushrooms

Preparation Time: 10 minutes

Cooking Time: 20 minutes

Servings: 3

Ingredients:

- ✓ 20 large mushrooms, washed
- ✓ 1 tablespoon extra-virgin olive oil
- ✓ 1 cup broccoli, chopped
- ✓ 1 medium red onion, diced
- ✓ 1 teaspoon garlic, minced
- ✓ ¼ cup capers
- ✓ ½ teaspoon dried oregano
- ✓ ½ teaspoon dried parsley
- ✓ 3 tablespoons feta cheese
- ✓ 1 tablespoon breadcrumbs
- ✓ Salt and pepper to taste

Directions:

- ☞ Preheat oven to 425 degrees F.
- ☞ Remove the stems from the mushrooms carefully and dice them.
- ☞ Place mushroom tops in a single layer on a baking sheet, with the hole facing up, and bake for 5 minutes.
- ☞ Heat olive oil in a pan with the diced mushrooms stems, broccoli, onion, garlic, capers, oregano, parsley, and salt and pepper. Cook for 5 – 10 minutes.
- ☞ Add feta and breadcrumbs.
- ☞ Stuff mushrooms with mixture and bake for 8 – 10 minutes.

Nutrition: Calories: 287, Total Fat: 11.2g, Carbs: 9.6g, Protein: 15.3g

185.   Roast Tomato and Parmesan Bruschetta with Capers

Preparation Time: 5 minutes

Cooking Time: 10 minutes

Servings: 4

Ingredients:

- ✓ 4 to 6 thick slices of whole-grain baguette, sliced on a diagonal
- ✓ 1 cup cherry tomatoes
- ✓ 2 tablespoons capers, drained
- ✓ 3 to 4 tablespoons extra virgin olive oil + 1 tablespoon extra
- ✓ ½ teaspoon sea salt
- ✓ 2/3 cup aged Parmesan, shaved

Directions:

- ☞ Preheat oven to 400 degrees F.
- ☞ Mix the cherry tomatoes, capers, and 3 to 4 tablespoons of olive oil together and pour

into an ovenproof dish. Roast for 10 to 15 minutes.

☞ While the tomatoes are roasting, toast the bread on both sides and drizzle the remaining 1 tablespoon of oil over the bread. Spoon the roast tomatoes and capers over the toasted bread, salt to taste and top with the shaved Parmesan to serve.

Nutrition: Calories: 286, Total Fat: 11.6g, Carbs: 8.7g, Protein: 15.4g

186. Herbed Tomato and Buffalo Mozzarella Appetizer

Preparation Time: 5 minutes

Cooking Time: 30 minutes

Servings: 4

Ingredients:

- ✓ 1 tablespoon parsley, minced
- ✓ ½ teaspoon dried basil
- ✓ ½ teaspoon dried lovage
- ✓ 1 tablespoon capers, drained
- ✓ 2 cloves garlic, minced
- ✓ 4 tablespoons extra virgin olive oil
- ✓ 1 ball of buffalo mozzarella cheese, sliced thinly
- ✓ 2 beefsteak tomatoes, sliced thinly
- ✓ 1 (7 ounces) jar roasted red peppers, drained
- ✓ Chili pepper flakes to taste (optional)

Directions:

☞ In a medium-sized bowl, mix together parsley, basil, lovage, capers, garlic, and olive oil.

☞ On a large plate or serving platter, layer slices of mozzarella cheese with tomato and top with a slice of roasted red pepper.

☞ Drizzle the herb and olive oil mixture over top of each stack. Cover and chill in the refrigerator for at least 30 minutes.

☞ Sprinkle with chili flakes before serving (optional).

Nutrition: Calories: 289, Total Fat: 11.2g, Carbs: 8.4g, Protein: 15.3g

187. Feta and Beet Stacked Appetizer

Preparation Time: 5 minutes

Cooking Time: 20 minutes

Servings: 4

Ingredients:

- ✓ 2 large fresh beets
- ✓ ½ teaspoon dried lovage
- ✓ ½ cup red wine vinegar
- ✓ ¼ cup lemon juice (optional)
- ✓ ½ cup feta cheese
- ✓ ½ cup walnuts, crushed

Directions:

☞ Soak the lovage in the red wine vinegar while you're preparing the rest of the appetizer.

☞ Bring a pot of water to a boil and cook the beets for 25 minutes, or until tender.

- Cool, peel, and slice in 1/3" thick slices.
- Place beets in a bowl with the lovage red wine vinegar and marinate for 15 minutes.
- Separate the beets from the vinegar and add the lemon juice to the liquid.
- Place a few beet slices on a microwave-safe dish and sprinkle them with some feta cheese and crushed walnuts. Drizzle with some of the lemon vinegar mixes.
- Top with more beet slices, and sprinkle again with feta, walnuts, and lemon vinegar. Repeat until you have no more beet slices left.
- Microwave on medium for 45 seconds to 1 minute.
- Cool slightly before serving.

Nutrition: Calories – 183; Fat – 4.3 g; Fiber – 7.6 g; Carbs – 26.2 g; Protein – 11.3 g; Sodium – 466 mg

188.   Blueberry Nut Bran Muffins

Preparation Time: 5 minutes

Cooking Time: 10 minutes

Servings: 4

Ingredients:

- ✓ Wheat bran – 1 cup
- ✓ Whole wheat flour – 1.5 cups
- ✓ Sea salt - .5 teaspoon
- ✓ Baking soda - .25 teaspoon
- ✓ Baking powder - .25 teaspoon
- ✓ Cinnamon – 1.5 teaspoons
- ✓ Eggs – 2
- ✓ Soy milk, unsweetened - .75 cup
- ✓ Apple cider vinegar – 1 tablespoon
- ✓ Apple sauce, unsweetened - .33 cup
- ✓ Date sugar – .5 cup
- ✓ Soybean oil - .33 cup
- ✓ Blueberries, fresh or frozen – 1 cup
- ✓ Walnuts, chopped - .5 cup

Directions:

- Begin by setting your standard or toaster oven to Fahrenheit four-hundred degrees. Line a twelve-cup muffin tin and then spray the paper liners with nonstick cooking spray.
- Whisk together the eggs, applesauce, date sugar, soybean oil, soy milk, and apple cider vinegar in a large bowl until fully combined. Set it aside. Stir together the whole wheat flour, wheat bran, cinnamon, sea salt, baking soda, and baking soda in another clean bowl. Once the dry ingredients are combined, fol them into the other prepared ingredients. Gently fold in the blueberries and walnuts, just until combined.
- Divide the blueberry nut bran muffin batter between the prepared muffin liners and allow them to cook until fully done and a toothpick once inserted is removed clean, about fifteen to eighteen minutes. Once removed from the oven allow the muffins to cool for five minutes before removing them from the pan.

189. Plum Oat Bars

Preparation Time: 5 minutes

Cooking Time: 10 minutes

Servings: 4

Ingredients:

- ✓ Rolled oats – 1.5 cups
- ✓ Baking powder – 1 teaspoon
- ✓ Almond meal - .5 cup
- ✓ Cinnamon – 1.5 teaspoon
- ✓ Soybean oil – 2 tablespoons
- ✓ Sea salt - .25 teaspoon
- ✓ Prunes – 2 cups

Directions:

- ☞ Begin by preheating the oven to Fahrenheit three-hundred and fifty degrees and preparing the prunes. Add the prunes to a large bowl and pour hot water over them until fully submerged. Allow the prunes to sit in the water for five minutes, until soft.

- ☞ Remove the prunes from the water and transfer them to a blender or food processor, reserving the water. Pour in a small amount of the water that you previously reserved from the prunes and blend until the prunes form a thick paste.

- ☞ Add two tablespoons of the prepared prune puree to a medium kitchen bowl along with the oil, sea salt, baking powder, cinnamon, almond flour, and rolled oats. Combine until the mixture resembles a crumble, slightly like wet sand. You can add more prune puree if it is too dry.

- ☞ Line a square baking dish with kitchen parchment and then press three-quarters of the oat mixture into the bottom to form a crust. Spread the remaining prune puree over the top of the crust, and then sprinkle the remaining oat mixture over the prune puree to add a crumble.

- ☞ Cook the bars in the oven until set and slightly toasted, about fifteen minutes. Remove the plum oat bars from the hot oven and let the pan cool completely. After the bars have reached room temperature slice them into nine bars and enjoy.

Nutrition: calories 274, fat 11.6, fiber 2.8, carbs 11.5, protein 15.4

190.   Spinach and Kale Mix

Preparation Time: 5 minutes

Cooking Time: 30 minutes

Servings: 4

Ingredients:

- ✓ 2 chopped shallots
- ✓ 1 c. no-salt-added and chopped canned tomatoes
- ✓ 2 c. baby spinach
- ✓ 2 minced garlic cloves
- ✓ 5 c. torn kale
- ✓ 1 tbsp. olive oil

Directions:

- ☞ Heat up a pan with the oil over medium-high heat, add the shallots, stir and sauté for 5 minutes.
- ☞ Add the spinach, kale and the other ingredients, toss, cook for 10 minutes more, divide between plates and serve.

Nutrition: Calories: 89, Fat:3.7 g, Carbs:12.4 g, Protein:3.6 g, Sugars:0 g, Sodium:50 mg

191.   Watermelon Juice

Preparation Time: 20 minutes

Cooking Time: 0 minutes

Servings: 1

Ingredients:

- ✓ 20g of young kale leaves
- ✓ 250g of watermelon chunks
- ✓ 4 mint leaves
- ✓ ½ cucumber

Directions:

- ☞ Remove the stalks from the kale and roughly chop them.
- ☞ Peel the cucumber, if preferred, and then halve it and seed it.
- ☞ Place all ingredients in a blender or juicer and process until you achieve the desired consistency. Serve immediately.

Nutrition: Calories 26 Fat 14,g Fiber 2g Carbs 14g Protein 20g

192.   Crunchy Potato Bites

Preparation Time: 15 minutes   **Cooking Time:** 30 minutes   **Servings:** 3 portions

Ingredients:

- ✓ 1 potato, sliced
- ✓ 2 bacon slices, already cooked and crumbled
- ✓ 1 small avocado, pitted and cubed
- ✓ 1 tbsp. of extra virgin olive oil

126

Directions:

- ☞ Spread potato slices on a lined baking sheet.
- ☞ Toss around with the extra virgin olive oil.
- ☞ Insert in the oven at 350 degrees F.
- ☞ Bake for 20 minutes.
- ☞ Arrange on a platter, top each slice with avocado and crumbled bacon, and serve as a snack.

Nutrition: Calories: 112 Cal Fat: 1 g Carbs: 0 g Protein: 0.2 g Fiber: 8 g

---

193.   Dates in a Parma Ham Blanket

Preparation Time: 5 minutes   **Cooking Time:** 5 minutes   **Servings:** 12 pieces

Ingredients:

- ✓ 12 Medjool dates
- ✓ 2 slices of Parma ham, cut into strips

Directions:

- ☞ Wrap each date with a strip of Parma ham. Can be served hot or cold.

Nutrition: Calories: 149 Cal Fat: 1 g Carbs: 0 g Protein: 0.2 g Fiber: 8 g

---

194.   Mung Beans Snack Salad

Preparation Time: 10 minutes   **Cooking Time:** 10 minutes   **Servings:** 6 portions

Ingredients:

- ✓ 2 cups tomatoes, chopped
- ✓ 2 cups cucumber, chopped
- ✓ 3 cups mixed greens
- ✓ 2 cups mung beans, sprouted
- ✓ 2 cups clover sprouts
- ✓ For the salad dressing:
- ✓ 1 tablespoon cumin, ground
- ✓ 1 cup dill, chopped
- ✓ 4 tablespoons lemon juice
- ✓ 1 avocado, pitted, peeled, and roughly chopped
- ✓ 1 cucumber, roughly chopped

Directions:

- ☞ In a salad bowl, mix tomatoes with 2 cups cucumber, greens, clover, and mung sprouts.
- ☞ In your blender, mix cumin with dill, lemon juice, 1 cucumber, and avocado and blend really well
- ☞ Add the blended cream to your salad, toss well, and serve as a snack.

Nutrition: Calories: 60 Cal Fat: 0 g Carbs: 0 g Protein: 0 g Fiber: 0 g

---

195.   Sprouts and Apples Snack Salad

Preparation Time: 10 minutes   **Cooking Time:** 10 minutes   **Servings:**   6   portion

Ingredients:

- ✓ 1 pound Brussels sprouts, shredded
- ✓ 1 cup walnuts, chopped
- ✓ 1 apple, cored and cubed
- ✓ 1 red onion, chopped

For the salad dressing:

- ✓ 3 tablespoons red vinegar
- ✓ 1 tablespoon mustard
- ✓ ½ cup olive oil
- ✓ 1 garlic clove, minced
- ✓ Black pepper to the taste

Directions:

- ☞ In a salad bowl, mix sprouts with apple, onion, and walnuts.
- ☞ In another bowl, mix vinegar with mustard, oil, garlic, and pepper and whisk really well.
- ☞ Add the dressing to your salad, toss well and serve as a snack.

Nutrition: Calories: 60 Cal Fat: 1 g Carbs: 0 g Protein: 0.1 g Fiber: 8 g

196.　　　Moroccan Snack Salad

Preparation Time: 10 minutes　　　**Cooking Time:** 10 minutes　　　**Servings:** 6 portions

Ingredients:

- ✓ 1 bunch radishes, sliced
- ✓ 3 cups leeks, chopped
- ✓ 1 and ½ cups olives, pitted and sliced
- ✓ A pinch of turmeric powder
- ✓ Black pepper to the taste
- ✓ 2 tablespoons olive oil
- ✓ 1 cup cilantro, chopped

Directions:

- ☞ In a bowl, mix radishes with leeks, olives, and cilantro.
- ☞ Add black pepper, oil, and turmeric, toss to coat, and serve as a snack.

Nutrition: Calories: 55 Cal Fat: 1 g Carbs: 10 g Protein: 1 g Fiber: 5 g

197.　　　Celery and Raisins Snack Salad

Preparation Time: 10 minutes　　　**Cooking Time:** 10 minutes　　　**Servings:** 1

Ingredients:

- ✓ ½ cup raisins
- ✓ 4 cups celery, sliced
- ✓ ¼ cup parsley, chopped
- ✓ ½ cup walnuts, chopped
- ✓ Juice of ½ lemon
- ✓ 2 tablespoons olive oil
- ✓ Salt and black pepper to the taste

Directions:

- ☞ In a salad bowl, mix celery with raisins, walnuts, parsley, lemon juice, oil, and black pepper and toss.
- ☞ Divide into small cups and serve as a snack.

Nutrition: Calories: 60 Cal Fat: 1 g Carbs: 0 g Protein: 0.2 g Fiber: 8 g

198.　　　Dill and Bell Peppers Snack Bowl

Preparation Time: 10 minutes　　　**Cooking Time:** 10 minutes　　　**Servings:** 4 portions

Ingredients:

- ✓ 2 tablespoons dill, chopped
- ✓ 1 yellow onion, chopped
- ✓ 1-pound multi-colored bell peppers, cut into halves, seeded, and cut into thin strips
- ✓ 3 tablespoons extra virgin olive oil
- ✓ 2 and ½ tablespoons white vinegar
- ✓ Black pepper to the taste

Directions:

- ☞ In a salad bowl, mix bell peppers with onion, dill, pepper, oil, and vinegar and toss to coat.

☞ Divide into small bowls and serve as a snack.

Nutrition: Calories: 68 Cal Fat: 1 g Carbs: 0 g Protein: 0.2 g Fiber: 8 g

199.   Spicy Pumpkin Seeds Bowl

Preparation Time: 0 minutes   **Cooking Time:** 30 minutes   **Servings:** 6 portions

Ingredients:

- ✓ ½ tablespoon chili powder
- ✓ ½ teaspoon cayenne pepper
- ✓ 2 cups pumpkin seeds
- ✓ 2 teaspoons lime juice

Directions:

- ☞ Spread pumpkin seeds on a lined baking sheet, add lime juice, cayenne, and chili powder, and toss well.
- ☞ Put it in the oven and roast at 275 degrees F for 20 minutes.
- ☞ Divide into small bowls and serve as a snack.

Nutrition: Calories: 50 Cal Fat: 1 g Carbs: 0 g Protein: 0.2 g Fiber: 8 g

200.   Apple and Pecan Bowls

Preparation Time: 10 minutes   **Cooking Time:** 10 minutes   **Servings:** 4 portions

Ingredients:

- ✓ 4 big apples, cored, peeled, and cubed
- ✓ 2 teaspoons lemon juice
- ✓ ¼ cup pecans, chopped

Directions:

- ☞ In a bowl, mix apples with lemon juice, and pecans and toss.
- ☞ Divide into small bowls and serve as a snack.

Nutrition: Calories: 60 Cal Fat: 1 g Carbs: 0 g Protein: 0.2 g Fiber: 8 g

201.   Cheesy mushrooms

Preparation Time: 10 minutes   **Cooking Time:** 40 minutes   **Servings:** 20 portions

Ingredients:

- ✓ 20 white mushroom caps
- ✓ 1 garlic clove, minced
- ✓ 3 tablespoons parsley, chopped
- ✓ 2 yellow onions, chopped
- ✓ Black pepper to the taste
- ✓ ½ cup low-fat parmesan, grated
- ✓ ¼ cup low-fat mozzarella, grated
- ✓ A drizzle of olive oil
- ✓ 2 tablespoons non-fat yogurt

Directions:

- ☞ Heat up a pan with some oil over medium heat, add garlic and onion, stir, cook for 10 minutes and transfer to a bowl.
- ☞ Add black pepper, garlic, parsley, mozzarella, parmesan, and yogurt, stir well, stuff the mushroom caps with the mix.
- ☞ Arrange them on a lined baking sheet and bake in the oven at 400 degrees F for 20 minutes.
- ☞ Serve them as an appetizer.

Nutrition: Calories: 60 Cal Fat: 1 g Carbs: 0 g Protein: 0.2 g Fiber: 8 g

202. Vegetable and nuts bread loaf

Preparation Time: 10 minutes **Cooking Time:** 1 h and 45 min **Servings:** 4 portions

Ingredients:

- ✓ 1 loaf
- ✓ 175g (6oz) mushrooms, finely chopped
- ✓ 100g (3½ oz) haricot beans
- ✓ 100g (3½ oz) walnuts, finely chopped
- ✓ 100g (3½ oz) peanuts, finely chopped
- ✓ 1 carrot, finely chopped
- ✓ 3 sticks celery, finely chopped
- ✓ 1 bird's-eye chili, finely chopped
- ✓ 1 red onion, finely chopped
- ✓ 1 egg, beaten
- ✓ 2 cloves of garlic, chopped
- ✓ 2 tablespoons olive oil
- ✓ 2 teaspoons turmeric powder
- ✓ 2 tablespoons soy sauce
- ✓ 4 tablespoons fresh parsley, chopped
- ✓ 100mls (3½ fl oz) water
- ✓ 60mls (2fl oz) red wine

Directions:

☞ Heat the oil in a pan and add the garlic, chili, carrot, celery, onion, mushrooms, and turmeric. Cook for 5 minutes.

☞ Place the haricot beans in a bowl and stir in the nuts, vegetables, soy sauce, egg, parsley, red wine, and water.

☞ Grease and line a large loaf tin with greaseproof paper. Spoon the mixture into the loaf tin, cover with foil and bake in the oven at 190C/375F for 60-90 minutes.

☞ Let it stand for 10 minutes then turn onto a serving plate.

Nutrition: Calories: 60 Cal Fat: 1 g Carbs: 0 g Protein: 0.2 g Fiber: 8 g

203. Cinnamon Apple Chips

Preparation Time: 10 minutes **Cooking Time:** 2 h 10 min **Servings:** 4 portions

Ingredients:

- ✓ Cooking spray
- ✓ 2 teaspoons cinnamon powder
- ✓ 2 apples, cored and thinly sliced

Directions:

☞ Arrange apple slices on a lined baking sheet, spray them with cooking oil, and sprinkle cinnamon on them.

☞ Put it in the oven and bake at 300 degrees F for 2 hours.

☞ Divide into bowls and serve as a snack.

Nutrition: Calories: 70 Cal Fat: 1 g Carbs: 0 g Protein: 0.2 g Fiber: 8 g

204. Chocolate Dessert with Dates and Walnuts

Preparation Time: 10 Minutes **Cooking time:** 15 Minutes **Servings:** 2

Ingredients:

- ✓ 4 Medjool dates, pitted
- ✓ 2 tbsp. cocoa powder
- ✓ 1 cup milk, skimmed
- ✓ 1 tsp. agar powder
- ✓ 1 tbsp. peanut butter
- ✓ 1 pinch of salt
- ✓ ½ tsp. cinnamon
- ✓ 2 walnuts
- ✓ 1 tsp whole wheat flour

Directions:

1. Blitz dates, peanut butter and 1tbsp. milk in a food processor. Put the mix in a pan; add cocoa, cinnamon, salt, flour, agar powder. Add the remaining hot milk bit by bit and mix well to obtain a smooth mixture.

2. Turn the heat on, bring to a boil and cook around 6-8 minutes until dense.
3. Divide in 2 cups, let cool and put in the fridge.
4. Add chopped walnuts before serving.

Nutrition: Calories 326, Carbs7 g, Protein: 25g, Fat3 g

205. Celery and Raisins Snack Salad

Preparation time: 10 minutes   **Cooking time:** 0 minutes   **Servings:** 4

Ingredients:
- ✓ ½ cup raisins
- ✓ 4 cups celery, sliced
- ✓ ¼ cup parsley, chopped
- ✓ ½ cup walnuts, chopped
- ✓ Juice of ½ lemon
- ✓ 2 tbsp. extra virgin olive oil
- ✓ Salt and black pepper to the taste

Directions:
1. In a salad bowl, mix celery with raisins, walnuts, parsley, lemon juice, oil, and black pepper, toss, divide into small cups and serve as a snack.

Nutrition: Calories 120 Fat 1g Carbohydrate 6 g Protein 5 g

206. Dijon Celery Salad

Preparation time: 10 minutes   **Cooking time:** 0 minutes   **Servings:** 4

Ingredients:
- ✓ 2 tsp. honey
- ✓ ½ lemon, juiced
- ✓ 1 tbsp. Dijon mustard
- ✓ 2 tsp. extra virgin olive oil
- ✓ Black pepper to taste
- ✓ 2 apples, cored, peeled and cubed
- ✓ 1 bunch celery roughly chopped
- ✓ ¾ cup walnuts, chopped

Directions:
1. In a salad bowl, mix celery and its leaves with apple pieces and walnuts. Add black pepper, lemon juice, mustard, honey, and olive oil, whisk well, add to your salad, toss, divide into small cups and serve as a snack.

Nutrition: Calories 125 Fat 2 Carbohydrate 7 g Protein 7 g

207. Mediterranean Tofu Scramble Snack

Preparation Time: 10 minutes   **Cooking Time:** 8 minutes   **Servings:** 2

Ingredients:
- ✓ 1 tsp. extra virgin olive oil
- ✓ ½ onion, chopped
- ✓ ½ zucchini, chopped
- ✓ 1 cup baby spinach
- ✓ ½ cup halved cherry tomatoes
- ✓ 1 tbsp. sundried tomatoes in oil
- ✓ 4 oz. tofu crumbled

Directions:
1. Place a pan on medium to low heat. Add oil.
2. When the oil is hot, add all vegetables until they are soft. Season with salt and pepper and cook for 5 minutes.
3. Add spinach along with tomatoes and cook for a few minutes until the spinach wilts. Add tofu and mix well. Heat thoroughly. Adjust the seasoning if necessary. Remove from heat and serve as snack.

Nutrition: Cal 134 Fat 9 g Carbs 5 g Fiber 1 g Protein 10 g

208. Salmon Fritters

Preparation time: 10 minutes   **Cooking time:** 20 minutes   **Servings:** 2

Ingredients:
- ✓ 6 oz. salmon, canned
- ✓ 1 tbsp. flour
- ✓ 1 clove garlic, crushed
- ✓ ½ red onion, finely chopped
- ✓ 2 eggs
- ✓ 2 tsp. olive oil
- ✓ Salt and pepper to taste
- ✓ 2 cups arugula

Directions:

1. Separate egg whites from yolks and beat them until very stiff. In a separate bowl mix salmon, flour, salt, pepper, onion, garlic, onion and yolks.
2. Add egg whites and slowly mix them together. Heat a pan on medium high. Add 1tsp. oil and when hot form salmon fritters with a spoon.
3. Cook until brown (around 4 minutes per side) and serve with arugula salad seasoned with salt, pepper and 1 tsp. olive oil.

Nutrition: Calories: 320 Carbs: 18g Fat: 7g Protein: 27g

209.   Mince Stuffed Eggplants

Preparation Time: 10 minutes   **Cooking Time:** 70 minutes   **Servings:** 6

Ingredients:

- ✓ 4 oz. lean mince
- ✓ 6 large eggplants
- ✓ 1 egg
- ✓ 3 tbsp. dry red wine
- ✓ ½ cup cheddar, grated
- ✓ Salt and pepper, to taste
- ✓ 1 red onion
- ✓ 2 tsp. olive oil
- ✓ 2 tbsp. tomato sauce
- ✓ 2 tbsp. parsley

Directions:

1. Preheat oven to 350°F. Meanwhile, slice eggplants in 2 and scoop out the center part, leaving ½ inch of meat. . Place eggplants in a microwavable dish with about ½" of water in the bottom.
2. Microwave on high for 4 minutes. In a saucepan, fry mince with onion for 5 minutes.
3. Add wine and let evaporate.
4. Add tomato sauce, salt, pepper, eggplant meat and cook around 20 minutes until done.
5. Combine, mince sauce, cheese, egg, parsley, salt and pepper in a large bowl and mix well. Pack firmly into eggplants.
6. Return eggplants to the dish you first microwaved them in and bake for 25 to 30 minutes, or until lightly browned on top.

Nutrition: Calories: 350 Carbs: 22g Fat: 10g Protein: 17g

210.   Easy Shrimp Salad

Preparation time: 5 minutes   **Cooking time:** 0 minutes   **Servings:** 2

Ingredients:

- ✓ 2 cups red endive, finely sliced
- ✓ 1 cup cherry tomatoes, halved
- ✓ 1 tsp. of extra virgin olive oil
- ✓ 1 tbsp. parsley, chopped
- ✓ 3 oz. celery, sliced
- ✓ 6 walnuts, chopped
- ✓ 2 oz. red onion-sliced
- ✓ 1 cup yellow pepper, cubed
- ✓ ½ lemon, juiced
- ✓ 6 oz. steamed shrimps

Directions:

1. Put red endive on a large plate. Evenly distribute on top finely sliced onion, yellow pepper, cherry tomatoes walnuts, celery and parsley.
2. Mix oil, lemon juice with a pinch of salt and pepper and distribute the dressing on top.

Nutrition: Calories: 353, Fat: 4.8g, Carbohydrate: 28.1g, Protein: 28.3g

211.   Red Onion Frittata with Chili Grilled Zucchini

Preparation time: 5 minutes   **Cooking time:** 30 minutes   **Servings:** 2

Ingredients:

- ✓ 1 ½ cups red onion, finely sliced
- ✓ 3 eggs
- ✓ 3 oz. cheddar cheese
- ✓ 2 tbsp. milk
- ✓ 2 zucchini
- ✓ 2 tbsp. oil
- ✓ 1 clove garlic, crushed
- ✓ ½ chili, finely sliced
- ✓ 1 tsp. white vinegar
- ✓ Salt and pepper to taste

Directions:

1. Heat the oven to 350°F. Cut the zucchini into thin slices; grill them and set them aside.

2. Add 3 eggs, shredded cheddar cheese, milk, salt, pepper, whisk well and pour in a silicone baking tray and cook 25-30 minutes in the oven.
3. Mix garlic, oil, salt, pepper and vinegar and pour the dressing on the zucchini. Serve the frittata alongside the zucchini.

Nutrition: Calories: 359, Fat: 7.8g, Carbohydrate: 18.1g, Protein: 21.3g

212.   Garlic Chicken Burgers

Preparation time: 10 minutes
Cooking time: 10 minutes
Servings: 2
Ingredients:
- ✓ 8 oz. chicken mince
- ✓ ¼ red onion, finely chopped
- ✓ 1 clove garlic, crushed
- ✓ 1 handful of parsley, finely chopped
- ✓ 1 cup arugula
- ✓ ½ orange, chopped
- ✓ 1 cup cherry tomatoes
- ✓ 3 tsp extra virgin olive oil

Directions:
1. Put chicken mince, onion, garlic, parsley, salt pepper in a bowl and mix well. Form 2 patties and let rest 5 minutes.
2. Heat a pan with olive oil and when very hot cook 3 minutes per part.
3. They are also very good when grilled, if you opt for grilling; just brush the patties with a bit of oil right before cooking.
4. Put the arugula on two plates; add cherry tomatoes and orange on top, dress with salt and the remaining olive oil. Put the patties on top and serve.

Nutrition: Calories: 353, Fat: 4.8g, Carbohydrate: 28.1g, Protein: 28.3g

213.   Turmeric Turkey Breast with Cauliflower Rice

Preparation Time: 5 Minutes   **Cooking time**: 25 Minutes   **Servings**: 2
Ingredients:
- ✓ 2 cups cauliflower, grated
- ✓ 8 oz. turkey breast, cut in slices
- ✓ 2 tsp. ground turmeric
- ✓ 1/2 pepper, chopped
- ✓ 1/2 red onion, sliced
- ✓ 2 tsp. extra virgin olive oil
- ✓ 1 large tomato
- ✓ 1 clove garlic, crushed
- ✓ 1 cup milk, skimmed
- ✓ 2 tsp. buckwheat flour
- ✓ 1 oz. parsley, finely chopped

Directions:
1. Coat turkey slices with flour.
2. Heat a pan on medium high with half the oil and when hot add the turkey.
3. Let the meat color on all sides, then add milk, salt, pepper, 1 tsp. turmeric. Cook 10 minutes until the turkey is soft and the sauce has become creamy.
4. In a different pan, add the remaining oil and heat on medium heat. Add pepper, onion and tomato, 1 tsp. turmeric and let cook 3 minutes.
5. Add the cauliflower and cook another 2 minutes. Add salt, pepper and let rest 2 minutes. Serve the turkey with the cauliflower rice.

Nutrition: Calories 107 Total Fat 2.9 g Total Carbs 20.6 g Protein 2.1 g

214.   Mustard Salmon with Baby Carrots

Preparation Time: 10 Minutes   **Cooking time**: 40 Minutes   **Servings**: 2
Ingredients:
- ✓ 8 oz. salmon fillet
- ✓ 2 tbsp. mustard
- ✓ 1 tbsp. white vinegar
- ✓ 1 tsp parsley, finely chopped
- ✓ 2 cups baby carrots
- ✓ 4 oz. buckwheat
- ✓ 2 tsp. extra virgin olive oil
- ✓ Salt and pepper to taste

Directions:
- ✓ Heat the oven to 400°F.

- ✓ Boil the buckwheat in salted water for 25 minutes then drain. Dress with 1 tsp olive oil. Set aside. Put the salmon over aluminum foil.
- ✓ Mix mustard and vinegar in a small bowl and brush the mixture over the salmon, close the foil in a packet. Cook in the oven 35minutes.
- ✓ While the salmon is cooking, steam baby carrots for 6 minutes then put them in a pan on medium heat with 1tsp. olive oil, salt and pepper until light brown.
- ✓ Serve the salmon with baby carrots and buckwheat on the side.

Nutrition: Calories 314, Fat 9.1g, Protein 41.5g, Carbohydrate 15.7g

215.   Turmeric Cous Cous with Edamame Beans

Preparation Time: 10 Minutes   **Cooking time**: 15 Minutes   **Servings**: 2

Ingredients:

- ✓ ½ yellow pepper, cubed
- ✓ ½ red pepper, cubed
- ✓ 1 tbsp. turmeric
- ✓ ½ cup red onion, finely sliced
- ✓ ¼ cup cherry tomatoes, chopped
- ✓ 2 tbsp. parsley, finely chopped
- ✓ 5 oz. cous cous
- ✓ 2 tsp. extra virgin olive oil
- ✓ ½ eggplant
- ✓ 1 ½ edamame beans

Directions:

1. Steam edamame for 5 minutes and set aside. Add 6 oz. salted boiling water to cous cous and let rest until it absorbs the water.
2. In the meantime, heat a pan on medium high heat.
3. Add oil, eggplant, peppers, onion and tomatoes, turmeric, salt and pepper. Cook for 5 minutes on high heat.
4. Add the cous cous and edamame.
5. Garnish with fresh parsley and serve.

Nutrition: Calories 342, Carbs 15 g, Fat 5 g, Protein: 32g

216.   Scrambled Eggs and Red Onion

Preparation time: 2 minutes   **Cooking time**: 2 minutes   **Servings**: 1

Ingredients:

- ✓ 2 Eggs
- ✓ 1 tbsp. Parmesan
- ✓ Salt and pepper
- ✓ ½ cup red onion
- ✓ 1 tbsp. parsley, finely chopped

Directions:

1. Put eggs and cheese with a pinch of salt and pepper and finely chopped onion in a bowl. Whisk quickly.
2. Cook the scrambled eggs in a skillet for 2 minutes, stirring continuously until done.

Nutrition: Calories: 278, Fat: 5.4g, Carbohydrate: 12.8g, Protein: 18.9g

217.   Pancakes with Caramelized Strawberries

Preparation time: 5 minutes   **Cooking time**: 15 minutes   **Servings**: 2

Ingredients:

- ✓ 1 egg
- ✓ 1 ½ oz. self-raising flour
- ✓ 1 ½ oz. buckwheat flour
- ✓ 1/3 cup skimmed milk
- ✓ 1 cup strawberries
- ✓ 2 tsp honey

Directions:

1. Mix the flours in a bowl; add the yolk and a bit of mix in a very thick batter. Keep adding the milk bit by bit to avoid lumps.
2. In another bowl, beat the egg white until stiff and then mix it carefully to the batter.
3. Put enough batter to make a 5-inch round pancake to cook 2 minutes per side until done. Repeat until all the pancakes are ready.
4. Put strawberries and honey in a hot pan until caramelized, the put half on top of each serving.

Nutrition: Calories: 272, Fat: 4.3g, Carbohydrate: 26.8g, Protein: 23.6g

CHAPTER 9: DESSERTS

218. Chocolate Waffles

Preparation Time: 15 minutes   **Cooking Time:** 24 minutes   **Servings:** 8

Ingredients:

- ✓ 2 cups unsweetened almond milk
- ✓ 1 tablespoon fresh lemon juice
- ✓ 1 cup buckwheat flour
- ✓ ½ cup cacao powder
- ✓ ¼ cup flaxseed meal
- ✓ 1 teaspoon baking soda
- ✓ 1 teaspoon baking powder
- ✓ ¼ teaspoons kosher salt
- ✓ 2 large eggs
- ✓ ½ cup coconut oil, melted
- ✓ ¼ cup dark brown sugar
- ✓ 2 teaspoons vanilla extract
- ✓ 2 ounces unsweetened dark chocolate, chopped roughly

Directions:

- ☞ In a bowl, add the almond milk and lemon juice and mix well.
- ☞ Set aside for about 10 minutes. In a bowl, place buckwheat flour, cacao powder, flaxseed meal, baking soda, baking powder, and salt, and mix well. In the bowl with the almond milk mixture, place the eggs, coconut oil, brown sugar, and vanilla extract, and beat until smooth.
- ☞ Now, place the flour mixture and beat until smooth. Gently, fold in the chocolate pieces. Preheat the waffle iron and then grease it.
- ☞ Place the desired amount of the mixture into the preheated waffle iron and cook for about 3 minutes, or until golden brown. Repeat with the remaining mixture.

Nutrition: Calories 295 Total Fat 22.1 g Carbs 1.5 g Sodium 302 mg Fiber 5.2 g Protein 6.3 g

219. Blueberry Muffins

Preparation Time: 15 minutes   **Cooking Time:** 20 minutes   **Servings:** 8

Ingredients:

- ✓ 1 cup buckwheat flour
- ✓ ¼ cup arrowroot starch
- ✓ 1½ teaspoons baking powder
- ✓ ¼ teaspoon of sea salt
- ✓ 2 eggs
- ✓ ½ cup unsweetened almond milk
- ✓ 2–3 tablespoons maple syrup
- ✓ 2 tablespoons coconut oil, melted
- ✓ 1 cup fresh blueberries

Directions:

- ☞ Preheat your oven to 350°F and line 8 cups of a muffin tin. In a bowl, place the buckwheat flour, arrowroot starch, baking powder, and salt, and mix well. In a separate bowl, place the eggs, almond milk, maple syrup, and coconut oil, and beat until well combined.
- ☞ Now, place the flour mixture and mix until just combined. Gently, fold in the blueberries.

Transfer the mixture into prepared muffin cups evenly.

- ☞ Bake for about 25 minutes or until a toothpick inserted in the center comes out clean. Remove the muffin tin from the oven and place it onto a wire rack to cool for about 10 minutes. Carefully invert the muffins onto the wire rack to cool completely before serving.

Nutrition: Calories 136 Fat 5.3 g Saturated Fat 3.4 g Cholesterol 41 mg Sodium 88 mg Carbs 20.7 g Fiber 2.2 g Sugar 5.7 g Protein 3.5 g

220.　Raw Vegan Chocolate Cashew Truffles

Preparation Time: 10 minutes　　**Cooking Time:** 35 minutes　　**Servings:** 4

Ingredients:

- ✓ 1 cup ground cashews
- ✓ 1 teaspoon of ground vanilla bean
- ✓ ½ cup of coconut oil
- ✓ ¼ cup raw honey
- ✓ 2 flax meal
- ✓ 2 hemp hearts
- ✓ 2 cacao powder

Directions:

- ☞ Mix all ingredients and make truffles.
- ☞ Sprinkle coconut flakes on top.

Nutrition: Calories: 87 Net carbs: 6g Fat: 6.5g Fiber: 0.5g Protein: 2.3g

221.　Raw Vegan Double Almond Raw Chocolate Tart

Preparation Time: 10 minutes　　**Cooking Time:** 35 minutes　　**Servings:** 4

Ingredients:

- ✓ 1½ cups of raw almonds
- ✓ ¼ cup of coconut oil, melted
- ✓ 1 raw honey or royal jelly
- ✓ 8 ounces dark chocolate, chopped
- ✓ 1 cup of coconut milk
- ✓ ½ cup unsweetened shredded coconut

Directions:

Crust:

- ☞ Ground almonds and add melted coconut oil, raw honey, and combine.
- ☞ Using a spatula, spread this mixture into the tart or pie pan.

Filling:

- ☞ Put the chopped chocolate in a bowl, heat coconut milk and pour over chocolate and whisk together. Pour filling into tart shell.
- ☞ Refrigerate.
- ☞ Toast almond slivers chips and sprinkle over tart.

Nutrition: Calories: 101 Net carbs: 3.4g Fat: 9.4g Fiber: 0.6g Protein: 2.4g

222.　Raw Vegan Bounty Bars

Preparation Time: 10 minutes　　**Cooking Time:** 35 minutes　　**Servings:** 4

Ingredients:

"Peanut" butter filling:

- ✓ 2 cups desiccated coconut
- ✓ 3 coconut oil - melted
- ✓ 1 cup of coconut cream - full fat
- ✓ 4 of raw honey
- ✓ 1 teaspoon ground vanilla bean
- ✓ Pinch of sea salt

Superfoods chocolate part:

- ✓ ½ cup cacao powder
- ✓ 2 raw honey
- ✓ 1/3 cup of coconut oil (melted)

Directions:

- ☞ Mix coconut oil, coconut cream, and honey, vanilla, and salt.
- ☞ Pour over desiccated coconut and mix well.
- ☞ Mold coconut mixture into balls, small bars similar to bounty and freeze.
- ☞ Or pour the whole mixture into a tray, freeze, and cut into small bars.
- ☞ Make superfoods chocolate mixture, warm it up and dip frozen coconut into the chocolate and put on a tray and freeze again.

Nutrition: Calories: 70 Net carbs: 6.7g Fat: 4.3g Fiber: 0.2g Protein: 1g

223. Raw Vegan Tartlets with Coconut Cream

Preparation Time: 10 minutes   **Cooking Time:** 35 minutes   **Servings:** 4

Ingredients:

Pudding:

- ✓ 1 avocado
- ✓ 2 coconut oil
- ✓ 2 raw honey
- ✓ 2 cacao powder
- ✓ 1 teaspoon ground vanilla bean
- ✓ Pinch of salt
- ✓ ¼ cup almond milk, as needed

Directions:

- ☞ Blend all the ingredients in the food processor until smooth and thick. Spread evenly into tartlet crusts.
- ☞ Optionally, put some goji berries on top of the pudding layer.
- ☞ Make the coconut cream, spread it on top of the pudding layer, and put it back in the fridge overnight.
- ☞ Serve with one blueberry on top of each tartlet.

Nutrition: Calories: 200 Net carbs: 25.2g Fat: 4.3g Fiber: 4.6g Protein: 12.8g

224. Raw Vegan "Peanut" Butter Truffles

Preparation Time: 10 minutes   **Cooking Time:** 30 minutes   **Servings:** 4

Ingredients:

- ✓ 5 sunflower seed butter
- ✓ 1 coconut oil
- ✓ 1 raw honey
- ✓ 1 teaspoon ground vanilla bean
- ✓ ¾ cup almond flour
- ✓ 1 flaxseed meal
- ✓ Pinch of salt
- ✓ 1 cacao butter
- ✓ Hemp hearts (optional)
- ✓ ¼ cup super-foods chocolate

Directions:

- ☞ Mix until all ingredients are incorporated.
- ☞ Roll the dough into 1-inch balls, place them on parchment paper and refrigerate for half an hour (yield about 14 truffles).
- ☞ Dip each truffle in the melted superfoods chocolate, one at a time.
- ☞ Place them back on the pan with parchment paper or coat them in cocoa powder or coconut flakes.

Nutrition: Calories: 94 Net carbs: 3.1g Fat: 8g Fiber: 1g Protein: 4g

225.   Raw Vegan Chocolate Pie

Preparation Time: 10 minutes   **Cooking Time:** 25 minutes   **Servings:** 4

Ingredients:

Crust:

- ✓ 2 cups almonds, soaked overnight, and drained
- ✓ 1 cup pitted dates, soaked overnight, and drained
- ✓ 1 cup chopped dried apricots
- ✓ 1½ teaspoon ground vanilla bean
- ✓ 2 teaspoon chia seeds
- ✓ 1 banana

Filling:

- ✓ 4 raw cacao powder
- ✓ 3 raw honey
- ✓ 2 ripe avocados
- ✓ 2 organic coconut oil
- ✓ 2 almond milk (if needed, check for consistency first)

Directions:

- ☞ Add almonds and banana to a food processor or blender.
- ☞ Mix until it forms a thick ball.
- ☞ Add the vanilla, dates, and apricot chunks to the blender.
- ☞ Mix well and optionally add a couple of drops of water at a time to make the mixture stick together. Spread in a 10-inch dis.
- ☞ Mix filling ingredients in a blender and add almond milk if necessary. Add filling to the crust and refrigerate.

Nutrition: Calories: 380 Net carbs: 50.2g Fat: 18.4g Fiber: 2.2g Protein: 7.2g

226.   Raw Vegan Chocolate Walnut Truffles

Preparation Time: 10 minutes   **Cooking Time:** 35 minutes   **Servings:** 4

Ingredients:

- ✓ 1 cup ground walnuts
- ✓ 1 teaspoon cinnamon
- ✓ ½ cup of coconut oil
- ✓ ¼ cup raw honey
- ✓ 2 chia seeds
- ✓ 2 cacao powder

Directions:

- ☞ Mix all ingredients and make truffles.
- ☞ Coat with cinnamon, coconut flakes, or chopped almonds.

Nutrition: Calories: 120 Fat: 13.6g Net carbs: 3.1g Fat: 8g Fiber: 1g Protein: 4g

227. Raw Vegan Carrot Cake

Preparation Time: 10 minutes
Cooking Time: 35 minutes
Servings: 4
Ingredients:

- carrot
- chopped

- ✓ 2 cups dates
- ✓ 1 teaspoon cinnamon
- ✓ ½ teaspoon nutmeg
- ✓ 1½ cups cashews
- ✓ 2 coconut oil
- ✓ Juice from 1 lemon
- ✓ 2 raw honey
- ✓ 1 teaspoon ground vanilla bean
- ✓ Water, as needed

- ✓ 1½ cups oats
- ✓ ½ cup dried coconut

Directions:
- ☞ Add all crust ingredients to the blender.
- ☞ Mix well and optionally add a couple of drops of water at a time to make the mixture stick together. Press in a small pan.
- ☞ Take it out and put it on a plate and freeze.
- ☞ Mix frosting ingredients in a blender and add water if necessary.
- ☞ Add frosting to the crust and refrigerate.

Nutrition: Calories: 241 Net carbs: 28.4g Fat: 13.4g Fiber: 0.8g Protein: 2.4g

228. Raw Vegan Chocolate Cream Fruity Cake

Preparation Time: 10 minutes   **Cooking Time:** 45 minutes   **Servings:** 4

Ingredients:

Chocolate cream:
- ✓ 1 avocado
- ✓ 2 raw honey
- ✓ 2 coconut oil

- ✓ 2 cacao powder
- ✓ 1 teaspoon ground vanilla bean

- ✓ Pinch of sea salt
- ✓ ¼ cup of coconut milk
- ✓ 1 coconut flakes

Fruits:
- ✓ 1 chopped banana

- ✓ 1 cup pitted cherries

Directions:
- ☞ Prepare the crust and press it at the bottom of the pan. Blend all chocolate cream ingredients, fold in the fruits, and pour in the crust.
- ☞ Whip the top layer, spread, and sprinkle with cacao powder. Refrigerate.

Nutrition: Calories: 106 Net carbs: 0.4g Fat: 5g Fiber: 0.1g Protein: 14g

229.   Chocolate Granola

Preparation Time: 10 minutes

Cooking Time: 38 minutes

Total time: 48 minutes

Servings: 8

Ingredients:

- ✓ ¼ cup cacao powder
- ✓ ¼ cup maple syrup
- ✓ 2 tablespoons coconut oil, melted
- ✓ ½ teaspoon vanilla extract
- ✓ 1/8 teaspoon salt
- ✓ 2 cups gluten-free rolled oats
- ✓ ¼ cup unsweetened coconut flakes
- ✓ 2 tablespoons chia seeds
- ✓ 2 tablespoons unsweetened dark chocolate, chopped finely

Directions:

- ☞ Preheat your oven to 300ºF and line a medium baking sheet with parchment paper.
- ☞ In a medium pan, add the cacao powder, maple syrup, coconut oil, vanilla extract, and salt, and mix well. Now, place the pan over medium heat and cook for about 2–3 minutes, or until thick and syrupy, stirring continuously.
- ☞ Remove from the heat and set aside.
- ☞ In a large bowl, add the oats, coconut, and chia seeds, and mix well.
- ☞ Add the syrup mixture and mix until well combined.
- ☞ Transfer the granola mixture onto a prepared baking sheet and spread in an even layer.
- ☞ Bake for about 35 minutes.
- ☞ Remove from the oven and set aside for about 1 hour.
- ☞ Add the chocolate pieces and stir to combine.
- ☞ Serve immediately.

Nutrition: Calories 193 Sodium: 24 mg Dietary Fiber: 1.7 g Total Fat: 3.1 g Total Carbs: 16.7 g Protein: 1.5 g

230.   Homemade Marshmallow Fluff

Preparation Time: 10 minutes   **Cooking Time:** 20 minutes   **Servings:** 2

Ingredients:

- ✓ 3/4 cup sugar
- ✓ 1/2 cup light corn syrup
- ✓ 1/4 cup water
- ✓ 1/8 teaspoon salt
- ✓ 3 little egg whites
- ✓ 1/4 teaspoon cream of tartar
- ✓ 1 teaspoon 1/2 tsp. vanilla extract

Directions:

- ☞ In a little pan, mix together sugar, corn syrup, salt, and water. Attach a candy thermometer into the side of this pan, but make sure it will not touch the underside of the pan.
- ☞ From the bowl of a stand mixer, combine egg whites and cream of tartar. Begin to whip on medium speed with the whisk attachment.
- ☞ Meanwhile, turn a burner on top and place the pan with the sugar mix onto heat. Put the mix

into a boil and heat to 240 degrees, stirring periodically.

☞ The aim is to have the egg whites whipped to soft peaks and also the sugar heated to 240 degrees at near the same moment. Simply stop stirring the egg whites once they hit soft peaks.

☞ Once the sugar has already reached 240 amounts, turn heat low, allowing it to reduce. Insert a little quantity of the popular sugar mix and let it mix. Insert still another little sum of the sugar mix. Add mix slowly and that means you never scramble the egg whites.

☞ After all of the sugar was added into the egg whites, then decrease the speed of the mixer and also keep mixing concoction for around 7- 9 minutes until the fluff remains glossy and stiff. At roughly the 5-minute mark, then add the vanilla extract.

☞ Use fluff immediately or store in an airtight container in the fridge for around two weeks.

Nutrition: Calories: 159 Sodium: 32 mg Dietary Fiber: 1.5 g Total Fat: 3.1 g Total Carbs: 15.3 g Protein: 1.4 g

231.   Ultimate Chocolate Chip Cookie N' Oreo Fudge Brownie Bar

Preparation Time: 10 minutes   **Cooking Time:** 50 minutes   **Servings:** 2

Ingredients:

- ✓ 1 cup (2 sticks) butter, softened
- ✓ 1 cup granulated sugar
- ✓ 3/4 cup light brown sugar
- ✓ 2 large egg
- ✓ 1 tablespoon pure vanilla extract
- ✓ 2 ½ cups all-purpose flour
- ✓ 1 teaspoon baking soda
- ✓ 1 teaspoon lemon
- ✓ 2 cups (12 oz) milk chocolate chips
- ✓ 1 package double-stuffed Oreo
- ✓ 1 family-size (9×1 3) brownie mixture
- ✓ 1/4 cup hot fudge topping

Directions:

☞ Preheat oven to 350 degrees F.

☞ Cream the butter and sugars in a large bowl, using an electric mixer at medium speed for 35 minutes.

☞ Add the vanilla and eggs and mix well to thoroughly combine. In another bowl, whisk together the flour, baking soda, and salt, and slowly incorporate in the mixer everything is combined.Stir in chocolate chips.

☞ Spread the cookie dough at the bottom of a 9×1-3 baking dish that is wrapped with wax paper and then coated with cooking spray.

☞ Shirt with a coating of Oreos. Mix brownie mix, adding an optional 1/4 cup of hot fudge directly into the mixture.

☞ Stir the brownie batter within the cookie-dough and Oreos. Cover with foil and bake at 350 degrees F for 30 minutes.

☞ Remove foil and continue baking for another 15 25 minutes.

☞ Let cool before cutting on brownies. They may be gooey at the while warm but will also set up perfectly once chilled.

Nutrition: Calories: 145Sodium: 33 mg Dietary Fiber: 1.4 g Total Fat: 4.1 g Total Carbs: 16.7 g Protein: 1.3 g.

232.   Crunchy Chocolate Chip Coconut Macadamia Nut Cookies

Preparation Time: 20 minutes   **Cooking Time:** 0 minute   **Servings:** 2

Ingredients:

- ✓ 1 cup yogurt
- ✓ 1 cup yogurt
- ✓ 1/2 teaspoon baking soda
- ✓ 1/2 teaspoon salt
- ✓ 1 tablespoon of butter, softened
- ✓ 1 cup firmly packed brown sugar
- ✓ 1/2 cup sugar
- ✓ 1 large egg
- ✓ 1/2 cup semi-sweet chocolate chips
- ✓ 1/2 cup sweetened flaked coconut
- ✓ 1/2 cup coarsely chopped dry-roasted macadamia nuts
- ✓ 1/2 cup raisins

Directions:

- ☞ Preheat the oven to 325°F. In a little bowl, whisk together the flour, oats and baking soda, and salt, then place aside.
- ☞ In your mixer bowl, mix the butter/sugar/egg mix. Mix in the flour/oats mix until just combined and stir in the chocolate chips, raisins, nuts, and coconut.
- ☞ Place outsized bits on a parchment-lined cookie sheet.
- ☞ Bake for 1-3 minutes before biscuits are only barely golden brown.
- ☞ Remove from the oven and then leave the cookie sheets to cool for at least 10 minutes.

Nutrition: Calories: 167 Sodium: 31 mg Dietary Fiber: 1.4 g Total Fat: 4.1 g Total Carbs: 16.5 g Protein: 1.3 g

233.   Walnut & Date Loaf

Preparation Time: 10 minutes   **Cooking Time:** 15 minutes   **Servings:** 12

Ingredients:

- ✓ 9 ounces of self-rising flour
- ✓ 4 ounces of Medrol dates, chopped
- ✓ 2 ounces of walnuts, chopped
- ✓ 8fl oz. milk
- ✓ 3 eggs
- ✓ 1 medium banana, mashed
- ✓ 1 teaspoon baking soda

Directions:

- ☞ Sieve the baking soda and flour into a bowl.
- ☞ Add in the banana, eggs, milk, and dates and combine all the ingredients thoroughly.
- ☞ Transfer the mixture to a lined loaf tin and smooth it out.
- ☞ Scatter the walnuts on top.
- ☞ Bake the loaf in the oven at 180C/360F for 45 minutes.
- ☞ Serve!

Nutrition: Calories: 204 Sodium: 33 mg Dietary Fiber: 1.7 g Total Fat: 3.1 g Total Carbs: 16.5 g Protein: 1.4 g

234.   Peach and Blueberry Pie

Preparation Time: 1 hour   **Cooking Time:** 0 minute   **Servings:** 2

Ingredients:

- ✓ 1 box of noodle dough

Filling:

- ✓ 5 peaches, peeled and chopped (I used roasted peaches)
- ✓ 3 cups strawberries
- ✓ 3/4 cup sugar
- ✓ 1/4 cup bread
- ✓ Juice of 1/2 lemon
- ✓ 1 egg yolk, beaten

Directions:

- ☞ Preheat oven to 400 degrees.
- ☞ Place dough on a 9-inch pie plate
- ☞ In a big bowl, combine tomatoes, sugar, bread, and lemon juice, then toss to combine. Pour into the pie plate, mounding at the center.
- ☞ Simply take some of the bread and then cut it into bits, then put a pie shirt and put the dough in addition to pressing on the edges.
- ☞ Brush crust with egg wash then sprinkles with sugar.
- ☞ Set onto a parchment paper-lined baking sheet.
- ☞ Bake at 400 for about 20 minutes, until crust is browned at borders.
- ☞ Turn oven down to 350, bake for another 40 minutes. Remove and let sit for at least 30minutes. Have with vanilla ice-cream.

Nutrition: Calories: 167 Sodium: 31 mg Dietary Fiber: 1.4 g Total Fat: 4.1 g Total Carbs: 16.6 g Protein: 1.2 g

235.   Pear, Cranberry and Chocolate Crisp

Preparation Time: 10 minutes
Cooking Time: 20 minutes
Servings: 3
Ingredients:
Crumble topping:

- ✓ 1/2 cup flour
- ✓ 1/2 cup brown sugar
- ✓ 1 tsp. cinnamon
- ✓ 1/8 teaspoon salt
- ✓ 3/4 cup yogurt
- ✓ 1/4 cup sliced peppers
- ✓ 1/3 cup butter, melted
- ✓ 1   teaspoon   vanill

Filling:

- ✓ 1 teaspoon lemon juice
- ✓ Two handfuls of milk chocolate chips

- ✓ 1 tablespoon brown sugar
- ✓ 3 teaspoons, cut into balls
- ✓ 1/4 cup dried cranberries

Directions:

- ☞ Preheat oven to 375.
- ☞ Spray a casserole dish with a butter spray.
- ☞ Put all of the topping ingredients - flour, sugar, cinnamon, salt, nuts, legumes, and dried

- ☞ Butter a bowl and then mix. Set aside.
- ☞ In a large bowl, combine the sugar, lemon juice, pears, and cranberries.
- ☞ Once the fully blended move to the prepared baking dish.
- ☞ Spread the topping evenly over the fruit.
- ☞ Bake for about half an hour.
- ☞ Disperse chocolate chips out at the top.
- ☞ Cook for another 10 minutes.
- ☞ Have with ice cream.

Nutrition: Calories: 324 Sodium: 33 mg Dietary Fiber: 1.4 g Total Fat: 4.1 g Total Carbs: 15.3 g Protein: 1.3 g

236. Apricot Oatmeal Cookies

Preparation Time: 10 minutes **Cooking Time:** 20 minutes **Servings:** 3

Ingredients:
- ✓ 1/2 cup (1 stick) butter, softened
- ✓ 2/3 cup light brown sugar packed
- ✓ 1 egg
- ✓ 3/4 cup all-purpose flour
- ✓ 1/2 teaspoon baking soda
- ✓ 1/2 teaspoon vanilla extract
- ✓ 1/2 teaspoon cinnamon
- ✓ 1/4 teaspoon salt
- ✓ 1 teaspoon 1/2 cups chopped oats
- ✓ 3/4 cup yolks
- ✓ 1/4 cup sliced apricots
- ✓ 1/3 cup slivered almonds

Directions:
- ☞ Preheat oven to 350°. In a big bowl, combine the butter, sugar, and egg until smooth.
- ☞ In another bowl, whisk the flour, baking soda, cinnamon, and salt together.
- ☞ Stir the dry ingredients into the butter-sugar bowl. Now stir in the oats, raisins, apricots, and almonds.
- ☞ I heard on the web that at this time, it's much better to cool with the dough (therefore, your biscuits are thicker). Afterward, I scooped my biscuits into some parchment-lined (easier removal and wash up) cookie sheet - around two inches apart. I sliced mine for approximately ten minutes - they were fantastic!

Nutrition: Calories: 132 Sodium: 33 mg Dietary Fiber: 1.4 g Total Fat: 3.1 g Total Carbs: 16.4 g Protein: 1.3 g

237. Guilt Totally Free Banana Ice-Cream

Preparation Time: 20 minutes **Cooking Time:** 0 minute **Servings:** 3

Ingredients:
- ✓ 3 quite ripe banana - peeled and chopped
- ✓ A couple of chocolate chips
- ✓ 2 tablespoons skim milk

Directions:
- ☞ Throw all ingredients into a food processor and blend until creamy.
- ☞ Eat: freeze and appreciate afterward.

Nutrition: Calories: 208 Sodium: 33 mg Dietary Fiber: 1.6 g Total Fat: 2.6 g Total Carbs: 14.6 g Protein: 1.8 g

238. Pomegranate Guacamole

Preparation Time: 10 minutes   **Cooking Time:** 30 minutes   **Servings:** 1

Ingredients:

- ✓ Flesh of 2 ripe avocados
- ✓ Seeds from 1 pomegranate
- ✓ 1 bird's-eye chili pepper, finely chopped
- ✓ ½ red onion, finely chopped
- ✓ Juice of 1 lime

Directions:

- ☞ Place the avocado, onion, chill, and lime juice into a blender and process until smooth.
- ☞ Stir in the pomegranate seeds. Chill before serving.
- ☞ Serve as a dip for chop vegetables.

Nutrition: Calories: 286 Sodium: 38 mg Dietary Fiber: 1.8 g Total Fat: 4.3 g Total Carbs: 16.5 g Protein: 1.7 g

---

239. Mascarpone Cheesecake With Almond Crust

Preparation Time: 10 minutes

Cooking Time: 0 minute

Servings: 2

Ingredients:

- ✓ **Crust:**
- ✓ 1/2 cup slivered almonds
- ✓ 8 teaspoons or 2/3 cup graham cracker crumbs
- ✓ 2 tablespoons sugar
- ✓ 1 tablespoon salted butter, melted
- ✓ **Filling:**
- ✓ 1 (8-ounce) packages cream cheese, room temperature
- ✓ 1 (8-ounce) container mascarpone cheese, room temperature
- ✓ 3/4 cup sugar
- ✓ 1 teaspoon fresh lemon juice (I needed to use imitation lemon-juice)
- ✓ 1 teaspoon vanilla extract
- ✓ 2 large eggs, room temperature

Directions:

For the crust:

- ☞ Preheat oven to 350 degrees F. You will need a 9-inch pan (I had a throw off). Finely grind the almonds, cracker crumbs sugar in a food processor (I used my Magical Bullet). Add the butter and process until moist crumbs form.
- ☞ Press the almond mixture on the base of the prepared pan (maybe not on the edges of the pan). Bake the crust until it's set and start to brown, about 1-2 minutes. Cool. Reduce the oven temperature to 325 degrees F.

For your filling:

- ☞ With an electric mixer, beat the cream cheese, mascarpone cheese, and sugar in a large bowl until smooth, occasionally scraping down the sides of the jar using a rubber spatula. Beat in the lemon juice and vanilla. Add the eggs, one at a time, beating until combined after each addition.

☞ Pour the cheese mixture on the crust from the pan. Put the pan into a big skillet or Pyrex dish, pour enough hot water into the roasting pan to come halfway up the sides of one's skillet. Bake until the middle of the filling moves slightly when the pan is gently shaken, about 1 hour (the dessert will get hard when it's cold). Transfer the cake to a stand; cool for 1 hour. Refrigerate until the cheesecake is cold, at least eight hours.

Topping:

☞ Squeeze just a small thick cream in the microwave using a chopped Lindt dark chocolate afterward, get a Ziplock baggie and cut out a hole at the corner, then pour the melted chocolate into the baggie and use this to decorate the cake!

Nutrition: Calories: 148 Sodium: 26 mg Dietary Fiber: 1.4 g Total Fat: 3.1 g Total Carbs: 11.2 g Protein: 1.6 g

---

240.   Chocolate Fondue

Preparation Time: 10 minutes   **Cooking Time:** 15 minutes   **Servings:** 1

Ingredients:

- ✓ 4 ounces of dark chocolate min 85% cocoa
- ✓ 11 ounces of strawberries
- ✓ 7 ounces of cherries
- ✓ 2 apples, peeled, cored, and sliced
- ✓ 3½ FL oz. double cream, heavy cream

Directions:

- ☞ In a fondue pot or saucepan, place the chocolate and cream then warm it until smooth and creamy.
- ☞ Serve in the fondue pot or transfer it to a serving bowl. Scatter the fruit in a serving dish ready to be dipped into the chocolate.

Nutrition: Calories: 220, Sodium: 43 mg, Dietary Fiber: 5.4 g, Fat: 2.1 g, l Carbs: 1.3 g Protein: 10.3 g.

---

241.   Choc Nut Truffles

Preparation Time: 10 minutes   **Cooking Time:** 15 minutes   **Servings:** 1

Ingredients:

- ✓ 5 ounces of desiccated shredded coconut
- ✓ 2 ounces of walnuts, chopped
- ✓ 1 ounce of hazelnuts, chopped
- ✓ 4 Medjool dates
- ✓ 2 tablespoons 100% cocoa powder or cacao nibs
- ✓ 1 tablespoon coconut oil

Directions:

- ☞ Place ingredients into a blender and process until smooth and creamy.
- ☞ Using a teaspoon, scoop the mixture into bite-size pieces, then roll it into balls.
- ☞ Place them into small paper cases, cover them, and chill for 1 hour before serving.

Nutrition: Calories: 220, Sodium: 43 mg, Dietary Fiber: 5.4 g, Total Fat: 2.1 g, Total Carbs: 1.3 g, Protein: 10.3 g.

---

242.   No-Bake Strawberry Flapjacks

Preparation Time: 10 minutes   **Cooking Time:** 0 minutes   **Servings:** 1

Ingredients:

- ✓ 3 ounces of porridge oats
- ✓ 4 ounces of dates
- ✓ 2 ounces of strawberries
- ✓ 2 ounces of peanuts, unsalted
- ✓ 2 ounces of walnuts
- ✓ 1 tablespoon coconut oil
- ✓ 2 tablespoons 100% cocoa powder or cacao nibs

Directions:

- ☞ Place the ingredients into a blender and process until they become a soft consistency.
- ☞ Spread the mixture onto a baking sheet or small flat tin.
- ☞ Press the mixture down and smooth it out.
- ☞ Cut it into 8 pieces, ready to serve.
- ☞ You can add an extra sprinkling of cocoa powder to garnish if you wish.

Nutrition: Calories: 123 Sodium: 30 mg Dietary Fiber: 1.4 g Total Fat: 2.1 g Total Carbs: 11.3 g Protein: 1.3 g

CONCLUSION

The Sirt Diet program includes two phases:

- **Phase 1:** This process will limit you to 1,000 calories a day for a week, and two of your meals will be green drinks rich in Sirtfoods such as lettuce, celery, parsley, green tea, and lemon. Even rich in Sirtfoods like beef, chicken, spinach, or buckwheat noodles you can have one meal per day.

- **Phase 2:** You are permitted to increase the caloric intake to 1,500 calories during this process and you are still consuming the two green drinks, but you are now permitted to add another meal to the day, allowing two meals and two beverages. This phase can last up to 14 days.

Generally, this diet is backed by science, as many case studies have been shown.

The Sirtfood Diet can be used to lose weight within a few days. Moreover, many sirt foods are quite healthy and should, therefore, be on the menu regularly. In general, the sirt food diet is less a short-term weight loss program than a long-term change in diet. The food recommended for the sirt food diet is also rated positively by nutrition experts because the plant-based meals primarily provide secondary plant substances, proteins, and good fats.

Sirt foods alone do not mean that those wanting to lose weight automatically lose large amounts of kilos. To do this, they would also have to pay attention to the calorie count and reduce it if necessary. A balanced diet combined with exercise is still the best way to live healthily and lose weight sustainably.

4-WEEK MEAL PLAN

That is an idea of a healthy way of eating in the next 4 weeks following the Sirtfood Diet. Here you will find out how easy it is to reach your goals besides making significant life changes that will guarantee an improved health condition and weight loss. You will not even notice this month because it will fly by just following these instructions.

Pantry basics: What I need?

Cooking basics: Spray, EVO Oil, Baking powder, Basmati rice, Sesame oil, Stock cubes, Breadcrumbs, Coconut Oil, Cooking, Flour, Honey, Brown Rice, Capers, Cocoa powder, Canned Tomatoes, Oats, Red wine, , Tomato sauce.

Dressings: Mustard, Salt, Balsamic Vinegar, Soy Sauce, Tamari.

Herbs and Spices: Pepper, Rosemary, Sage, Thyme, Bay, Basil, Chili, Cinnamon, Garlic, Ginger, Marjoram, Nutmeg, Oregano, Paprika, Turmeric, Cumin, Curry, Dill, Garam Masala, Vanilla Extract.

Nuts and Seeds: Sesame seeds, Walnuts, Almonds, Pumpkin seed.

WEEK 1 – PHASE I

Shopping List

NB - Necessary: You can choose your favorite Sirtfood Green Juices Recipes each week. Remember to include the related ingredients in this list accordingly.

- ✓ Artichokes
- ✓ Arugula Avocado
- ✓ Baby Spinach Bird's eye chili
- ✓ Broccoli
- ✓ Buckwheat
- ✓ Buckwheat flour
- ✓ Carrots
- ✓ Celeriac
- ✓ Celery
- ✓ Chicken
- ✓ Breast
- ✓ Chicken
- ✓ Thighs
- ✓ Chicken
- ✓ Wings
- ✓ Chicory
- ✓ Coconut cream
- ✓ Dates

- ✓ Goat
- ✓ Cheese
- ✓ Kale
- ✓ Lettuce
- ✓ Leeks
- ✓ Lemons
- ✓ Orange Parmesan
- ✓ Parsley
- ✓ Red Onions
- ✓ Red Peppers Salmon
- ✓ Shrimps
- ✓ Smoked Salmon Spinach
- ✓ Sweet potatoes Tomatoes
- ✓ Tuna
- ✓ Steak
- ✓ Turkey Breast Turnips
- ✓ Yellow   Peppers

Meal Plan

Quick Recap: This week is divided into two moments: Day 1-3 with 3 juices a day, 1 optional snack, and a full meal. Day 4-7 with 2 juices a day, 2 optional snacks, and a full meal.

DAY	BREAKFAST	SNACK	LUNCH	SNACK	DINNER
1	Sirtfood Green Juice	2 squares of dark chocolate	Sirtfood Green Juice	Sirtfood Green Juice	Tomato Soup & Meatballs
2	Sirtfood Green Juice	2 squares of dark chocolate	Sirtfood Green Juice	Sirtfood Green Juice	Lemon Paprika Chicken with Vegetables
3	Sirtfood Green Juice	2 squares of dark chocolate	Sirtfood Green Juice	Sirtfood Green Juice	Sweet Potato and Salmon Fishballs and Artichoke Salad
4	Sirtfood Green Juice	Sirtfood Green Juice	Goat Cheese Salad with Cranberries and Walnut	2 squares of dark chocolate	Seared Tuna in Soy Sauce and Black Pepper
5	Sirtfood Green Juice	Sirtfood Green Juice	Shrimp Tomato Hotpot	2 squares of dark chocolate	Spicy Chicken Hotpot
6	Sirtfood Green Juice	Sirtfood Green Juice	Salmon Salad	2 squares of dark chocolate	Turkey Breast with Peppers
7	Sirtfood Green Juice	Sirtfood Green Juice	Chicken with Kale and Chili Salsa	2 squares of dark chocolate	Veggies Curry

Recipes

243.   Seared Tuna in Soy Sauce and Black Pepper

Preparation Time: 15 minutes   **Cooking Time: 8 minutes**   **Servings: 1**

Ingredients:

- ✓ 5 ounces tuna, 1-inch thick
- ✓ 1 teaspoon sesame seeds
- ✓ 2 teaspoon EVO oil
- ✓ 2 cups baby spinach
- ✓ 1 red onion, chopped

- ✓ 2 tablespoons soy sauce
- ✓ ¼ teaspoon ground black pepper
- ✓ ½ tablespoon grated ginger
- ✓ 1 tablespoon orange juice

Directions:

Marinate tuna with soy sauce (1 tablespoon), oil and black pepper for 30 minutes. Place a skillet over high heat and when very hot, add tuna and quickly cook 1 minute per side. Cut the tuna in slices, dress them with soy sauce (1 tablespoon) mixed with grated ginger. Finally, add green onion and sesame seeds on top. Serve with a baby spinach salad dressed with olive oil (1 teaspoon), salt, pepper and orange juice.

Nutrition Facts: Calories: 154 Fats 4.1 g Carbohydrate 3g Protein 15 g

244.   Artichoke Salad

Preparation time: 5 minutes   **Cooking time:** 15 minutes   **Servings: 2**

Ingredients:

- ✓ 2 Roman artichokes
- ✓ 1 lemon, juice
- ✓ 1 teaspoon EVO oil
- ✓ Salt and pepper

Directions:

- ☞ Wash and peel the artichokes by removing all the hardest leaves. Cut them in two and gently remove the hair inside the artichoke. Cut them very finely. Put them in water and lemon so that they do not turn brown.
- ☞ When ready to serve, drain the artichokes, mix them with olive oil, a few drops of lemon, salt and pepper and they are ready to be served.

Nutrition Facts: Calories: 100 Fat: 10.9g Protein: 13.3g Carbohydrate: 3.4g

245.   Salmon Salad

Preparation time: 5 minutes   **Cooking time: 30 minutes**   **Servings: 2**

Ingredients:

- ✓ 1 large Medjool date, thinly chopped
- ✓ 3 oz. celery, sliced
- ✓ 6 walnuts, chopped
- ✓ 1 tablespoon capers
- ✓ 1 cup chicory leaves
- ✓ ½ cup arugula
- ✓ 1 teaspoon of EVO oil
- ✓ 1 tablespoon parsley, chopped
- ✓ 2 oz. red onion-sliced
- ✓ ½ avocado-peeled, stoned, and sliced
- ✓ Juice of ¼ lemon
- ✓ 6 oz. smoked salmon

Directions:

- ☞ Mix chicory and arugula and put them on a large bowl. Evenly distribute on top finely sliced onion, avocado, walnuts, capers, celery and parsley.
- ☞ Mix oil, lemon juice with a pinch of salt and pepper and distribute the dressing on top.

Nutrition Facts: Calories: 353, Fat: 4.8g, Carbohydrate: 28.1g, Protein: 28.3g

246.   Tomato Soup & Meatballs

Preparation time: 15 minutes   **Cooking time: 30 minutes**   **Servings: 2**

Ingredients:

- ✓ 8 oz. lean mince
- ✓ 1 egg
- ✓ 1 red pepper, chopped
- ✓ 1 can tomatoes or 3 ripe large tomatoes
- ✓ 2 cups stock
- ✓ 1 tablespoon parmesan
- ✓ 1 tablespoon breadcrumbs
- ✓ 2 teaspoons of EVO oil
- ✓ 1 red onion finely chopped
- ✓ 1 yellow pepper, chopped
- ✓ 1 clove of garlic, crushed
- ✓ 1 chili, finely sliced
- ✓ 4 oz. buckwheat
- ✓ salt and pepper to taste

Directions:

- ☞ Put mince, egg, breadcrumbs, parmesan, salt and pepper in a bowl and mix well, then create small meatballs. Heat a pan, add oil and gently sauté onion and garlic until transparent.
- ☞ Add the meatballs and cook another 5 minutes.

☞ Add peppers and chili and let flavors mix together, then add the tomatoes (canned or roughly chopped if fresh), add the broth and let it simmer for 20-25 minutes. While the soup cooks, boil buckwheat for 25 minutes, drain it and add it to the soup right before serving it.

Nutrition Facts: Calories: 348, Fat: 7.6g, Carbohydrate: 28.4g, Protein: 23.2g

247.   Veggies Curry

Preparation Time: 15 minutes.   **Cooking Time: 25 minutes**   **Servings: 2**

Ingredients:

- ✓ 3 tablespoons coconut oil
- ✓ ¼ small red onion, chopped
- ✓ 1 cup broccoli florets
- ✓ 1 teaspoon garlic, minced
- ✓ ½ cup coconut cream
- ✓ 2 teaspoons low-sodium soy sauce
- ✓ ½ chili
- ✓ 1 teaspoon fresh parsley, chopped finely
- ✓ 1 teaspoon fresh ginger, minced
- ✓ 1 tablespoon red curry paste or powder
- ✓ 2 cups spinach

Directions:

☞ In a large skillet, melt the coconut oil (2 tablespoons) over medium-high heat and sauté the onion for about 3-4 minutes. Add the garlic, chili and ginger and sauté for about 1 minute. Add the broccoli and stir to combine well. Immediately reduce the heat to medium-low and cook for about 1-2 minutes, stirring continuously. Stir continuously in the curry paste and cook for about 1 minute.

Then, stir frequently in the spinach and cook or about 2 minutes. Add the coconut cream and remaining coconut oil and stir until smooth.

☞ Stir in the soy sauce and simmer for about 5-10 minutes, stirring occasionally or until curry reaches the desired thickness.

☞ Remove from the heat and serve hot, topped with parsley.

Nutrition Facts: Calories 324 Fat 24.5 g Carbs 8 g Protein 17.5 g

248.   Goat Cheese Salad with Cranberries and Walnut

Preparation time: 20 minutes   **Cooking time: 30 minutes**   **Servings: 2**

Ingredients:

- ✓ 4 oz. goat cheese
- ✓ 2 teaspoons EVO oil
- ✓ 1 cup lettuce
- ✓ ½ cup arugula
- ✓ ½ cup baby spinach
- ✓ 1 tablespoon dried cranberries
- ✓ 10 walnuts, chopped
- ✓ 1 tablespoon balsamic vinegar
- ✓ 1 teaspoon mustard
- ✓ Salt and pepper to taste

Directions:

Mix lettuce, arugula and baby spinach. Whisk oil, mustard, salt, pepper and vinegar, put the dressing on the salad and mix well. Transfer to a serving bowl. Crumble goat cheese over. Add cranberries and walnuts on top and serve.

Nutrition Facts: Calories: 250 Fat: 20.9g Protein: 20.3g Carbohydrate: 3.4g

249. Shrimp Tomato Hotpot

Preparation time: 35--40 min   **Cooking time:** 20-30 min   **Servings: 1**

Ingredients:

- ✓ 8 oz. shrimps
- ✓ 1 tablespoon EVO oil
- ✓ 2 cups tomatoes
- ✓ 2 cups stock
- ✓ 2 leeks, finely chopped
- ✓ 1 Garlic clove, finely chopped
- ✓ 1 tablespoon parsley, chopped
- ✓ 1 Bird's eye chili, thinly sliced
- ✓ 2 tablespoons wine
- ✓ 1 large carrot, finely chopped
- ✓ 1 celery stick, finely chopped
- ✓ Salt and pepper to taste

Directions:

Fry garlic, onion, celery, carrot and chili with oil over a low heat for 5 minutes. Add the leeks. Turn up the heat to medium, add the wine and let evaporate. Add tomatoes and cook for 5 minutes, then add the stock and let simmer for 20 minutes. Add shrimps and let cook for 4-5 minutes until they become opaque. Don't overcook! Serve warm.

Nutrition Facts: Calories: 213 kCal Fat: 13.1 g Protein: 80.62 g Sugar: 51.67 g

250. Lemon Paprika Chicken with Vegetables

Preparation time: 10 minutes   **Cooking time:** 45 minutes   **Servings: 2**

Ingredients:

- ✓ 2 carrots, chopped
- ✓ 3 turnips, peeled and chopped
- ✓ 8 oz. of chicken wings
- ✓ 2 bay leaves
- ✓ 2 tablespoons paprika
- ✓ 2 cups stock
- ✓ 2 tablespoons red wine
- ✓ Juice of 1 lemon
- ✓ ½ celeriac, peeled and chopped
- ✓ 3 tablespoons EVO oil
- ✓ Sprigs of rosemary and thyme
- ✓ 2 cups kale, chopped

Directions:

☞ Heat the oil with a tight-fitting lid inside a large saucepan. Add the carrots, paprika, celeriac, turnips and chicken wings to the saucepan and cook for a few minutes. Add the wine, mix and let it evaporate. Stir in the pan the stock, spices, salt, pepper and lemon juice and bring to the boil. Turn the heat down, cover it with a lid and gently simmer for 40 minutes.

☞ Add the kale and cook until the kale and the chicken are both cooked.

Nutrition Facts: Calories 154.0 Total Fat 2.2 g Carbohydrate: 32.1 Protein 21.4

251.   Chicken with Kale and Chili Salsa

Preparation time: 5 minutes   **Cooking time: 40 minutes**   **Servings: 3**

Ingredients:

- ✓ 3 oz. buckwheat
- ✓ 1 teaspoon fresh ginger
- ✓ 1 oz. onion, sliced
- ✓ 8 oz. chicken breast
- ✓ 1 tomato

- ✓ 1 handful parsley
- ✓ ½ lemon, juiced
- ✓ 1 bird's eye chili, chopped
- ✓ 1 teaspoon turmeric

- ✓ 2 cups kale, chopped
- ✓ 2 teaspoons EVO oil
- ✓ 1 teaspoon paprika

Directions:

Finely chop the tomato, mix it with chili, parsley, lemon juice, salt, pepper and 1 teaspoon olive oil.

Heat the oven to 220F.

Marinate the chicken with oil (1teaspoon), turmeric, paprika and let it rest for 10 minutes.

Heats a backing pan over medium heat until it is hot then add marinated chicken and allow it to cook for a minute on both sides until golden. Transfer the chicken to the oven (and bake for 8 to 10 minutes or until it is cooked through. In a little oil, fry the ginger and red onions until they are soft and then add in the kale and sauté it for 5-10 minute until it's done. Cook the buckwheat in 25 to 30 minutes, dress it with the chili tomato sauce and serve with kale and chicken.

Nutrition Facts: Calories: 290, Fat: 3.8g, Carbohydrate: 24.3g, Protein: 22g

252.   Spicy Chicken Hotpot

Preparation time: 10 minutes   **Cooking time: 30 minutes**   **Servings: 2**

Ingredients:

- ✓ 2 red peppers, chopped
- ✓ 2 large onion, sliced
- ✓ 3 teaspoons EVO oil
- ✓ 4 chicken tights
- ✓ 4 oz. buckwheat

- ✓ 2 garlic cloves, minced
- ✓ 1 ½ cups vegetable broth
- ✓ ½ teaspoon ground nutmeg

- ✓ 1 tablespoon paprika
- ✓ 1 chili, sliced
- ✓ 1 tomato, chopped
- ✓ 1 tablespoon parsley

Directions:

Boil the buckwheat for 25 minutes then drain it and set it aside. Put the oil in a pan and heat, add onion, garlic, chili and spices and cook for 5 minutes until soft. Add the chicken and let it turn golden brown on medium high heat for 5 minutes. Add the peppers and the tomato, salt and pepper and cook another 3-5 minutes until they start softening. Add the stock, turn the heat down and let simmer for 25 minutes. Then, add the buckwheat and let it absorb all the spicy flavors for 2-3 minutes. Serve hot.

Nutrition Facts: Calories: 305, Fat: 9.5g, Carbohydrate: 14.2g, Protein: 3.7g

253.   Sweet Potato and Salmon Fishballs

Preparation time: 10 minutes   **Cooking time: 30 minutes**   **Servings: 2**

Ingredients:

- 8oz wild salmon, cooked or tinned
- 3 tablespoons Buckwheat flour
- 8oz sweet potato cooked and mashed
- 1 tablespoon EVO oil
- 1 tablespoon balsamic vinegar
- 1 tablespoon dill
- 1 head red endive

Directions:

Preheat the oven up to 325°F. Mix the sweet potato, salmon, dill, salt and pepper together. Then, take a small handful of mixture and shape it into a ball. Flatten into a shape of burger then dip into the flour on each side. Place it on a lined baking tray. Repeat until the blend is used up.

Bake only turning once for 20 minutes. Serve with a salad made with finely sliced red endive seasoned with vinaigrette made with olive oil, salt, pepper and vinegar.

Nutrition Facts: Calories: 316 kcal, Fat: 6.3g, Carbohydrate: 18.3g, Protein: 19.2g

---

254.   WEEK 2- PHASE II: 'MAINTENANCE PHASE'

Shopping List

NB - Necessary: You can choose your favorite Sirtfood Green Juices Recipes each week. Remember to include the related ingredients in this list accordingly.

- Almond Milk unsweetened
- Arugula Asparagus
- Avocado
- Baby Spinach
- Banana Bird's eye chili
- Blueberries
- Broccoli
- Buckwheat puffed
- Carrots
- Cauliflower
- Celeriac
- Celery
- Cherry tomatoes
- Chicken Wings
- Chicory
- Chocolate 85%
- Coconut milk full fat
- Cucumber
- Eggs
- Greek yoghurt
- Kale
- Lean
- Mince
- Lettuce
- Lemons
- Lentils canned
- Lime
- Milk skimmed
- Mixed Berries frozen
- Mozzarella
- Mushrooms
- Oats
- Orange
- Parmesan
- Parsley
- Parsnip
- Red Onions
- Red Peppers
- Salmon fillets
- Scallions
- Shrimps
- Sirloin
- Strawberries
- Tomatoes

Meal Plan

Quick Recap: this week, you will have 1 juice a day, 2 optional snacks, and 2 full meals.

DAY	BREAKFAST	SNACK	LUNCH	SNACK	DINNER
8	Vanilla Semifreddo with Berries	Sirtfood Green Juice	Lemon Ginger Shrimp Salad	2 squares of dark chocolate	Indian Vegetarian Patties Meatballs
9	Sautéed Mushrooms and Poached Eggs	2 squares of dark chocolate	Spicy Salmon with Turmeric and Lentils	Blueberry Smoothie	Creamy Turkey and Asparagus
10	Banana Vanilla Pancake	Sirtfood Green Juice	Arugula Salad with Turkey and Italian Dressing	2 squares of dark chocolate	Chicken and Broccoli Casserole
11	Scrambled Eggs and Cherry Tomatoes	Sirtfood Green Juice	Caprese Skewers	Banana Strawberry Smoothie	Lemon Chicken Skewers with Peppers
12	Overnight Oats with Strawberries and Chocolate	Sirtfood Green Juice	Trout with Roasted Vegetables	2 squares of dark chocolate	Mushroom Soup with Chicken
13	Kale and Mushroom Frittata	Sirtfood Green Juice	Shredded Chicken Bowl	2 squares of dark chocolate	Mince Stuffed Peppers
14	Blueberry Pancakes	Sirtfood Green Juice	Oriental Beef Salad	2 squares of dark chocolate	Baked Salmon with Sautéed Vegetables

Recipes

255.   Vanilla Semifreddo with Berries

Preparation time: 5 minutes   **Cooking time: 0 minutes**   **Servings: 1**

Ingredients:

- ✓ 4 oz. Greek yogurt
- ✓ ½ teaspoon Vanilla extract
- ✓ 1 cup mixed berries, frozen is perfect
- ✓ 1 teaspoon honey or maple syrup
- ✓ 1 tablespoon buckwheat granola

Directions:

Mix yoghurt, vanilla extract and honey. Alternate yogurt and berries in a jar and top with granola.

Frozen berries are perfect if the Semifreddo is made in advance because they release their juices in the yoghurt.

Nutrition Facts: Calories: 318, Fat: 5.4g, Carbohydrate: 22.8g, Protein: 21.9g

256.   Caprese Skewers

Preparation time: 5 minutes   **Cooking time: 30 minutes**   **Servings: 2**

Ingredients:

- ✓ 4 oz. cucumber, cut in 8 pieces
- ✓ 8 cherry tomatoes
- ✓ 8 basil leaves
- ✓ 2 teaspoons of balsamic vinegar
- ✓ salt and pepper to taste
- ✓ 8 small balls of mozzarella or 4 oz. mozzarella cut in 8 pieces
- ✓ 1 teaspoon of EVO oil

Directions:

Use two medium skewers per person or four small ones. Alternate the ingredients in the following order: tomato, mozzarella, basil, yellow pepper, cucumber and repeat.

Mix oil, vinegar, salt and pepper and pour the dressing over the skewers.

Nutrition Facts: Calories: 280kcal, Fat: 8g, Carbohydrate: 14.g, Protein: 17

---

257.   Scrambled Eggs and Cherry Tomatoes

Preparation time: 2 minutes   **Cooking time: 2 minutes**   **Servings: 1**

Ingredients:

- ✓ 2 Eggs
- ✓ 1 tablespoon Parmesan or other shredded cheese
- ✓ Salt and pepper
- ✓ ½ cup cherry tomatoes

Directions:

Put eggs and cheese with a pinch of salt and pepper in a jar. Microwave for 30 seconds, then quickly stir with a spoon. Then, put back in the microwave for 60 seconds and they are a ready to eat with cherry tomatoes.

In case you <u>don't own a microwave</u>, cook the scrambled eggs in a small pan for 2 minutes, stirring continuously until done.

Nutrition Facts: Calories: 278, Fat: 5.4g, Carbohydrate: 12.8g, Protein: 18.9g

---

258.   Kale and Mushroom Omelet

Preparation time: 15 minutes   **Cooking time:** 30 minutes   **Servings: 4**

Ingredients:

- ✓ 8 eggs
- ✓ 1 red onion, chopped
- ✓ 1 garlic clove, minced
- ✓ 1 cup fresh mushrooms, chopped
- ✓ ½ cup unsweetened almond milk
- ✓ Salt and ground black pepper, to taste
- ✓ 1 tablespoon EVO oil
- ✓ 1½ cups fresh kale, chopped

Directions:

Preheat oven to 350°F. In a large bowl, place the eggs, coconut milk, salt, and black pepper, and beat well. Set aside. In a large ovenproof pan, heat the oil over medium heat and sauté the onion and garlic for about 3–4 minutes. Add the kale salt, and black pepper, and cook for about 8–10 minutes.

Stir in the mushrooms and cook for about 3–4 minutes. Place the egg mixture on top evenly and cook for about 4 minutes, without stirring. Transfer the pan in the oven and bake for about 12–15 minutes or until desired doneness.

Remove from the oven and let rest for about 3–5 minutes before serving.

Nutrition Facts: Calories 151, Total Fat 10.2 g, Total Carbs 5.6 g, Protein 10.3 g

259.   Banana Strawberry Smoothie

Preparation time: 5 minutes   **Servings: 1**

Ingredients:

- ✓ 1 cup strawberries
- ✓ ½ banana
- ✓ ½ cup almond milk, unsweetened
- ✓ ½ teaspoon cocoa powder
- ✓ 3 cubes ice (optional)

Directions:

Blend all ingredients together and serve immediately. Use a mixer.

Nutrition Facts: Calories: 92kcal, Fat: 1.3g, Carbohydrate: 12.8g, Protein: 3.6g

---

260.   Blueberry Pancakes

Preparation time: 5 minutes   **Cooking time: 15 minutes**   **Servings: 2**

Ingredients:

- ✓ 1 egg
- ✓ 1 cup blueberries
- ✓ 2 teaspoons honey
- ✓ 2 oz. self-raising flour
- ✓ 1 oz. buckwheat flour
- ✓ 1/3 cup skimmed milk

Directions:

Mix the flours in a bowl, add the yolk and a bit of mix in a very thick batter. Keep adding the milk bit by bit to avoid lumps.

In another bowl, beat the egg white until stiff and then mix it carefully to the batter. Put enough batter to make a 5-inch round pancake to cook 2 minutes per side until done. Repeat until all the pancakes are ready.

Put honey (1 teaspoon) and ½ cup blueberries on top of each serving.

Nutrition Facts: Calories: 272, Fat: 4.3g, Carbohydrate: 26.8g, Protein: 23.6g

---

261.   Mince Stuffed Peppers

Preparation Time: 15 minutes   **Cooking Time: 60 minutes**   **Servings: 4**

Ingredients:

- ✓ 4 oz. lean mince
- ✓ 2 red bell peppers
- ✓ 1 tablespoon parmesan
- ✓ 2 tablespoons breadcrumbs
- ✓ ¼ cup brown rice, cooked
- ✓ 2 larges yellow
- ✓ Salt and pepper, to taste
- ✓ 2 cups Arugula
- ✓ 2 teaspoons EVO oil
- ✓ 3 oz. mozzarella
- ✓ 1 egg
- ✓ ¼ cup walnuts, chopped
- ✓ Few drops Lemon juice
- ✓ Cooking spray

Directions:

Preheat oven to 350° F. In a bowl mix mince, parmesan, brown rice, egg and mozzarella. Mix well and set aside. Cut peppers lengthwise, remove the seeds, fill them with the mince mix and put them on a baking tray.

Distribute breadcrumbs on top and lightly spray with cooking spray to have a crunchy top without adding calories to the recipe.

Cook for 50-60 minutes until peppers are soft. Let cool for a few minutes.

Serve stuffed peppers with an arugula salad dressed with olive oil, salt and a few drops of lemon.

Nutrition Facts: Calories 375.1 Fat 8.2g Carbohydrate 24.7g Protein 15.3g

262. Arugula Salad with Turkey and Italian Dressing

Preparation time: 5 minutes   **Cooking time: 30 minutes**   **Servings: 2**

Ingredients:

- ✓ 8oz. turkey breast
- ✓ 1 cup arugula
- ✓ 2 teaspoons oregano
- ✓ 1/4 cup scallions, sliced
- ✓ 2 teaspoons EVO oil
- ✓ 1 cup lettuce
- ✓ 2 teaspoons Dijon mustard
- ✓ 1 tablespoon cumin
- ✓ 1/2 cup celery, finely diced
- ✓ Salt and pepper to taste

Directions:

Grill the turkey and shred it. Set aside. Mix lettuce and arugula on a plate. Evenly distribute shredded turkey, celery and scallions.

In a bowl mix all dressing ingredients: mustard, oil, lemon juice, oregano, salt and pepper and pour it over the salad just before serving.

Nutrition Facts: Calories: 165 kcal, Fat: 2.9g, Carbohydrate: 13.6g, Protein: 26.1g

263. Overnight Oats with Strawberries and Chocolate

Preparation time: 5 minutes+8h   **Cooking time: 0 minutes**
Servings: 2

Ingredients:

- ✓ 2 oz. rolled oats
- ✓ 1 cup strawberries
- ✓ 1 teaspoon honey
- ✓ 1 square 85% chocolate
- ✓ 4 oz. almond milk, unsweetened
- ✓ 2 tablespoons plain yoghurt

Directions:

Mix the oats and the milk in a jar and leave overnight. In the morning top the jar with yoghurt, honey, strawberries and chocolate cut in small pieces.

It can be prepared in advance and left up to 3 days in the fridge.

Nutrition Facts: Calories: 258, Fat: 3.3g, Carbohydrate: 29.8g, Protein: 13.6g

264. Mushroom Soup with Chicken

Preparation Time: 10 minutes   **Cooking Time**: 40 minutes   **Servings**: 3

Ingredients:

- ✓ 2 cups vegetable stock
- ✓ 8 oz. mixed mushrooms, sliced
- ✓ 1 red onion, finely diced
- ✓ 1 carrot, finely diced
- ✓ 1 tablespoon EVO oil
- ✓ 3 leaves sage
- ✓ 1 stick celery, finely diced
- ✓ 4 oz. chicken breast, cubed

Directions:

Put 1 tablespoon oil in a skillet and cook chicken until lightly brown. Set aside.

Put the mushrooms in a hot pan with 1 tablespoon oil, celery, carrot, onion and sage and cook for 3 to 5 minutes. Add the stock and let it simmer for another 5 minutes, then using a hand blender, blend the soup until smooth. Add the chicken and cook for another 8 to 10 minutes until creamy.

Nutrition Facts: Calories 302.0 Fat 3.5 g Carbohydrate 16.3 Protein 15 g

265.   Chocolate Mousse

Preparation time: 5 minutes   **Servings: 1**

Ingredients:

- ✓ ½ avocado
- ✓ 1 teaspoon cocoa powder
- ✓ 1 teaspoon honey

Directions:

Blend all ingredients together and serve immediately.

Nutrition Facts: Calories: 87, Fat: 1.1g, Carbohydrate: 11.8g, Protein: 1.6g

266.   Lemon Ginger Shrimp Salad

Preparation time: 15 minutes   **Cooking time: 5 minutes**   **Servings: 2**

Ingredients:

- ✓ 1 cup chicory leaves
- ✓ 2 teaspoons of EVO oil
- ✓ ½ cup arugula
- ✓ ½ cup baby spinach
- ✓ Juice of ½ lemon
- ✓ 8 oz. shrimps
- ✓ 6 walnuts, chopped
- ✓ 1 avocado-peeled, stoned, and sliced
- ✓ 1 pinch chili

Directions:

Mix chicory, baby spinach and arugula and put them on a large plate. Heat a skillet on medium high temperature, put 1 tablespoon oil and cook shrimps with garlic, chili, salt and pepper until they are not transparent anymore (5 minutes)

Blend avocado with oil, lemon juice with a pinch of salt and pepper and distribute the dressing on top. Then, chop the walnuts, put them on the plate as last ingredient and serve.

Nutrition Facts: Calories: 353, Fat: 4.8g, Carbohydrate: 28.1g, Protein: 28.3g

267.   Blueberry Smoothie

Preparation time: 5 minutes   **Servings: 1**

Ingredients:

- ✓ 1 cup blueberries
- ✓ ½ cup orange juice
- ✓ ½ banana
- ✓ 3 cubes ice (optional)

Directions:

Blend all ingredients together and serve immediately.

Nutrition Facts: Calories: 87, Fat: 1.1g, Carbohydrate: 11.8g, Protein: 1.6g

268.   Sautéed Mushrooms and Poached Eggs

Preparation time: 10 minutes   **Cooking time: 15 minutes**   **Servings: 2**

Ingredients:

- ✓ 2 eggs
- ✓ 1 onion, sliced
- ✓ 10 oz. tomatoes, chopped
- ✓ 1 teaspoon EVO oil
- ✓ 10 oz. mushrooms, sliced
- ✓ 1 teaspoon marjoram (or thyme)

Directions:

Sauté the onions in a frying pan with the oil for 5 minutes. Add mushrooms, tomatoes, herbs and season with salt and pepper to taste.

While the mushrooms are cooking, bring some water to a boil, crack one egg per time and poach it. Put the poached egg on top of mushrooms and serve.

Nutrition Facts: Calories: 270, Fat: 4.3g, Carbohydrate: 19.8g, Protein: 22g

269.   Lemon Chicken Skewers with Peppers

Preparation time: 5 minutes   **Cooking time:** 15 minutes   **Servings: 8**

Ingredients:

- ✓ 8 oz. chicken breast
- ✓ ½ teaspoon paprika
- ✓ ½ teaspoon turmeric
- ✓ 3 teaspoons EVO oil
- ✓ 2 cups peppers, chopped
- ✓ 1 cup tomatoes, chopped
- ✓ 1 garlic clove
- ✓ ½ lemon, juiced
- ✓ 1 handful parsley, chopped
- ✓ Salt and pepper

Directions:

Cut the breast in small cubes and let it marinate with oil and spices for 30 minutes.

Prepare the skewers and set aside. Heat a pan with oil. When hot add garlic and cook 5 minutes, the remove the clove. Then, add peppers, tomatoes, salt and pepper and cook on high heat for 5-10 minutes.

Heat another pan to high heat, when very hot, put the skewers in and cook 10-12 minutes until golden on every side. Serve the skewers alongside the peppers.

Nutrition Facts: Calories: 315 Fat: 20.9g Protein: 15.8g Carbohydrate: 5.4g

270.   Baked Salmon with Sautéed Vegetables

Preparation time: 20 minutes   **Cooking time: 30 minutes**   **Servings: 2**

Ingredients:

- ✓ 8 oz. wild salmon fillets
- ✓ Grated zest and juice of 1 lemon
- ✓ 1 teaspoon sesame oil
- ✓ 2 teaspoons EVO oil
- ✓ 2 carrots cut into matchsticks
- ✓ Bunch of kale, chopped
- ✓ 2 teaspoons of root ginger, grated
- ✓ Salt and pepper to tast

Directions:

Mix ginger lemon juice and zest together. Place the salmon in an oven proof dish and pour over the lemon ginger mixture. Cover with foil and leave for 30-60 minutes to marinate.

Then, bake the salmon at 375°F in the oven for 15 minutes. While cooking heat up a wok or frying pan then add sesame oil and olive oil. Add the vegetables, and cook, stirring constantly for a few minutes.

Once the salmon are cooked spoon some of the salmon marinade onto the vegetables and cook for a few more minutes. Serve the vegetables onto a plate and top with salmon.

Nutrition Facts: Calories 458kcal, Fat 13.2 g Carbohydrate 15.3 Protein 21.4

271.   Spicy Salmon with Turmeric and Lentils

Preparation Time: 5 Minutes   **Cooking time:** 30 Minutes   **Servings: 4**

Ingredients:

- ✓ 8 oz. Skinned salmon
- ✓ 1 teaspoon EVO oil
- ✓ 1 teaspoon turmeric
- ✓ 1/4 juice of a lemon
- ✓ ½ red onion, finely chopped
- ✓ 1 garlic clove, finely chopped
- ✓ 1 large tomato, cut into 8 wedges

- ✓ 1 cup chicken or vegetable stock
- ✓ 1 bird's eye chili, finely chopped
- ✓ 3 oz. lentils, canned
- ✓ 5 oz. celery cut into 2cm sticks
- ✓ 1 teaspoon Mild curry powder
- ✓ 1 tablespoon parsley, chopped

Directions:

Heat the oven to 400°F. Heat a frying pan over a medium–low heat; add the olive oil, then onion, garlic, ginger, chili, and celery. Fry gently for 2–3 minutes or until softened, then add the curry powder and cook for another minute. Add the tomatoes, then stock and lentils, and simmer gently for 10 minutes.

You may want to increase or decrease the cooking time depending on how crunchy you like your celery. Meanwhile, mix the turmeric, oil, and lemon juice and rub over the salmon. Place on a baking tray and cook for 8–10 minutes.

To finish, spread parsley on top of the celery and serve with the salmon.

Nutrition Facts: Calories: 177kcal Carbohydrates: 4g Protein: 12g

272.   Trout with Roasted Vegetables

Preparation time: 25 minutes   **Cooking time: 20 minutes**   **Servings: 2**

Ingredients:

- ✓ 2 turnips, peeled and chopped
- ✓ EVO oil
- ✓ 2 trout fillets
- ✓ 2 parsnips, peeled and cut into wedges

- ✓ 2 tablespoons Tamari
- ✓ Dried dill
- ✓ 1 lemon, juiced
- ✓ 2 carrots cut into sticks

Directions:

Put the sliced vegetables into a baking tray. Sprinkle with a dash of tamari and olive oil. Heat the oven to 400°F. Take the vegetables out of the oven after 25 minutes and stir well. Put the fish over it. Sprinkle with the dill and lemon juice. Cover with foil and go back to the oven.

Turn down the oven to 375°F and cook till the fish is cooked through for 20 minutes.

Nutrition Facts: Calories 154.0 Total Fat 2.2 g Carbohydrate 14.5 Protein 23.6

---

273.   Chicken and Broccoli Casserole

Preparation time: 15 minutes   **Cooking time: 30 minutes**   **Servings: 2**

Ingredients:

- ✓ 3 cups broccoli
- ✓ 8 oz. chicken breast, cubed
- ✓ 1/2 onion
- ✓ 2 tablespoons wine
- ✓ 1 tablespoon flour
- ✓ 1 cup mushrooms
- ✓ ½ cup broth
- ✓ 2 tablespoons Parmesan

Directions:

Heat the oven to 350°F. Steam the broccoli for 5 minutes, drain and cool in water and ice to set the bright green color. Cut the chicken breast in medium sized cubes. Mix chicken and broccoli and put them in a baking tray.

Now, prepare the creamy sauce. Sauté the onion with olive oil on a low heat, then set to high heat, put in the mushrooms, a pinch of salt and pepper, flour and mix. Add the wine and mix until it has evaporated. Add the broth, cook for 5 minutes, then hand blend until smooth.

Pour the sauce over the chicken and broccoli, spread 2 tablespoons of Parmesan and cook in the oven for 30-35 minutes. Turn on the broiler for the last 5 minutes.

Nutrition Facts: Calories: 353, Fat: 4.8g, Carbohydrate: 28.1g, Protein: 28.3

---

274.   Creamy Turkey and Asparagus

Preparation time: 10 minutes   **Cooking time: 30 minutes**   **Servings: 2**

Ingredients:

- ✓ 8 oz. turkey breast
- ✓ 2 cups asparagus
- ✓ 2 cloves garlic
- ✓ 2 teaspoons EVO oil
- ✓ ½ cup full fat coconut milk
- ✓ ½ red onion
- ✓ ½ bird's eye chili
- ✓ Salt and pepper

Directions:

Heat a skillet over medium high heat, put oil, onion, garlic, chili and let cook for 5 minutes. Then, add turkey, cut in strips, and cook it another 5 minutes until golden on all sizes. Add the asparagus, cut in 2-inch pieces and after 2 minutes add the coconut milk. Let it simmer for 25 minutes until the sauce is creamy.

Nutrition Facts: Calories: 353, Fat: 4.8g, Carbohydrate: 28.1g, Protein: 28.3g

---

275.   Oriental Beef Salad

Preparation time: 15 minutes   **Cooking time: 8 minutes**   **Servings: 2**

Ingredients:

- ✓ 3 teaspoons EVO oil
- ✓ 8 oz. sirloin steaks
- ✓ ½ red onion, finely sliced
- ✓ 1 tablespoon soy sauce
- ✓ ½ bird's eye chili
- ✓ ½ cucumber, sliced
- ✓ ½ cup cherry tomatoes, halved
- ✓ 2 cups lettuce
- ✓ 1 handful parsley
- ✓ 3 tablespoons lemon juice

163

Directions:

Crush the garlic, mix it with finely sliced chili and parsley, 2 teaspoons olive oil and soy sauce. This will be the dressing. Prepare the salad in a bowl placing lettuce on the bottom, then onion, cherry tomatoes and cucumber.

Heat a skillet until very hot. Brush the steaks with remaining oil, season them with salt and pepper and cook them to your taste. Transfer the steaks onto a cutting board for 5 minutes before slicing. Drizzle the dressing on the salad and mix well.

Place steak slices on top and serve.

Nutrition Facts: Calories 262, Total Fat 12 g , Total Carbs 15.2 g Protein 25.2 g

276.   Banana Vanilla Pancake

Preparation time: 10 minutes   **Cooking time: 15 minutes**   **Servings: 2**

Ingredients:

- ✓ 1 Egg
- ✓ 1 Egg White
- ✓ 1 Banana
- ✓ 2 teaspoons honey

- ✓ 1 cup Rolled Oats
- ✓ ½ cup almond milk, unsweetened
- ✓ ¼ teaspoon Baking Powder

- ✓ A pinch of salt
- ✓ 1 teaspoon Vanilla extract

Directions:

First, put half banana, eggs, oats, vanilla, baking powder, salt and almond milk in a blender and blend until smooth. Heat a small pan and when hot but batter in to form pancakes.

Top with honey and the other half banana.

Nutrition Facts: Calories: 232, Fat: 5.3g, Carbohydrate: 22.8g, Protein: 18.6g

277.   Indian Vegetarian Patties

Preparation time: 5 minutes   **Cooking time: 30 minutes**   **Servings: 2**

Ingredients:

- ✓ 1 cup cauliflower
- ✓ Cooking spray
- ✓ ¼ cup breadcrumbs
- ✓ 1 egg
- ✓ 1 cup brown rice
- ✓ 1 teaspoon smoked paprika
- ✓ 1 ½ tablespoon garam masala
- ✓ 1 teaspoon ginger
- ✓ 1 tablespoon parsley, chopped
- ✓ 1 cup tomato sauce
- ✓ Broth (if needed)
- ✓ 1 teaspoon of extra virgin olive oil
- ✓ 1 cloves garlic crushed

- ✓ ½teaspoon turmeric
- ✓ 1 tablespoon EVO oil
- ✓ 1 red onion-diced
- ✓ 6oz full fat coconut milk

Directions:

Steam cauliflower for 5 minutes then blend it with rice. Use pulse in order to get a result similar to mince. Add egg, breadcrumbs, 1 clove garlic, salt, pepper, turmeric, paprika and finely chopped parsley. Mix well until you can form patties. Not: if it's too dry, add 1 tablespoon egg white and mix. If it's too runny, add 1 tablespoon breadcrumb and mix. Spray a pan with cooking spray, heat it and gently cook the patties for 5 minutes until golden. Be careful when you turn them so that they don't break. Put them aside

In a different pan, put oil, onion ginger garlic salt and pepper and cook on low heat until the onion is done, add tomato sauce and coconut milk and let it simmer around 15 minutes until dense. Put the patties in the sauce and cook another 5 minutes before serving.

Nutrition Facts: Calories: 412, Fat: 7.8g, Carbohydrate: 39.1g, Protein: 18.3g

---

278. Shredded Chicken Bowl

Preparation Time: 10 minutes　　　　**Cooking time:** 35 minutes　　　　**Servings 2**

Ingredients:

- 8 oz. chicken breast
- 1teaspoon onion powder
- 1 teaspoon garlic powder
- 2 cups broth

- 2 cups baby spinach
- ½ Lime
- 2 teaspoons extra virgin olive oil

- 2 ripe avocados
- 1 cup cherry tomatoes

Directions:

Put the chicken breasts in a saucepan with salt, pepper, onion and garlic powder. Add the broth, bring to a boil and cook 30 to 40 minutes with a lid until the meat starts to shred. Remove the chicken from the broth move the chicken and shred it with a fork. Then, put the baby spinach as base in a serving bowl. Add the shredded chicken into the bowl, sliced avocado and cherry tomatoes.

Prepare the dressing with lime, oil, salt and pepper and drizzle it over the salad just before serving.

Nutrition Facts: Calories 420, Fat: 5.6g, Carbohydrate 12.5 g, Protein: 21.4

---

279. WEEK 3- PHASE II: 'MAINTENANCE PHASE'

Shopping List

NB - Necessary: You can choose your favorite Sirtfood Green Juices Recipes each week. Remember to include the related ingredients in this list accordingly.

- Almond Milk unsweetened
- Artichokes
- Arugula
- Avocado
- Banana Bird's eye chili
- Blueberries
- Brussels Sprouts
- Buckwheat
- Carrots

- Celery
- Cheddar
- Cherry tomatoes
- Chicken Breast
- Chickpeas canned
- Cilantro
- Eggplants
- Eggs
- Feta cheese
- Greek yoghurt

- Kale
- Lettuce
- Lemons
- Milk, skimmed
- Mint
- Mixed Berries, frozen
- Miso
- Paste
- Mozzarella
- Mushrooms

- ✓ Oats
- ✓ Orange
- ✓ Parmesan
- ✓ Parsley
- ✓ Plain
- ✓ Yoghurt
- ✓ Red Onions

- ✓ Ricotta cheese
- ✓ Salmon fillets
- ✓ Scallions
- ✓ Sirloin
- ✓ Spinach
- ✓ Sweet potatoes
- ✓ Tomato paste

- ✓ Tomatoes
- ✓ Tortillas, wholegrain
- ✓ Tuna Steak
- ✓ Turkey
- ✓ Bacon
- ✓ Turkey Breast

Meal Plan

Quick Recap: this week, you will have 1 juice a day, 2 optional snacks, and 2 full meals.

DAY	BREAKFAST	SNACK	LUNCH	SNACK	DINNER
15	Brussels Sprouts Egg Skillet	Sirtfood Green Juice	Brussels Sprouts and Ricotta Salad	Blueberry Smoothie	Sesame Chicken with Ginger and Chili Stir-Fried Greens
16	Blueberry and Walnut Bake	Sirtfood Green Juice	Roasted Butternut and Chickpeas Salad	2 squares of dark chocolate	Greek Omelet with Garlic Grilled Eggplant
17	Blueberry Pancakes	Sirtfood Green Juice	Arugula Salad with Turkey and Italian Dressing	Buckwheat Granola	Turkey Bacon Fajitas
18	Sautéed Mushrooms and Poached Eggs	Sirtfood Green Juice	Shrimp Tomato Hotpot	2 squares of dark chocolate	Sesame Tuna with Artichoke Hearts
19	Banana Vanilla Pancake	Sirtfood Green Juice	Baked Salmon with Sautéed Vegetables	Mango Mousse with Chocolate Chips	Eggplant Pizza Towers
20	Scrambled Eggs and Cherry Tomatoes	Sirtfood Green Juice	Orange Cumin Sirloin and Simple Arugula Salad	2 squares of dark chocolate	Spicy Hotpot with Potatoes and Spinach
21	Vanilla Semifreddo with Berries	Sirtfood Green Juice	Indian Vegetarian Patties Meatballs	Chocolate Mousse	Garlic Salmon with Brussel Sprouts and Rice

Recipes

Recipes of Week 1 &2	Banana Vanilla Pancake; Indian Vegetarian Patties; Blueberry Smoothie; Shrimp Tomato Stew; Scrambled Eggs and Cherry Tomatoes; Chocolate Mousse; Sautéed Mushrooms and Poached Eggs; Vanilla Semifreddo with Berries; Arugula Salad with Turkey and Italian Dressing

280. ⬚ Brussels Sprouts and Ricotta Salad

Preparation time: 15 minutes   **Cooking time: 0 minutes**   **Servings: 2**

Ingredients:

- ✓ 1 ½ cups Brussel sprouts, thinly sliced
- ✓ 1 green apple cut "à la julienne"
- ✓ 1 tablespoon lemon juice
- ✓ 1 tablespoon orange juice
- ✓ ½ red onion
- ✓ 8 walnuts, chopped
- ✓ 1 teaspoon extra virgin olive oil
- ✓ 4 oz. ricotta cheese

Directions:

Put the red onion in cup and cover it with boiling water. Let it rest 10 minutes, then drain and pat with kitchen paper. Now, slice Brussel sprouts as thin as you can, cut the apple à la julienne.

Mix Brussel sprouts, onion and apple and season them with oil, salt, pepper, lemon juice and orange juice and spread it on a serving plate. Spread small spoons of ricotta cheese over the serving plate and top with chopped walnuts.

Nutrition Facts: Calories: 353, Fat: 4.8g, Carbohydrate: 28.1g, Protein: 28.3g

---

281. Buckwheat Granola

Preparation time: 15 minutes   **Cooking time: 30 minutes**   **Servings: 10**

Ingredients:

- ✓ 2 cups buckwheat, puffed
- ✓ ¾ cup pumpkin seeds
- ✓ ¾ cup walnuts, chopped
- ✓ 1 teaspoon ground cinnamon
- ✓ 1 ripe banana, mashed
- ✓ 2 tablespoons honey
- ✓ 2 tablespoons coconut oil

Directions:

Preheat your oven to 350°F. In a bowl, place the buckwheat groats, pumpkin seeds, walnuts, cinnamon and vanilla and mix well. Add banana, honey and coconut oil to the buckwheat mixture and mix until well combined.

Transfer the mixture onto a baking tray and spread in an even layer. Bake for about 25–30 minutes, stirring once halfway through. Remove the baking tray from oven and set aside to cool.

Nutrition Facts: Calories 252 Total Fat 14.3 g Total Carbs 27.6 g Protein 7.6 g

---

282. Blueberry and Walnut Bake

Preparation time: 5 minutes   **Cooking time: 30 minutes**   **Servings: 4**

Ingredients:

- ✓ 4 oz. rolled oats
- ✓ 1 banana, ripe and mashed
- ✓ ½teaspoon vanilla extract
- ✓ 1 oz. walnuts, chopped
- ✓ 12 oz. almond milk, unsweetened
- ✓ 1 cup blueberries
- ✓ To serve: ½ cup plain yoghurt

Directions:

Heat the oven to 400°F. Mix the oats, milk, vanilla, banana, blueberries and walnuts in a bowl. Put on a baking tray lined with parchment paper and cook around 30 minutes. It can be eaten alone or served with ½ cup plain yoghurt.

Nutrition Facts: Calories: 308, Fat: 5.3g, Carbohydrate: 35.8g, Protein: 15.6g

283. Turkey Bacon Fajitas

Preparation time: 5 minutes   **Cooking time: 20 minutes**   **Servings: 2**

Ingredients:

- ✓ 3 eggs, lightly beaten
- ✓ 2 wholegrain tortillas
- ✓ ½ cup cherry tomatoes
- ✓ 1 red onion
- ✓ 2 turkey bacon slices
- ✓ 2 oz. cup shredded cheddar
- ✓ 1 teaspoon extra virgin olive oil

Directions:

Sauté the onion with olive oil on medium heat for 5 minutes, add the eggs and stir continuously until they are done. Add turkey bacon, finely sliced and cheddar cheese on top so that it starts to melt.

Quick heat the tortillas on a pan (keep them soft), divide the egg mixture between them and serve immediately.

Nutrition Facts: Calories: 353, Fat: 4.8g, Carbohydrate: 28.1g, Protein: 28.3g

284. Eggplant Pizza Towers

Preparation time: 15 minutes   **Cooking time: 40 minutes**   **Servings: 2**

Ingredients:

- ✓ 1 ½ eggplants
- ✓ 1 tablespoon tomato paste
- ✓ 2 cups tomato sauce
- ✓ ½ red onion
- ✓ 1 clove garlic
- ✓ ½ cup mozzarella
- ✓ 4 basil leaves
- ✓ 1 teaspoon extra virgin olive oil
- ✓ 1 tablespoon Parmesan
- ✓ Salt and pepper

Directions:

Cut the eggplants into thick slices, add some salt and let them rest so that they let their bitter water out. In the meantime, prepare the salsa. Heat a pan with oil, when hot add onion and garlic and cook 5 minutes. Then, add tomato sauce, tomato paste, salt and pepper and cook on low heat for about 15-18 minutes. Add a few leaves of basil. Pat the eggplants with kitchen paper and grill them. Heat the oven at 350°F.

Compose the towers: put a slice of eggplant, sauce, a few dices of mozzarella and again eggplant, sauce, mozzarella. Three layers per tower are best. Distribute parmesan on top.

When done, put the tray in the oven for about 10 minutes until the mozzarella is melted.

Nutrition Facts: Calories: 353, Fat: 4.8g, Carbohydrate: 28.1g, Protein: 28.3g

285. Arugula Salad

Preparation Time: 10 minutes.   **Cooking Time: 0 minutes**   **Servings: 4**

Ingredients:

- ✓ 1 white onion, peeled and chopped
- ✓ 1 tablespoon vinegar
- ✓ 1 bunch baby arugula
- ✓ ¼ cup walnuts, chopped
- ✓ 2 tablespoons fresh cilantro, chopped
- ✓ 2 garlic cloves, peeled and minced
- ✓ 2 tablespoons extra virgin olive oil
- ✓ 1 tablespoon lemon juice

Directions:

In a bowl, mix the water and vinegar, add the onion, set aside for 5 minutes, and drain well.

In a salad bowl, mix the arugula with the walnuts and onion, and stir. Add the garlic, salt, pepper, lemon juice, cilantro, and oil, toss well, and serve.

Nutrition Facts: Calories 200 Fat 2 g Carbs 5 g Protein 7 g

286.   Sesame Tuna with Artichoke Hearts

Preparation time: 5 minutes　　　**Cooking time: 30 minutes**　　　**Servings: 2**

Ingredients:

- ✓ 8 oz. tuna steaks
- ✓ 1 clove garlic
- ✓ 2 artichokes
- ✓ 2 teaspoon extra virgin olive oil
- ✓ ½ lemon, juiced
- ✓ 2 tablespoons white sesame
- ✓ 2 tablespoons black sesame
- ✓ 1 teaspoon sesame oil
- ✓ 1 handful parsley

Directions:

Discard the outer leaves, and then slice artichokes very finely. Heat a pan with olive oil, put garlic and cook for a couple of minutes, then remove the clove. Add artichokes, lemon, salt pepper and cook 5-10 minutes until tender. Set aside. Mix sesame seeds and press them on tuna until it is completely covered.

Heat a pan, add sesame oil and when it's very hot cook tuna 1-2 minutes per side. Serve tuna alongside artichokes.

Nutrition Facts: Calories: 353, Fat: 4.8g, Carbohydrate: 28.1g, Protein: 28.3g

---

287.   Sesame Chicken with Ginger and Chili Stir-Fried Greens

Preparation time: 10 minutes　　　**Cooking time: 25 minutes**　　　**Servings: 4**

Ingredients:

- ✓ 1 mirin
- ✓ 1 oz. celery
- ✓ 2 oz. red onion
- ✓ 1tablespoon miso paste
- ✓ 2 zucchini
- ✓ 1 Thai chili
- ✓ 2 garlic cloves
- ✓ 1 teaspoon fresh ginger
- ✓ 6 oz. chicken breast
- ✓ 1 teaspoon ground turmeric
- ✓ 1 teaspoon EVO oil
- ✓ 1 teaspoon tamari
- ✓ 1 cup spinach
- ✓ 2 teaspoons sesame seeds
- ✓ 3 oz. buckwheat

Directions:

Heat the oven to 400 °F. Line a roasting pan with parchment-paper. Mix in the mirin and the miso. Lengthwise cut the chicken and marinate it with the miso mix for 15 minutes.

Place the chicken in the roasting pan, sprinkle it with the sesame seeds, and roast in the oven for 15 to 20 minutes until it has been beautifully caramelized.

Wash the buckwheat in a sieve, and then place it along with the turmeric in a saucepan of boiling water. Cook 25-30min until done, and then drain. Chop celery, red onion, and zucchini to medium pieces. Chop the chili, garlic, and ginger very thinly, and set aside.

Heat the oil in a frying pan; add the celery, onion, zucchini, chili, garlic, and ginger and fry over high heat for 1 to 2 minutes, then reduce to medium heat for 3 to 4 minutes until the vegetables are cooked through but are still crunchy. If the vegetables begin to stick to the pan, you can need to add a cup of water. Add the tamari and spinach and cook for 2 minutes.

Serve with chicken and buckwheat.

Nutrition Facts: Calories: 417, Fat: 6.5g, Carbohydrate: 34.8g, Protein: 32.1g

288. Spicy Stew with Potatoes and Spinach

Preparation time: 10 minutes   **Cooking time: 30**   **Servings: 2**

Ingredients:

- ✓ 2 sweet potatoes
- ✓ 1 cup spinach
- ✓ 8 oz. chicken breast
- ✓ ½ bird's eye chili
- ✓ 2 tablespoons paprika
- ✓ 1 cup tomatoes, chopped
- ✓ 2 teaspoons EVO oil
- ✓ 1 red onion, finely chopped
- ✓ 1 cup stock
- ✓ Salt and pepper to taste

Directions:

Peel and cut sweet potatoes in 1-inch cubes and boil them 12 minutes. Drain and set aside. Heat a pan on medium high heat, add onion and cook for 5 minutes. Then, add chicken cubes and spices and let the meat color on all sides for 5 minutes. Add tomatoes and stock and let cook 15 minutes on low heat. Add sweet potatoes and spinach, let mix the flavors 5 minutes then turn the heat off.

Let rest 10 minutes then serve.

Nutrition Facts: Calories: 213 Cal Fat: 13.1 g Protein: 80.62 g Sugar: 51.67 g

---

289. Garlic Salmon with Brussel Sprouts and Rice

Preparation time: 5 minutes   **Cooking time**: 30 minutes   **Servings**: 2

Ingredients:

- ✓ 3 oz. basmati rice
- ✓ 8 oz. salmon fillet slices
- ✓ 1 cup Brussel sprouts
- ✓ 1 cup cherry tomatoes
- ✓ 1 teaspoon extra virgin olive oil
- ✓ 1 clove garlic, crushed
- ✓ 2 tablespoons wine
- ✓ 3 tablespoons stock (or water), if needed

Directions:

Boil the basmati rice until tender and set aside. Crush the garlic and coat the top of the salmon. Put a skillet on medium high heat and when hot put the salmon fillets skin down. Cook for 5 minutes than turn them. Cook them until it becomes brown and crispy (around 5-6 more minutes).

Remove the salmon from the pan and add Brussel sprouts, tomatoes, wine and salt and cook them around 10 minutes. Add stock or water if needed. When done, add the basmati rice and mix to combine the flavors. Add the parmesan and serve putting the salmon on top.

Nutrition Facts: Calories: 353, Fat: 4.8g, Carbohydrate: 28.1g, Protein: 28.3g

---

290. Roasted Butternut and Chickpeas Salad

Preparation time: 15 minutes   **Cooking time:** 35 minutes   **Servings:** 2

Ingredients:

- ✓ 1 cup chickpeas, drained
- ✓ ½ teaspoon honey
- ✓ 2 cups kale
- ✓ 2 teaspoon EVO oil
- ✓ 1 green apple
- ✓ ½ lemon, juiced
- ✓ 2 cloves of garlic
- ✓ Salt and pepper to taste

Directions:

Heat the oven at 400°F. Cut the squash into medium cubes, put them in a baking tray, add drained chickpeas, garlic 1 tablespoon EVO oil, salt and pepper and mix. Cook for 25 minutes. Mix the kale with the dressing: salt, pepper, lemon, EVO oil and honey so that while the squash is cooking it becomes softer and more pleasant to eat.

When squash and chickpeas are done, put them aside 10 minute and in the meantime chop the apple and mix it with kale. Add squash and chickpeas on top and serve warm.

Nutrition Facts: Calories: 353, Fat: 4.8g, Carbohydrate: 28.1g, Protein: 28.3g

291.   Orange Cumin Sirloin

Preparation time: 5 min + 8h   **Cooking time: 10 minutes**   **Servings: 2**

Ingredients:

- ✓ 8 oz. sirloin
- ✓ ½ teaspoon cumin
- ✓ ½ bird's eye chili
- ✓ 2 tablespoons soy sauce
- ✓ 2 tablespoons EVO oil
- ✓ ½ lime juice
- ✓ ½ orange juice
- ✓ 2 cloves garlic, crushed
- ✓ ¼ cup parsley
- ✓ Salt and pepper

Directions:

Prepare the marinade combining all the ingredients, reserve 2 tablespoons for later and put the rest on the sirloin in a small tray. Turn the meat several times so that the marinade covers it completely. Cover with aluminum foil and put in the fridge for 8 hours. Drain the meat from the marinade; pat it with kitchen paper in order to dry it. Heat the grill or a skillet until very hot and cook to your taste.

Let the cooked meat sit on a plate for 5 minutes then slice it and dress it with the 2 tablespoons of marinade you kept aside.

Nutrition Facts: Calories: 353, Fat: 4.8g, Carbohydrate: 28.1g, Protein: 28.3g

292.   Mango Mousse with Chocolate Chips

Preparation time: 5 minutes   **Servings: 1**

Ingredients:

- ✓ 1 cup mango
- ✓ 2 squares dark chocolate, chopped
- ✓ ½ cup Greek yoghurt
- ✓ ¼ teaspoon vanilla extract

Directions:

Blend mango, yoghurt and vanilla together, add chocolate chips and serve immediately.

Nutrition Facts: Calories: 87, Fat: 1.1g, Carbohydrate: 11.8g, Protein: 1.6g

293.   Greek Omelet with Garlic Grilled Eggplant

Preparation time: 5 minutes   **Cooking time: 30 minutes**   **Servings: 2**

Ingredients:

- ✓ 2 tablespoons milk
- ✓ 3 eggs
- ✓ 2 leaves mint, finely chopped
- ✓ 1 eggplant

- ✓ 1 ½ cups shredded zucchini
- ✓ 1 clove garlic, crushed
- ✓ 1 teaspoon balsamic vinegar
- ✓ 3 oz. feta cheese
- ✓ 2 tablespoons oil
- ✓ Salt and pepper to taste

Directions:

Heat the oven to 350°F. Cut the eggplant into thin slices; mix with a pinch of salt and let rest.

Mix the shredded zucchini with a pinch of salt and let it rest in a colander until they lost some water. After 10 minutes, squeeze them out and put them in a bowl. Add 3 eggs, crushed feta cheese, milk, salt, pepper, mint, whisk well and pour in a silicone baking tray and cook 25-30 minutes in the oven.

Pat the eggplant slices dry and grill them. Mix garlic, oil, salt, pepper and balsamic vinegar and pour the dressing on the eggplants. Serve the omelet alongside the eggplant.

Nutrition Facts: Calories: 359, Fat: 7.8g, Carbohydrate: 18.1g, Protein: 21.3g

294.   WEEK4-PHASEIII: TRANSITION

Phase 3 will allow you to transition to normal healthy eating that keeps including various Sirtfoods in daily meals.

Shopping List

NB - Necessary: You can choose your favorite Sirtfood Green Juices Recipes each week. Remember to include the related ingredients in this list accordingly.

- ✓ Almond Milk, unsweetened
- ✓ Almond
- ✓ Flour
- ✓ Arugula
- ✓ Avocado
- ✓ Baby potatoes
- ✓ Baby Spinach
- ✓ Banana
- ✓ Blueberries
- ✓ Broccoli
- ✓ Brussels Sprouts
- ✓ Buns, whole wheat
- ✓ Butternut
- ✓ Squash

- ✓ Buckwheat
- ✓ Cheddar
- ✓ Chicken
- ✓ Breast
- ✓ Chicken
- ✓ Mince
- ✓ Chickpeas, canned
- ✓ Chicory
- ✓ Coconut, shredded
- ✓ Eggs
- ✓ Lamb, shoulder
- ✓ Lean
- ✓ Mince
- ✓ Lettuce
- ✓ Lentils, canned

- ✓ Mozzarella
- ✓ Mushrooms
- ✓ Oats
- ✓ Parmesan
- ✓ Peanut
- ✓ Butter P
- ✓ Red Onions
- ✓ Red Peppers
- ✓ Ricotta cheese
- ✓ Shrimps
- ✓ Spinach
- ✓ Strawberries
- ✓ Sweet potatoes
- ✓ Tomatoes

Meal Plan

Quick Recap: this week, you will have 1 juice a day, 2 snacks, and 3 full meal

DAY	BREAKFAST	SNACK	LUNCH	SNACK	DINNER
22	Vanilla Semifreddo with Berries	Mango Mousse with Chocolate Chips	Chicken and Broccoli Casserole and Baked Sweet Potato	Sirtfood Green Juice	Spicy Indian Dahl with Basmati Rice
23	Brussels Sprouts Egg Skillet	Sirtfood Green Juice	Baked Salmon with Sautéed Vegetables	Cocoa Balls	Tex-Mex Chicken Casserole
24	Overnight Oats with Strawberries and Chocolate	Chocolate Mousse	Shredded Chicken Bowl	Sirtfood Green Juice	Sesame Tuna with Artichoke Hearts and Baked Sweet Potato
25	Banana Vanilla Pancake	Sirtfood Green Juice	Lemon Tuna Steaks with Baby Potatoes	Chocolate Mousse	Spinach Quiche
26	Blueberry Pancakes	Sirtfood Green Juice	Creamy Turkey and Asparagus	Buckwheat Granola and ½ cup plain yoghurt	Creamy Broccoli and Potato Soup
27	Blueberry and Walnut Bake	Sirtfood Green Juice	Sirt Chicken Burgers	Chocolate Mousse	Sesame Tuna with Artichoke Hearts and Baked Sweet Potato
28	Chickpea Flapjacks	Sirtfood Green Juice	Brussels Sprouts and Ricotta Salad	Walnut Bar	Lamb, Butternut Squash and Date Tagine

Recipes

Recipes of Week 2 &3	Vanilla Semifreddo with Berries; Sesame Tuna with Artichoke Hearts; Blueberry and Walnut Bake; Mango Mousse with Chocolate Chips; Shredded Chicken Bowl; Chocolate Mousse; Blueberry Pancakes; Lemon Ginger Shrimp Salad; Mince Stuffed Peppers; Overnight Oats with Strawberries and Chocolate; Chicken and Broccoli Casserole; Baked Sweet Potato; Buckwheat Granola; Banana Vanilla Pancake; Brussels Sprouts and Ricotta Salad

295.   Lemon Tuna Steaks with Baby Potatoes

Preparation time: 5 minutes   **Cooking time: 30 minutes**   **Servings: 2**

Ingredients:

- ✓ 10 oz. tuna steaks
- ✓ ½ tablespoon oregano
- ✓ 1 tablespoon rosemary
- ✓ 12 oz. baby potatoes, chopped
- ✓ 1 garlic clove, crushed

- ✓ 1 tablespoon thyme
- ✓ 1 lemon
- ✓ 2 teaspoons extra virgin olive oil
- ✓ Salt and pepper to taste

Directions:

Heat the oven to 400°F. Marinate the tuna for 20 minutes with 1 teaspoon oil, herbs, salt, pepper and the juice of half lemon. Chop the baby potatoes and season them with oil, salt, pepper and rosemary.

Then, put potatoes in a baking tray, spreading the potatoes so that they are in a single layer. Cook them for 12 minutes. Cut the remaining half lemon in slices in put them on the tuna steaks. Take the tray out of the oven and add tuna steaks. Cook for another 10 minutes and serve immediately.

Nutrition Facts: Calories: 305, Fat: 5.5g, Carbohydrate: 34.2g, Protein: 23.7g

296.   Sirt Chicken Burgers

Preparation time: 10 minutes   **Cooking time: 10 minutes**   **Servings: 2**

Ingredients:

- ✓ 8 oz. chicken mince
- ✓ ¼ onion, finely chopped
- ✓ 1 clove garlic, crushed
- ✓ ½ tomato

- ✓ 2 teaspoons EVO oil
- ✓ 2 whole wheat buns
- ✓ 1 handful of parsley, finely chopped

- ✓ Juice and zest of ¼ lemon
- ✓ 2 leaves Lettuce

Directions:

Put chicken mince, onion, garlic, parsley, salt pepper, lemon zest and juice in a bowl and mix well. Form 2 patties and let rest 5 minutes.

Heat a pan with olive oil and when very hot cook 3 minutes per part.

They are also very good when grilled, if you opt for grilling, just brush the patties with a bit of oil right before cooking. Put the patties in the buns with lettuce and tomato and enjoy.

Nutrition Facts: Calories: 353, Fat: 4.8g, Carbohydrate: 28.1g, Protein: 28.3g

297.   Tex-Mex Chicken Casserole

Preparation time: 5 minutes   **Cooking time: 40 minutes**   **Servings: 4**

Ingredients:

- ✓ 2 cups spinach
- ✓ ½ cup buckwheat
- ✓ ½ red onion

- ✓ 8 oz. chicken mince
- ✓ 4 oz. black beans, rinsed
- ✓ 1 cup shredded cheddar

- ✓ 1 tablespoon paprika
- ✓ ½ chili
- ✓ 1 clove garlic

Directions:

Boil buckwheat for 25 minutes then rinse and put aside. Then, heat a pan with oil, when hot add onion, garlic and chili and cook for 5 minutes. Add mince and spices and cook for 10 minutes stirring repeatedly. Add spinach and cook another 3 minutes.

Take a baking dish and put buckwheat as first layer, then add chicken mince. Spread the cheese on top and bake for 10 minutes until the cheese is melted.

Nutrition Facts: Calories: 353, Fat: 4.8g, Carbohydrate: 28.1g, Protein: 28.3g

298.   Baked Sweet Potato

Preparation time: 5 minutes   **Cooking time: 50 minutes**   **Servings: 1**

Ingredients:

- ✓ 1 medium sweet potato
- ✓ 1 teaspoon butter

Directions:

Heat the oven to 425°C. Clean the potato very well under running water to get rid of the dirt.

Prick it several times and put it in the oven for 50minutes. Always remember to test if it's done using a stick. Make a cut in the upper part and put the butter over.

Nutrition Facts: Calories: 353, Fat: 4.8g, Carbohydrate: 28.1g, Protein: 28.3g

---

299.   Chickpea Flapjacks

Preparation time: 5 minutes   **Cooking time: 30 minutes**   **Servings: 3**

Ingredients:

- ✓ 1 can chickpeas, drained
- ✓ 1 teaspoon ginger
- ✓ ½ teaspoon black pepper salt, to taste
- ✓ 2 chicken breasts, cooked and shredded
- ✓ 2 egg whites
- ✓ ½ cup fresh parsley leaves, very finely cut
- ✓ 2 tablespoons coconut oil, for frying

Directions:

Blend the chickpeas in a food processor and combine them with the chicken, egg whites, parsley, and ginger into a smooth batter. At this point, heat the oil in a frying pan over medium heat. Using a large spoon, scoop the batter into fritters.

Cook each one for 2-3 minutes each side or until golden and cooked through.

Nutrition Facts: Calories: 207, Net carbs: 35.6g, Fat: 3.1g, Protein: 10.3g

---

300.   Creamy Broccoli and Potato Soup

Preparation time: 5 minutes   **Cooking time: 30 minutes**   **Servings: 3**

Ingredients:

- ✓ 3 cups broccoli, chopped
- ✓ 3 cups vegetable broth
- ✓ 3 teaspoons. extra virgin olive oil
- ✓ 3 garlic cloves, minced
- ✓ 1 cup raw cashews
- ✓ 2 potatoes, peeled and chopped
- ✓ 1 large onion, chopped
- ✓ ½teaspoon ground nutmeg

Directions:

First, soak cashews in a bowl with boiling water and let rest for at least 4 hours. Drain them and blend them with 1 cup of vegetable broth until smooth. Now, set aside. This will make the soup super creamy.

Gently heat olive oil in a large saucepan over medium-high heat. Cook onion and garlic for 3-4 minutes until tender. Add in broccoli, potato, nutmeg and water. Cover and bring to the boil, then reduce heat and simmer for 20 minutes, stirring from time to time.

Remove from heat and stir in cashew mixture. Blend until smooth, return to pan and cook until heated through.

Nutrition Facts: Calories: 305, Fat: 9.5g, Carbohydrate: 14.2g, Protein: 3.7g

---

301. Lamb, Butternut Squash and Date Tagine

Preparation time: 15 minutes Cooking time: 1 hour 15 minutes **Servings: 4**

Ingredients:

- ✓ 1 cup basmati rice
- ✓ 3 garlic cloves, crushed
- ✓ 1 teaspoon chili flakes
- ✓ 2 teaspoons cumin seeds
- ✓ 2 tablespoons extra virgin olive oil
- ✓ 1 red onion, chopped
- ✓ 1-inch ginger, grated
- ✓ 1 cinnamon stick
- ✓ 2 teaspoons ground turmeric
- ✓ 2 cups tomatoes
- ✓ 1 cup broth
- ✓ 2 cups butternut squash, cubed
- ✓ 16 oz. lamb shoulder, cut into pieces
- ✓ ½teaspoon salt
- ✓ 2 oz. dates, pitted and sliced
- ✓ 1 can chickpeas, drained
- ✓ 2 tablespoons fresh coriander

Directions:

First, heat the oven at 325°F. Add oil into a tagine pot or an ovenproof saucepan with lid, heat on low heat and when hot gently cook the onions until they are soft. Then, add the grated ginger and garlic, chili, cumin, cinnamon and turmeric. Stir well and cook 1 minute. Add a dash of water if it becomes too dry. Add the lamb and stir to coat it with spices and onions. Add dates, tomatoes and 1 cup broth.

Bring the tagine into the boil, set the lid and place on your preheated oven for about 1 hour and 15 minutes. Steam the basmati rice and put aside. After 45 minutes, add butternut squash and drained chickpeas to the tagine. Stir everything together, place the lid back on and go back to the oven for 30 minutes. Serve with basmati rice on the side.

Nutrition Facts: Calories: 380 Cal Fat: 13.1 g Protein: 80.62 g Sugar: 51.67 g

---

302. Spicy Indian Dahl with Basmati Rice

Preparation time: 10 minutes **Cooking time: 15 minutes** **Servings: 1**

Ingredients:

- ✓ 1 cup red lentils
- ✓ 2 oz. onion, nicely chopped
- ✓ 1 chili, nicely chopped
- ✓ 2 garlic cloves, nicely chopped
- ✓ 1 teaspoon fresh ginger
- ✓ 1 teaspoon of mild curry powder
- ✓ teaspoon of ground turmeric
- ✓ 1 medium tomato, chopped
- ✓ 1tsp cinnamon stick
- ✓ ½teaspoon cardamom seeds
- ✓ ½teaspoon cumin seeds
- ✓ 1 oz. basmati rice

- ✓ 1 teaspoon EVO oil

Directions:

Cook the lentils in boiling water for 20 to 25 minutes until almost done. In the meantime, cook the rice in a separate pot for 20 minutes and drain. Put cinnamon, onion, garlic, ginger, and chili in a hot pan with olive oil. Cook until tender, for about 5 minutes then discard the cinnamon.

Drain the lentils and put them in the pan. Add tomato, turmeric, curry, cardamom and cumin and cook for a few minutes until all the flavors have mixed together.

Serve Dahl with steamed rice.

Nutrition Facts: Calories: 272, Fat: 4.3g, Carbohydrate: 26.8g, Protein: 23.6g

---

303.   Spinach Quiche

Preparation time: 10 minutes   **Cooking time: 40 minutes**   **Servings: 4**

Ingredients:

- ✓ 3 oz. almond flour
- ✓ ½ cup water
- ✓ 5 oz. all purposes flour
- ✓ 2 oz. buckwheat flour
- ✓ 3 Eggs
- ✓ 1 cup ricotta cheese
- ✓ 1 tablespoon Parmesan
- ✓ 2 tablespoons EVO oil
- ✓ 1 small pinch of baking soda
- ✓ 3 cups spinach

Directions:

Mix the flours, salt and baking soda. Add the water and mix until you get a dough. If needed add some more water. Let the dough rest for 30 minutes. Heat the oven at 350°F. Heat a pan with oil, put spinach and a bit of salt and let cook 5 minutes on low heat. Set aside.

When the dough is ready, roll the dough to 1/8 Inch and put it in a baking tin. Mix ricotta, eggs, salt, pepper and spinach and put the filling in the tin.

Remove the excess dough with a knife. Bake 35 minutes. Let cool 10 minutes and serve.

Remaining dough can be stored in the fridge or freezer in an airtight container.

Nutrition Facts: Calories: 353, Fat: 4.8g, Carbohydrate: 28.1g, Protein: 28.3g

---

304.   Cocoa Balls

Preparation time: 5 min +30 min + 4 h   **Servings: 2**

Ingredients:

- ✓ 20 almonds
- ✓ 4 dates, pitted
- ✓ 1 tablespoon peanut butter
- ✓ Cocoa powder for coating

Directions:

Blend all the ingredients then put the mix in the fridge for 30 minutes. Form the balls and coat them with cocoa powder. Put them back in the fridge for 4 hours before eating.

Nutrition Facts: Calories: 132, Fat: 5.3g, Carbohydrate: 22.8g, Protein: 4.6g

ACKNOWLEDGEMENTS

Thank you for reading this book!

I hope the recipes could help you to enjoy this diet for delicious meals and reach your goals!

As I said at the beginning of this book, this diet is thought of as a **lifestyle and not as a diet to lose only weight**. Like other diets, i.e., the ketogenic one, the Sirtfood diet is based on **scientifically proven activation mechanisms for the body's natural slimming and burning fat.**

The Sirtfood Diet consists of eating foods that contain high levels of sirtuins. **Sirtuins** are particular proteins **in everyday foods like wine and chocolate** that can **boost your metabolism for a long time** by activating your "skinny gene." **Making the Sirtfood diet a lifestyle will experience a noticeable change in your health with high benefits.** It has been proven to be not only easy to follow but **very effective.** Indeed, it can be usefully employed to slow down the aging process.

This **Sirtfood diet offers a flexible approach that adapts to your needs.** The diet allows delicious foods like chocolate and red wine, which, combined with other sirtuin-rich foods, will take your body and health to the next level!

You deserve to live quietly! If you **no longer** want to live by **counting calories** and **becoming crazy,** cooking different dishes for each family member. You will not need to look any further for a **comfortable, healthy weight loss and a healthy diet.**

Thanks very much for reading, and I wish you to achieve your goals and start a new lifestyle!

Eleanor Fields
&
Susan Wilma Cooper

Printed in Great Britain
by Amazon